In Spite of . . .
Everything

A Young Lady's Guide to
Those Who Came Before

Tom Barnaba

authorHOUSE®

AuthorHouse™
1663 Liberty Drive
Bloomington, IN 47403
www.authorhouse.com
Phone: 1 (800) 839-8640

Published by AuthorHouse 04/09/2018

ISBN: 978-1-5462-3238-4 (sc)
ISBN: 978-1-5462-3237-7 (e)

Library of Congress Control Number: 2018903044

Print information available on the last page.

For Valyri and Adriana and Carli...

in the hope that this may be of some help to you, and other young ladies, as well.

All of the ladies in this book are listed in groups and are in alphabetical order, beginning with Abigail Adams and ending with "Babe" Didrikson Zaharias, with the exception of the following:

Anne Bradford is in the Prologue

Kalpana Chawla is listed in Group Seven, # 80, under Christa McAuliffe

Laurel Clark is listed in Group Seven, #80, under Christa McAuliffe

Hillary Rodham Clinton is in the Afterward

Anne Hutchinson is in the Prologue

Tsuyako Kitishima is listed in Group Four, #45, under Mitsuye Endo

Pocahontas is in the Prologue

Judith Resnick is listed in Group Seven, #80, under Christa McAuliffe

Elizabeth Cady Stanton is listed in Group One, #7, under Susan B. Anthony

Gloria Steinem is in the Afterward

Meryl Streep is listed in the Afterward

Anne Sullivan is listed in Group Six, #68, under Helen Keller

Serena Williams is in the Afterward

Oprah Winfrey is in the Afterward

Also by Tom Barnaba is East Of The Cross Island: Stretch'd and Basking

Contents

Preface..xv
Prologue xvii

Group One

1. Abigail Adams (1744-1818) 1
2. Maude Adams (1872-1953) 2
3. Jane Addams (1860-1935) 4
4. Louisa May Alcott (1832-1888) 5
5. Marian Anderson (1897-1993) 7
6. Maya Angelou (1928-2014) 9
7. Susan B. Anthony and Elizabeth Cady Stanton 11
8. Virginia Apgar (1909-1974) 15

Group Two

9. Alice Ball (1892-1916) 19
10. Lucille Ball (1911-1989) 20
11. Clara Barton (1821-1912) 22
12. Ruth F. Benedict (1887-1948) 23
13. Mary McLeod Bethune (1875-1955) 25
14. Antoinette Brown Blackwell (1825-1921) 27
15. Elizabeth Blackwell (1821-1910) 29
16. Amelia Bloomer (1818-1894) 30
17. Nellie Bly (1864-1922) 32
18. Evangeline Booth (1865-1950) 34
19. Gwendolyn Brooks (1917-2000) 35
20. Pearl Buck (1892-1973) 37
21. Frances Burnett (1849-1924) 38

Group Three

22. Frances X. (Mother) Cabrini (1850-1917) 43
23. Rachel Carson (1907-1964) 44
24. Mary Cassatt (1844-1926) 46
25. Willa Cather (1873-1947) 47
26. Carrie Chapman Catt (1859-1947) 49
27. Shirley Chisholm (1924-2005) 51
28. Alice Coachman (1923-2014) 53
29. Jacqueline Cochran (1906-1980) 54
30. Bessie Coleman (1893-1926) 56
31. Miriam Colon (1936-2017) 58
32. Mary Colter (1869-1958) 59
33. Maureen Connolly (1934-1969) 61
34. Gerty Cori (1896-1957) 62
35. Susan Ahn Cuddy (1915-2015) 64

Group Four

36. Bette Davis (1908-1989) 69
37. Dorothy Day (1897-1980)..71
38. Julia de Burgos (1914-1953) 74
39. Ruby Dee (1922-2014) 76
40. Emily Dickinson (1830-1886)..77
41. Dorothea Dix (1802-1887) 79
42. Amelia Earhart (1897-1937) 80
43. Gertrude Ederle (1905-2003) 82
44. Gertrude Belle Elion (1918-1999) 84
45. Mitsuye Endo and Tsuyako Kitashima 85
46. Edna Ferber (1887-1968) 87
47. Geraldine Ferraro (1935-2011) 89
48. Ella Fitzgerald (1917-1996) 91
49. Betty Friedan (1921-2006) 93
50. Margaret Fuller (1810-1850)... 94
51. Althea Gibson (1927-2003) 95
52. Lillian M. Gilbreth (1878-1972) 98
53. Katherine Graham (1917-2001)..99

Group Five

54. Alice Hamilton (1869-1970) 105
55. Lorraine Hansberry (1930-1965) 106
56. Helen Hayes (1900-1993) 108
57. Lillian Hellman (1905-1984) 109
58. Katherine Hepburn (1907-2003).. 111
59. Billie Holiday (1915- 1959) 113
60. Jeanne M. Holm (1921-2010)... 114
61. Grace Murray Hopper (1906-1992) 116
62. Lena Horne (1917-2010) 118
63. Whitney Houston (1963-2012)...120
64. Julia Ward Howe (1819-1910)...122
65. Mahalia Jackson (1911-1972) 124
66. Mother Jones (1830s-1930) 126
67. Florence Griffith Joyner (1959-1998)...128

Group Six

68. Helen Keller and Anne Sullivan...133
69. Stephanie Kwolek (1923-2014) 137
70. Hedy Lamarr (1914-2000)..138
71. Dorothea Lange (1895-1965) 139
72. Estee Lauder (1908-2004)..141
73. Emma Lazarus (1849-1887) 142
74. Lydia Liliuokakani (1838-1917) 144
75. Belva Lockwood (1830-1917) 146
76. Juliet Gordon Low (1860-1927) 148
77. Amy Lowell (1874-1925) 149
78. Clare Boothe Luce (1903-1987) 150
79. Mary Lyon (1797-1849) 152

Group Seven

80. Astronauts Christa McAuliffe, Judith Resnik, Laurel Clark & Kalpana Chawla 157
81. Carson McCullers (1917-1967)...161
82. Dolley Madison (1768-1849)...162

83. Helene Madison (1913-1970) 164

84. Wilma Mankiller (1945-2010) 165

85. Julia Marlowe (1865-1950) 166

86. Maria Mayer (1906-1972) 168

87. Margaret Mead (1901-1978) 169

88. Edna St. Vincent Millay (1892-1950) 170

89. Patsy Mink (1927-2002) 172

90. Margaret Mitchell (1900-1949) 174

91. Maria Mitchell (1818-1889) 175

92. Marianne Moore (1887-1972) 176

93. Mary Tyler Moore (1936-2017) 178

94. Julia Morgan (1872-1957) 180

95. "Grandma" Moses (1860-1961) 181

96. Lucretia Mott (1793-1880) 183

Group Eight

97. Louise Nevelson (1899- 1988) 187

98. Georgia O'Keeffe (1887-1986) 188

99. Annie Oakley (1860-1926) 190

100. Antonia Pantoja (1922-2002) 191

101. Dorothy Parker (1893-1967) 193

102. Rosa Parks (1913-2005) 194

103. Alice Paul (1885-1977) 197

104. Annie Smith Peck (1850-1935) 199

105. Frances Perkins (1882-1965) 200

106. Molly Pitcher (Mary Hays and Margaret Corbin) 202

107. Rosa Ponselle (1897-1981) 204

Group Nine

108. Ma Rainey (1886-1939) 209

109. Jeannette Rankin (1880-1973) 210

110. Janet Reno (1938-2016) 211

111. Sally Ride (1951-2012) 213

112. Felisa Rincon de Gautier (1897-1994) 215

113. Mary Roberts Rinehart (1876-1958) 216

114. Lola Rodriguez de Tio (1842-1924) 217

115. Eleanor Roosevelt (1884-1962) 218
116. Wilma Rudolph (1940-1994) 220
117. Maria Amparo Ruiz de Burton (1832-1895) 222
118. Lillian Russell (1861-1922) 223

Group Ten
◇◇◇◇◇◇◇◇◇◇◇◇◇◇◇◇

119. Sacajawea (1788-1884) 229
120. Margaret Sanger (1879-1966) 230
121. Selena (1971-1995) 232
122. Elizabeth Ann Seton (1774-1821) 234
123. Beverly Sills (1929-2007) 235
124. Bessie Smith (1898-1937) 237
125. Margaret Chase Smith (1897-1995) 238
126. Gertrude Stein (1874-1946) 240
127. Lucy Stone (1818-1893) 241
128. Harriet Beecher Stowe (1811-1896) 243

Group Eleven
◇◇◇◇◇◇◇◇◇◇◇◇◇◇◇◇◇◇◇◇◇◇

129. Maria Tallchief (1925-2013) 247
130. Ida M. Tarbell (1857-1944) 248
131. Elizabeth Taylor (1932-2011) 250
132. Laurette Taylor (1883-1946) 252
133. Shirley Temple (1928-2014) 253
134. Sojourner Truth (1797-1883) 255
135. Harriet Tubman (1820-1913) 256
136. Lillian Wald (1867-1940) 258
137. Madam C. J. Walker (1867-1919 259
138. Edith Wharton (1862-1937) 261
139. Phillis Wheatley (1753-1784) 263
140. Victoria Claflin Woodhull (1838-1927) 264
141. Chien-Shuing Wu (1912-1997) 266
142. Rosalyn Yalow (1921-2011) 267
143. Babe Didrikson Zaharias (1911-1956) 269

Afterward 271

Preface

In Spite of . . . Everything
A Young Lady's Guide to Those Who Came Before

It is an understatement to say that women are real people with true and great abilities, just like men, but yet It does seem that forever we have been debating the rights of women and how they match up against the rights of men. By every reckoning there is no blockage to the total equality of women to men, but yet there it is.... In spite of everything that we have professed to do with the laws that do exist, there always seems those who still feel that there are things only men should do and things only women should do. Women really do have the right to expect fair and unbiased treatment in all matters. But even within governmental agencies and corporations, tests and examinations are sometimes geared or tilted to skew a higher rate of success to male applicants. Whether acknowledged or not, it is nothing more than a veiled bias, intolerance and disregard.

In spite of all this prejudice, young women need to know about those great, sometimes not too well-known, women who have pushed and prodded and fought like crazy to get today's women to a spot that would have been thought unheard of only a relatively short time ago. There are so many women of great accomplishment in America today, but, again, this book is to showcase the deeds of those women who have gone before, and are now gone. Hopefully, within these pages it will show that these women who have come and gone, have been great and real and true Americans, worthy of highest praise and placed in the eschelons of respect and honor.

If it is a woman's ambition to go into the grind and competiveness of the business world, she should be given all the same chances and choices that a man gets, without the snears of behind-the-back comments. And if she wishes to be a housewife, she should be greeted warmly by all, and not looked down upon because of her decision. In spite of everything... the women in this book persevered anyway to pave the way.

It has to be acknowledged that by opening up the world of more choices to women, it guarantees more applicants for prestigious jobs, and, truthfully, more competition for men to attain certain positions. What it means is more qualified candidates to do a job.

Even in politics women have been able to bring more choices to the voters. More women have been elected recently as mayors, to state legislatures and executive offices, and Congress, and beyond. And despite the hectic pace and all the in-fighting, yet there have been far fewer who have been forced to resign because of incompetence or criminality.

Many of the women mentioned in these pages could have been even more useful and helpful had they not had to face that word, "tradition." Elizabeth Cady Stanton and Susan B. Anthony did so much. So much criticism was leveled against them, but they showed their worth and far-sightedness and kept fighting for an ideal that did not climax until after they were dead, with the passage of the "Anthony" amendment in 1920. They were some team! If they did not have to spend their entire adult lives fighting for rights that should have been theirs without struggle, the organizational ability and tireless effort of these two could have been applied to any other field, and had they been allowed, could not have been met with failure. To a great extent, it goes back to Stanton's calling a women's rights convention in Seneca Falls, New York in 1848.

Had Phillis Wheatley been free and able to pursue knowledge and literary technique further than her daring and unique master allowed, her fine, but imitative poetry could have developed into some of the deepest this nation has produced. And who knows what medical advances could have been brought forth by Elizabeth Blackwell had she not had to spend such a precious and an inordinate amount of time just getting into medical schools, and then fighting to keep her hospital open.

So, in spite of everything, it is important to know and remember those who brought about the gains. Just think of Jane Addams giving up a life of wealth and comfort to help the poor; Sacajawea, along with a baby on her back, showing America the mountains and rivers that would become the basis for one of the greatest migrations ever; Margaret Mead traveling among primitive people to further the knowledge of mankind; Eleanor Roosevelt choosing not to sit back and just be a president's wife; or Clara Barton putting herself in danger aiding wounded soldiers on battlefields. They certainly helped this nation so very much, in spite of the fact that people opposed them and their capabilities.

Were these women exceptions? Of course they were. But so were George Washington, Abraham Lincoln and Martin Luther King, Jr. And so were Benedict Arnold, John Wilkes Booth and the Timothy McVeigh.

Someday we will be a truly be a land of equality, practicing what it preaches, and the women will get us there. Not all women (or men) are great, talented, ambitious, but the women of this book were, and what they did was amazing and worthwhile, and should be remembered. Just a last bit of tiniest advice: it probably is best to loosen the male grip on reality before the gentle female hand rips it away.

Prologue

Even before we were a nation, there were women, here in colonial America, possessing true and great abilities. A spotlight here is on only three, though there were more: Anne Hutchinson, Pocahontas, and Anne Bradstreet.

A. Anne Hutchinson (1591-1643)

"Courageous exponent of civil liberties and religious toleration"

In 1591 in Alford, England, one Anne Marbury, daughter of an Anglican cleric Francis and his wife Bridget, and a distant descendent of both English and French royalty, was born, later to be Anne Hutchinson. Her father gave her a very good education, which was rare for a daughter at that time. In 1612 she married her merchant husband William, and began raising a family. In 1633 her eldest son followed preacher John Cotton to Massachusetts. Anne, also an admirer of Cotton, followed the next year with the family. Once in Boston they were admitted into the church membership.

William became an important member of the Boston community and soon Anne was having informal meetings on Thursdays for the women of the congregation in her home. As a spiritual advisor, she discussed church doctrine and the most recent preaching. This was probably the first woman's club in America. Eventually men were invited.

These gatherings led Anne to be the first woman in America to stand up and challenge government officials. This was beyond the what her gender was permitted. She voiced her opinion that the Holy Spirit was in everyone, and that salvation would come by the individual's interpretation of God's will. To Anne Hutchinson, religion was personal, and was not subject to the obedience of the laws of the church, which she felt was too obsessed with formalities and legalities. There seemed to be no room for true morality.

This was not orthodoxy, and has been called the Antinomian Controversy (also known as the Free Grace Controversy), and she was accused of flouting moral law, heresy and creating a schism in the church, disagreeing with most preachers. She had been too assertive and too highly visible according to those preachers. The church said good deeds were needed for salvation, but Anne disagreed. She felt only a good heart was necessary. The controversy spread throughout Massachusetts and citizens began taking sides. John Cotton, preacher John Wheelwright and Governor Vane were on her side, but influential ex-governor John Winthrop opposed her.

In 1637 and 1638 frail and sickly midwife Anne Hutchinson was brought before a church synod and her doctrines were denounced. She went through a second trial and lost that also. Winthrop had became governor again, and viewed Anne as a threat to his political prowess. She was banished from Massachusetts, and in 1638, excommunication for defying Puritan orthodoxy was added. John Winthrop had been both prosecutor and judge. Winthrop used the Hutchinson controversy as the blame for all the colony's woes.

The Hutchinsons, encouraged by founder Roger Williams, left for Aquidnek (Rhode Island), and they helped found Portsmouth, Rhode Island. She and her family traveled six days in the snow to get there. Her husband William for a while became a leader here, but died in 1641. Soon after, when it seemed like Massachusetts might take control over this area, she left with sixteen followers and settled very briefly in the northern Bronx in New York which was then under Dutch control.

As a result of a war between the Dutch and the Siwanoy tribe over disputed land ownership, Anne's home was attacked in 1643, and Anne and most of her family were massacred. Only one daughter, nine year old Susanna survived, captured by the tribe, and later ransomed.

Anne Hutchinson's story has been told many times. She is the heroine of Theda Kenyon's epic poem, Scarlet Anne, is in the play, Goodly Creatures, the opera, Anne Hutchinson, and in a 1770 tribute poem by America's first African American poet, Jupiter Hammon. It was also rumored that Nathaniel Hawthorne used Hutchinson as a model for his Hester Prynne character in The Scarlet Letter. She is also the ancestor of Thomas Hutchinson, a Tory governor of Massachusetts, and of presidents Franklin D. Roosevelt, and both George Bush Sr. and Jr., presidential candidates Stephan Douglas, and George and Mitt Romney, also a chief justice of the Supreme Court Melville W. Fuller, and an associate justice, Oliver Wendell Holmes, Jr. Near Quincy, Massachusetts is a memorial to Anne, and in Boston, the city that banished her, stands a 1922 statue of her in Boston Common. The quote at the top of this biography is from there. She is in the National Women's Hall of Fame and the Rhode Island Women's Hall of Fame. The Hutchinson River and Hutchinson River Parkway in lower New York State are named for her. In Portsmouth, Rhode Island there is the Anne Hutchinson/ Mary Dyer Memorial Herb Garden. There are any number of schools named in her honor. The Episcopal Church of America has declared February 5 the feast of Roger Williams and Anne Hutchinson.

Anne Hutchinson dared to defy the powers that were and was punished unmercifully for it. She was and is a key figure in the development of religious freedom and of women in the ministry, possibly the most important woman of colonial America. In 1987 the governor of Massachusetts pardoned Anne and revoked her banishment.

B. Pocahontas (1596-1617)

"Civilized Savage"

In the Tidewater region of Virginia, near the Chickahominy River, around 1596 a baby daughter, Matoaka, meaning "Bright Stream Between the Hills" (later called Amonute), was born to Wahunsenakok, a paramount chief of Tsenacommacah, part of an alliance with in the Algonquin confederacy. This chief became known to the settlers as "Powhatan" which was really his title meaning "great chief." His daughter was given the nickname "Pocahontas," which loosely translated means "playful tomboy."

The main Native American village of Werowocomoco overlooked the James River and Pocahontas' people numbered about eight thousand and controlled six hundred square miles. She often visited the Jamestown colony where Captain John Smith would make the young girl toys of wood.

The most well-known incident in the life of Smith and Pocahontas had him captured and brought to the village with the aim of him being executed. Two warriors stood over the prone Smith with clubs. Pocahontas stayed the execution by adopting the much older captive, as was an allowable custom. This story is probably fiction or a misinterpretation, but Pocahontas' contribution to America was not. What came later was what was really important. She and her father, it seemed, had different viewpoints. Whereas she helped the settlers in a number of ways, saving even others from execution, and bringing food such as corn, pumpkins and squash to a starving Jamestown. Her father, however, only tolerated them, many times taking villagers prisoner, even killing some. The settlers were beginning to be aggressive and wanting to expand their territory. The chief would not stand for that.

In 1613 Pocahontas was kidnaped and held as prisoner, in hopes of curtailing her father's antagonistic attitude toward them. She was, however, free to roam about the community, actually being taught, and accepting their religion. After her baptism her Christian name became Rebecca. When given the opportunity to return to her people, she did not.

Actually, Pocahontas had been married to a fellow tribesman, but in April 1614 she married Jamestown widower John Rolfe, who is somewhat credited with the beginnings of the tobacco industry in America. The governor of the colony was pleased because this could be seen as a move to bind the colonists closer to the Algonquin confederacy. And it did keep the peace for a while. This stretch of time has come to be known as the Peace of Pocahontas.

Pocahontas, now Rebecca Rolfe, gave birth to a son Thomas in 1615, and in 1616, the family and some tribal members sailed for England. Not only did she again meet John Smith, but was also introduced to King James, not only as a "civilized savage," but also a princess, and was treated accordingly by most. She was a hit of society, even attending a masque at Whitehall Palace.

The purpose of the trip was to get investors in the Jamestown colony. Rolfe's tobacco had been a great boon to the settlement. They remained in England awhile, but unfortunately Pocahontas contracted what might have been smallpox, while still on the River Thames at the very beginning of her trip home to America. She was buried in Gravesend, England. She was only twenty-two years of age.

Her son Thomas was educated in England, left with relatives, never seeing his father again, but returned to Virginia and through his tobacco holdings was a wealthy man. Among Pocahontas' descendants is Virginia founding father John Randolph, first ladies Edith Bolling Galt Wilson and Nancy Reagan, Robert E. Lee, famous aviator and admiral Richard Byrd and governor and senator Harry F. Byrd. There is a statue of her in restored Jamestown, and a painting of her in the United States Capitol in Washington, D. C. There exists cities named in her honor in at least four states, a Pocahontas County in West Virginia, and four ships launched as the USS Pocahontas. In 1907 a postage stamp was issued in her likeness.

There has been a ballet, Pocahontas, and at least eight films with her as the main character. A 1995 animated film, as well as 1953's Captain John Smith and Pocahontas, and 2005's The New World are mostly fictionalized accounts. In 2017, on the four hundredth anniversary of her death. Smithsonian Channel did Pocahontas: Beyond the Myth.

Without Pocahontas Jamestown most probably would have met the same fate as the mysterious vanished Roanoke. How would all of that have affected American history? She is probably the most famous female in colonial America, and an inductee and member of Virginia Women of History.

C. Anne Bradstreet (1612-1672)

America's First Published Poet

Anne Dudley Bradstreet, the first woman published in America, was born in England on March 20, 1612, growing up on the estate of the Earl of Lincoln in Sempringham. She had access to the earl's library, and was allowed to read many of the classics, such as Dryden, Vergil, Ovid and Homer and others, as well as the Bible. She was the daughter of Thomas Dudley, the estate's manager, and eventual governor of Massachusetts and one of the founders of Harvard, and Dorothy Yorke Dudley. In 1625 Charles I became king, and with his ascendency, all Puritans knew their peaceful existence was soon to be at an end, even though her family were not strict Puritans. It did not matter.

In 1628, at the age of sixteen, she married Simon Bradstreet, who also became a governor of Massachusetts and a founder of Harvard. She also contracted smallpox, and later tuberculosis, and would ever after lead a life harried by illness after illness. In 1630, with both her husband and her parents, she sailed on John Winthrop's ship, Arabella, for a voyage that brought her to Salem, Massachusetts. They moved to Charlestown and then to Boston and Ipswich. She gave birth to her first child in 1633, and a second in 1634. They moved to what is now North Andover at about 1645, where she would spend the rest of her days, writing her poetry and raising eight children.

Although a good wife, nevertheless she was shaken by the controversy swarming about her friend, the religiously rebellious Anne Hutchinson in 1637. Anne Bradford was also a unique and free thinker and she understood Hutchinson. However, she said nothing due to the feelings on the matter by her own prominent and influential husband and father. But her own feelings would surface in her poetry. She did not approve or accept the 1600's tradition that women were inferior to men.

In 1650 her brother-in-law, Reverend John Woodbridge, had a collection of her poems published while on a trip to England, entitled, The Tenth Muse Lately Sprung Up in America. And so, frail, sickly Anne Bradford became the first woman poet published in the English language. The poems were a great success, even though she complained that she had not been able to edit or rewrite her work. She was shown to be a woman with a voice. Even though she was not some primitive colonial writer, unfortunately she was overshadowed by many who came later. Bradford's work was just about ignored until the twentieth century rediscovered her worthwhile sensitive and lyrical poetry. She was a great poet nurtured on those classics.

Her poetry is a simple, restrained mystical Puritan song. They are historical, political, religious, on mortality, on love, on the role of women, elegies, dialogues, and some with a dash of sarcasm and irony. The rather long Contemplations is probably her best. "In Honour of that High and Mighty Princess Queen Elizabeth of Happy Memory" has Bradford pointing out that a woman can do what a man can do, and sometimes better. Was there ever a better example than Queen Elizabeth? Her later poetry was deeper, more personal and original.

In 1666 her house burned down, but she survived. She died, probably from tuberculosis, in North Andover, Massachusetts on September 16, 1672. In 1997 Harvard University erected the Bradstreet Gate to honor America's first published poet. In 2000 North Andover erected a marker noting the three hundred and fiftieth anniversary of the publication of her poems. In 2012 North Andover also celebrated Ann Bradstreet's four hundredth birthday. These are possibly the only posthumous honors she has ever received. Oliver Wendell Holmes, Jr.

is a descendent. Despite this ill-treatment, it does not take away that she was America's first published poet, and a very good one.

Her influence can be seen in the works of Shelley, Coleridge, Wordsworth and other romantic poets.

These three women, all dead more than a century before the Declaration of Independence, each in their own way, paved a way for future women. They, without realizing it, told us all what America could and should be, for everyone, in spite of everything.

Group One

#1- *Abigail Adams* (*1744-1818*)

"Remember the Ladies..."

Abigail Smith Adams, one of only two women to be the wife of a president and mother of another, was born in Weymouth, Massachusetts on November 11, 1744 to minister William Smith and his wife Elizabeth. She had no formal education, but read voraciously, especially John Milton, William Shakespeare and other poets. She met John Adams, a distant cousin, when she was fifteen years old, and married him before she was twenty. They lived in Braintree and Boston, but after their return from diplomatic service in France and England in 1788, they made their home in Quincy, Massachusetts. They had six children, the second being John Quincy Adams, sixth President of the United States. In addition to raising her own children, she also took care of John Quincy's family when he was a minister to Russia.

Possibly her greatest contribution was to take a constantly self-doubting man, John Adams, and boost him, support him, encourage him to be the gifted individual he was. Her letters to him while he was helping shape the United States were invaluable. They exchanged well over one thousand letters. John thought Abigail superior to him in erudition and intellect.

On March 31, 1776, Abigail wrote to John Adams in Philadelphia,"....in the new Code of Laws which I assume it will be necessary for you to make, I desire you would remember the Ladies and be more generous and favorable to them than your ancestors. Do not put such unlimited power in the hands of the Husbands...If particular care and attention is not paid to the Ladies, we are determined to foment a rebellion, and will not hold ourselves bound by any Laws in which we have no voice, or Representation." Not much later she went on, "I can not say that I think you very generous to the Ladies, for whilst you are proclaiming peace and good will to Men...you insist upon retaining an absolute power over wives. But you must remember that Arbitrary power is like most other things which are very hard, very liable to be broken-- and not withstanding all your wise Laws and Maxims we have it in our power not only to free ourselves but to subdue our Master, and without violence throw both your natural and legal authority at our feet." Abigail was also critical of Washington and Jefferson because they were slave holders, and told her husband so, indicating how could they, therefore, be for freedom!

John Adams was impressed. Although nothing was done for women at that time, he did write her, "I think you shine as a Stateswoman, of late as well as a Farmeress." She, however, was not impressed, writing back in August of that same year, "If we mean to have Heroes, Statesmen and Philosophers, we should have learned women. The world would perhaps laugh at me, and accuse me of vanity, But you know I have a mind so enlarged and liberal to disregard the Sentiment. If much depends on as is allowed upon the early Education of youth and the first principals which are instilled take the deepest root, great benefit must arrive from accomplishment in women." She was dedicated to the education of women and to the property rights of married women. Some have even referred to her as a "Founder of the United States." While John was much away helping to found the fledgling United States of America, she ran the family farm and finances. She even gave their pewter to the Minutemen to melt down and make bullets.

Abigail also had a soothing and beneficial effect on John's sometimes prickly attitude and temper, especially while as a diplomat with England's King George III and in France. Abigail Adams was the first "First Lady" to live in the brand new White House, and there were some of the congressional delegation who referred to her sarcastically as "Mrs. President," noting her determination. Later she even managed to bring about a reconciliation between her husband and Thomas Jefferson. Again, she was an extraordinary woman of passion and principle, well-versed in poetry, philosophy, national affairs and politics, an advocate for the property rights of women, an abolitionist, and sought more educational opportunities for women.

Abigail Adams died of a stroke on October 28, 1818 in Quincy, never having seen her son, John Quincy Adams, elected president. Her grandson, historian Charles Francis Adams, published her letters. The home in Quincy, Massachusetts is part of the Adams National Historical Park. In nearby New Hampshire there is a Mount Adams named for her husband, and another named for her. She was represented in the 1969 Broadway musical and 1972 film, 1776. She was also depicted on television in both PBS's 1976 Adams Chronicles and HBO's 2008 John Adams, and has been inducted into the National Women's Hall of Fame. Abigail Adams was a remarkable woman and as much a patriot as any for the Founding Fathers.

#2- *Maude Adams (1872-1953)*

Peter Pan

Maude Ewing Adams Kiskadden, who became the mysterious, bewitchingly beautiful Maude Adams, was born in Salt Lake City on November 11, 1872, daughter of Asaneth Adams and James Kiskadden, and a descendant of the political Adamses, and of a passenger on the Mayflower. At two months of age she appeared at the Brigham Young Theatre in The Lost Baby with her mother, known as actress Annie Adams. Although Mormons were in her family, she herself never was one. At the age of two the family moved to Virginia City, Nevada.

At sixteen she appeared in The Paymaster and then joined the E. H. Sothern Company and appeared in Lord Chumley in Boston, then toured with the show. At eighteen she became associated with the Charles Frohman Stock Company as an apprentice. By 1892 she was Frohman's leading lady, appearing opposite the noted John Drew in The Masked Ball and was a sensation, overshadowing the more famous Drew. This was followed by The Imprudent Young Couple, and Rosemary. She received very high praise.

But it was 1897 that propelled Maude Adams into the category of the most popular actress of her time, and the most successful. She opened as Lady Babbie in James M. Barrie's The Little Minister in the Empire Theatre in New York City. It was a record-breaking, spectacular success: 300 performances (almost all sold out), and setting an all-time box office record. It was revived in 1905 and again in 1916.

In 1899 she appeared in Romeo and Juliet, and the next year in L'Aiglon, in New York. In 1901 she appeared as Miss Phoebe in Quality Street.

Commencing in 1905, in a play written by James M. Barrie, especially for her, Maude Adams appeared over fifteen hundred times in Peter Pan: or The Boy Who Wouldn't Grow Up, the role for which she is most remembered. Any number of actresses have played this part, but Adams was not only the first, but for whom the part was written. It made her the highest paid actress of her day. She played this role for over ten years in New York and on tour. During this time, though, she also appeared in What Every Woman Knows, and in the masterpiece of her career, The Maid of Orleans. She was considered overwhelming. In 1911 she starred in Chantecler, and was such a rousing success that she once had twenty-two curtain calls. This was her favorite play, even moreso than Peter Pan. By 1916 she was at her peak, and starred in A Kiss for Cinderella. Her tiara from this show now sits in the Museum of the City of New York. Maude Adams was delicate, was charming, was winsome.

In 1918 she came down with an intense case of influenza, causing her to take time off, which became retirement. She spend much of the 1920s working on improvements in lighting stage technology. Ladies' Home Journal published her biography in 1926 after she officially retired. She did come out of retirement in the 1930s for The Merchant of Venice, and her final performance in Twelfth Night in 1934. Some other of her plays were: the hugely successful The Midnight Bell, Men and Women, and The Legend of Leonora. She also did some radio broadcasts of her more well-known roles and became head of the drama department at Stephens College in Missouri from 1937 to 1943, and also did some teaching.

In the novel, Bid Time Return, and its film version, Somewhere in Time, there is performance of The Little Minister being performed within the story, with the main character, Elise, based on Maude Adams, and portrayed by actress Jane Seymour.

During her career, Maude Adams would take long breaks from her acting, and stay in Catholic facilities. In 1922 she donated her Lake Ronkonkoma, Long Island, New York estate to the

Sisters of St. Regis for a novitiate and retreat house. Maude Adams died on July 17, 1953 in Tannersville, New York, and is buried at the Lake Ronkonkoma property.

#3- *Jane Addams* (1860-1935)

Hull House

Activist, reformer, social worker, philosopher, sociologist, author, role model, leader, humanitarian! Jane Addams was all of these, one of the greatest givers in history. She was born in Cedarville, Illinois on September 6, 1860, daughter of a wealthy Quaker businessman John H. Adams, and friend of Abraham Lincoln. Her mother, Sarah, died when Jane was two years old, but she was very well looked after. She graduated Rockford Seminary as president of her class in 1881, deciding then to go on to study medicine at the Woman's Medical College of Philadelphia.

However, due to illness she was unable to continue her studies. At the suggestion of her doctor and her father, she traveled. She went to at least eight countries in Europe, where she stayed twenty-one months. While on these journeys she witnessed terrible living conditions, especially in London, which reminded her of the slums of Chicago. But Jane Addams was much impressed with Toynbee Hall, a social services center that aided the poor.

When she finally returned home she founded Hull House on Halsted Street in Chicago in 1889, assisted by her friend Ellen Gates Starr. It was a run-down mansion once owned by Charles Hull, needing furniture, painting and some roofing. But with Addams' efforts it provided recreation and kindergarten for the children of working mothers. Also there were rooms for working girls, summer country trips for children, and an attempt to acclimatize the Italian, Irish, German, Polish, Jewish, Russian, Greek, Bohemian and French Canadian immigrants of Chicago's nineteenth ward. It had an employment bureau, a school for adults, drama group, girls club, art gallery, library, gymnasium, book bindary, and bathhouse. Her perseverance corrected or improved the horrible conditions in the area, working on housing, truancy, prostitution, drug problems and working conditions. Eventually Hull House expanded to thirteen buildings.

All this, and more, Jane Addams accomplished, despite the fact that she was not physically fit from four years of age, often having to wear a steel brace on her back due to a curved spine. She had to deal with the greed and corruption of politicians, but with help from people like Frances Perkins, she influenced the regulation of child labor, improved factory conditions, forced the creation of more sanitary conditions, and established playgrounds. She did this through sheer willpower and by becoming a sanitation inspector and a member of the Chicago Board of Education. In addition, she became president of the National Conference of Charities and Correction, chair of the American Sociologists Society, and first vice president of the Playgrounds Association of America. She even helped found the NAACP (National Association for the Advancement of Colored People) in 1909 and was a co-founder of the ACLU (American Civil Liberties Union) in 1920.

But Chicago was only the beginning. Addams also dedicated herself to peace and attended peace conferences all over the world from 1907 to 1921. She stood her ground even after the United States entered World War I. This cost her, some denouncing her as unAmerican, even going so far as being called a traitor and a communist. She was even expelled from membership in the Daughters of the American Revolution. This did not stop her. Even after the war was over, she continued her peace work, presiding over the Women's International League for Peace and Freedom, the American Friends Service Committee and was a member of the Anti-Imperialistic League. Appropriately, in 1931 she was awarded the Nobel Peace Prize, and has been inducted into the National Women's Hall of Fame and the Hall of Fame of Great Americans.

Jane Addams did not just give money to causes, she worked hard for the down-trodden reaching out to all people to improve the lot of everyone, including lecturing on college campuses. In 1926 she had a heart attack. She died in Chicago on May 21, 1935 following an operation that indicated she had cancer. December 10 is Jane Addams Day in Chicago.

Among her books are: Twenty Years at Hull House, A New Conscience and an Ancient Evil, The Spirit of Youth and the City, Peace and Bread in Time of War, The Second Twenty Years at Hull House, and The Newer Ideals of Peace and a novel, Shoes. There are schools, college buildings, parks and roadways named in her honor. In 1940 a ten-cent stamp was issued with her likeness. In 1943 the Jane Addams Children's Book Awards was founded to "foster a better understanding between the people of the world toward the end that wars may be avoided and a lasting peace enjoyed."

#4- Louisa May Alcott (1832-1888)

Little Women

The author of Little Women, the most successful girls' book ever written, Louisa May Alcott, was born in the Philadelphia suburb of Germantown on November 29, 1832. Her mother Abby May was married to her father, the poor, but famous A. Bronson Alcott, transcendentalist, abolitionist and schoolteacher, and friend to Ralph Waldo Emerson, Henry David Thoreau, Nathaniel Hawthorne, Margaret Fuller and Henry Wadsworth Longfellow. All had a hand in helping educate her, although her father was her prime teacher, but she constantly borrowed books from Emerson's library. This upbringing made her a lifelong abolitionist and feminist. Emerson was really a good friend and helped them financially, even with the purchase of the final home.

The family moved briefly to Boston, Massachusetts, then for a short while lived in the Utopian Fruitland's community, but finally to Concord and the home she would love forever. The family even served as "station masters" on the Underground Railroad helping runaway slaves. The second oldest of four daughters, she was high-spirited, always running, climbing and leaping. She wrote Flower Fables when sixteen for Ellen, Emerson's daughter, but these were not published until much later, and she received thirty-two dollars.

Alcott left home when she was nineteen to ease the financial burdens and began teaching in Boston. She also was a governess, did sewing, and wrote for magazines, such as Gleason's Pictorial and the Boston Saturday Gazette. However, by 1860 her short stories and poems were appearing in The Atlantic Monthly.

During the Civil War she assisted Dorothy Dix as a nurse at Union Hospital in Georgetown, in the District of Columbia, eventually becoming head nurse. However, she caught typhoid fever and was ill many months. These experiences led to Hospital Sketches, written in 1863 and published in 1865, following the publication of her first novel, Moods. The latter reflected her work and time in the hospital. These successes were enough to pay off all the family's debts. After the war she became editor of Merry's Museum, a children's magazine.

For a while she wrote under the pen name A. M. Barnard, creating sensationalistic, romantic, but vengeful female characters.

Also in 1865 and 1866 Alcott traveled to Europe as a nurse and companion to an invalid. While in Switzerland she met and fell in love with Ladislaw Wisniewsky (Laddie), a Pole, who was much younger than herself. For some unknown reason they never married. Her character Laurie was based on him.

But it was in 1868 that Little Women appeared (and that character Laurie), whose original intended title was The Pathetic Family. It was an immediate success and Louisa May Alcott became a celebrated author. It was the story of Jo the tomboy, Amy the artist, Meg the homebody, and sickly Beth--the March sisters, who, in reality were the Alcott sisters, growing into adulthood in Concord.

Little Women has sold millions upon millions of copies and at numerous times been made into a motion picture, the 1933 version with Katherine Hepburn as Jo, and a 1949 version with

Elizabeth Taylor as Amy. The success of this book made it possible for her parents to live in comfort, and for her to take her artistic sister to Europe.

In 1871 she published Little Men. It was as successful in its day, but did not have the continuous popularity of Little Women. She wrote a number of sequels: Jo's Boys, Aunt Jo's Scrap Bag, and Eight Cousins. Louisa May Alcott also wrote A Modern Mephestopheles, Under the Lilacs, Jack and Jill, An Old-Fashioned Girl and Work, which was semi-autobiographical.

Louisa May Alcott never married, many believing she never got over "Laddie," but she did raise her sister's daughter. She spent much of her later life traveling in Europe. Over her life she suffered from both vertigo and typhoid fever, and died from a stroke in Boston on March 6, 1888. Her home in Concord, "The Alcott House, Home of the Little Women," is a museum. Her home in Boston is on the Boston Women's Heritage Trail. She has been inducted into the National Women's Hall of Fame. In 1940 a five cent cent stamp was issued with her likeness.

#5- *Marian Anderson (1897-1993)*

"...once in a hundred years"

Marian Anderson was born in Philadelphia on February 17, 1897, to John B. and Annie Anderson, and by age six was singing in the Union Baptist Church's junior choir, and by thirteen was singing in the senior choir, demonstrating her phenomenal range. Only at sixteen did she begin taking voice lessons. After high school she applied to the Philadelphia Music Academy, but was rejected because of color. At nineteen her congregation and some neighbors made the effort to allow her to study under Giuseppi Boghetti.

In 1925 she won a contest over three hundred others and was given the opportunity to sing with the New York Philharmonic Orchestra. She received a music scholarship from the National Association of Negro Musicians and a Rosenwald Fellowship. Due to racial prejudice Marian Anderson was unable to sing in the best of venues in the United States. In 1930 she made her European debut and went on to perform in England, Germany and seventy-six concerts in the Scandanavian countries where the fans there had "Marian fever'". There was no racial problem in Europe. On a second trip to Europe she sang for the crowned heads of Sweden, Denmark and Italy. Anderson also sang in England, Norway and Russia. It was In 1935 when acclaimed conductor Arturo Toscanini said, "A voice like yours is heard once in a hundred years." She soon came under the management of Sol Hurok who booked her into New York's Town Hall. She was magnificent.

In 1939 the Daughters of the American Revolution denied her a booking at their Constitution Hall in Washington, D. C. because of her race. Eleanor Roosevelt, wife of the president, resigned from that organization, and was instrumental in sponsoring Marian Anderson's concert on Easter Sunday, 1939, on the steps of the Lincoln Memorial. Over seventy-five thousand people stretched from the Lincoln Memorial almost to the Washington Monument to hear her sing "America" ("My Country 'Tis of Thee"), "Ave Maria" and "Nobody Knows the Trouble I've Seen." In 1940 she was given the Bok Award as the most distinguished citizen of Philadelphia. With the money obtained from the award she started the Marian Anderson Scholarship Fund for "talented American artists without regard to race or creed."

In 1943 this contralto did get to sing in Constitution Hall, and to a non-segregated audience. Marian Anderson also sang at the White House before the Roosevelts and the king and queen of England, and again for President John F. Kennedy. In 1955, late in her career, at the request of Rudolf Bing, she became the first African American to sing at the Metropolitan Opera House. She played Ulrica in Verdi's Un ballo in maschera.

Although she married architect Orpheus Fisher in the 1940s, and the bought a sprawling property in Danbury, Connecticut, she continued her storied career. But that would be her home for most of the rest of her life. It is on Connecticut's Freedom Trail. But her home in Philadelphia is also listed on the National Register of Historic Places. During World War II and the Korean War she spent time entertaining the troops. In 1956 she wrote her autobiography, My Lord, What A Morning, which later was made into a musical play performed at Kennedy Center. She went on tour to India and the Orient in 1957 for the state department and the United Nations. The next year she served as alternate delegate for the United States to the United Nations. She sang at Dwight D. Eisenhower's inauguration and, again, at John F. Kennedy's presidential inauguration, where Marian Anderson was chosen to sing the national anthem. She performed not only before President Kennedy, but also before past presidents Eisenhower and Truman and future presidents Johnson and Nixon.

She retired in 1965, but continued to make appearances, and was chosen to read the Declaration of Independence at the Bicentennial Celebration in Philadelphia in 1976 in the presence of President Gerald Ford. Needless to say, she was one of the most famous and celebrated performers of the twentieth century.

Marian Anderson's voice was grand, dramatic, versatile, rich, and interpretive. Poet Gwedolyn Brooks praised Marian Anderson with a poem entitled, "When I hear Marian Anderson sing".

Marian Anderson died in Portland, Oregon of congestive heart failure on April 8. 1993. She had suffered a stroke a short time earlier. Her accomplishments can only partially be appreciated through the enormity of her awards: Springarn Medal (1939), Bok Award (1940), Fellow of the American Academy of Arts and Sciences (1957), Presidential Medal of Freedom (1963), University of Pennsylvania Glee Club Award of Merit (1973), United Nations Peace

Prize (1977), New York City's Handel Medallion (1977), Congressional Gold Medal (1977), Kennedy Center Honors (1978), George Peabody Medal (1981), first recipient of the Eleanor Roosevelt Human Rights Award (1984), National Medal of Arts (1986), Grammy Lifetime Achievement Award (1991),and induction into the National Women's Hall of Fame and the Connecticut Women's Hall of Fame. She was awarded honorary doctorates from Smith College, Temple University and Howard University. In 1980 the United States Treasury struck a commemorative gold medal in her honor. In 2006 a postage stamp in her likeness was issued. In 2020 Anderson, Eleanor Roosevelt and some of the suffragettes will be honored on the reverse of the new five dollar bill. She is also listed in Molefi Kete Asante's 100 Greatest African Americans.

In 1999, that one-act play, My Lord What A Morning: the Marian Anderson Story, was presented at the Kennedy Center, and 2008 the documentary, Marian Anderson: the Lincoln Memorial concert.

#6- Maya Angelou (1928-2014)

"Still I Rise"

Marguerite Anne Johnson, daughter of doorman Bailey and nurse Vivian, was born on April 4, 1928 in St. Louis, Missouri. In her tumultuous lifetime she did everything and anything. A biographer (seven autobiographies), a poet, an essayist, a journalist, a screenwriter, a director, a professor, a lecturer, a producer, a civil rights activist...all yes. But also a cook, a dancer, a cable car conductor, an actress, and a "sex worker." "Maya" was her brother's shortened form of Marguerite. "Angelou" came from her 1951-1954 marriage to Greek sailor Anastasios ("Tosh") Angelopulos ("Angelous"). She later married (and divorced) Paul du Feu, 1974-1983.

Her family split up when she was still a young child and she was sent to live with her paternal grandparents in Stamps, Arkansas. After a while she went back to her mother in St. Louis, and there was raped by her mother's boyfriend. She returned to Arkansas, but was so traumatized by not only the rape, but the brutal killing of her rapist that she remained mute for five years after, thinking her saying his named killed him. The one positive of all this was that that she began to become an avid reader. As an adolescent she moved to Oakland, California with her mother, where, a short time later, she became the first African American cable car conductor in nearby San Francisco. And while there attended the California Labor School. Also, however, at seventeen, she gave birth to a son.

By the 1950s and into the early 1960s she was into entertainment, appearing in Porgy and Bess, Calypso Hot Wave and The Blacks. She teamed with dance partner Alvin Ailey as "Al and Rita," but they were not so very successful. Then on to Africa where she did some writing and journalistic work in both Egypt (The Arab Observer) and Ghana (The African Review and Ghanaian Times), and worked at the University of Ghana. She returned home and eventually became northern coordinator and fundraiser for Martin Luther King, Jr.'s Southern Christian Leadership Conference, and became a supporter of Malcolm X. In 1968 she wrote, produced and narrated Blacks, Blues, Black, a documentary tying the blues to African American culture.

But 1969 was the turning point. When I Know Why the Caged Bird Sings was published in 1969 it made her an instant and international celebrity, and was the first non-fiction book by an African American woman to make it to the best seller list. This did make her famous, but always her themes would be about identity, family racism.

In the 1970s she wrote Georgia Georgia, and was the first African American woman to have a screenplay produced. In 1973 she was nominated for Broadway's Tony Award for Look Away, and in 1977 was nominated for a television Emmy for Roots. In 1982 she was the first Reynolds Professor of American Studies at Wake Forest University in Winston-Salem, North Carolina.

In 1993 she was chosen to read at president Bill Clinton's inauguration, and she read her "On the Pulse of Morning." It brought Maya Angelou an exalted status she had not had before. The sales of all her books skyrocketed. She later received a Grammy award for the spoken word for reading the same.

In the late 1990s she wrote and directed Down in the Delta. She received the NAACP (National Association for the Advancement of Colored People) Image Award, once for her inspirational Letter to My Daughter, and once for a cookbook (Hallelujah! The Welcome Table). In the opening pages of Letter, she says, "I gave birth to one child, a son, but I have thousands of daughters. You are Black and White, Jewish and Muslim, Asian, Spanish-speaking, Native American and Aleut. You are fat and thin and pretty and plain, gay and straight, educated and unlettered, and I am speaking to you all."

Other books by Maya Angelou: Just Give Me A Cool Drink of Water 'Fore I Die, All God's Children Need Traveling Shoes, Singin' and Swingin' and Gettin' Merry Like Christmas, Gather Together In My Name, The Heart of a Woman, A Song Flung Up to Heaven, Mom & Me & Mom, I Shall Not Be Moved, and Shaker, Why Don't You Sing.

Maya Angelou passed away on May 28, 2014 in Winston-Salem, North Carolina. Not only is she in the National Women's Hall of Fame, but a postage stamp has been issued in her likeness. In 2017 PBS television showed the documentary "Maya Angelou: And Still I Rise" as part of their American Masters series. She had also been granted over fifty honorary degrees, and was awarded the Presidential Medal of Freedom. In 1978 she published Still I Rise. A middle stanza is so very much Maya Angelou:

"You may shoot me with your words, You may cut me with your eyes, You may kill me with your hatefulness, But still, like air, I'll rise."

7. Susan B. Anthony and Elizabeth Cady Stanton

In 2020 a statue of both these women will be erected in Central Park, New York City

#7A- Susan B. Anthony (1820-1906)

The "Anthony" Amendment

Susan Brownell Anthony, the patient planner, the factual figurer, the enormously hard-working co-leader of the early women's suffrage movement, was born on February 15, 1820 in Adams, Massachusetts, but at age six moved with her activist Quaker father, Daniel and non-Quaker mother, Lucy, to Battenville in western New York, and then to Rochester. Even as a teenager she was out collecting signatures on petitions against slavery. The Panic of 1837 left her parents struggling, so at about this time she left home to help them out and became a teacher and then, for a while, the headmistress of girls at the Quaker Canojaharie Academy.

She was very much influenced by the reformers of the day, particularly William Lloyd Garrison and William Ellery Channing, and was elected president of the Canojaharie Daughters of Temperance. By 1840 she had begun to shed some of her Quaker ways, and becoming acutely aware of sex discrimination, since, as a teacher, knew the men were making triple her salary. She then ran the family farm for a while. Anthony also knew from her experience in an 1849 temperance meeting that women were not allowed to speak. Anthony was now convinced that America could not advance as a socially enlightened nation until women were granted equal rights. In 1852 she attended her first women's rights convention in Syracuse and also helped found the New York Women's State Temperance Society, where women could speak. She would really now become the social reformer and women's rights advocate.

11

And then it happened! Her friend Amelia Bloomer (whose "bloomers" Anthony wore for a while) introduced Anthony to Mrs. Elizabeth Cady Stanton, and they would be friends and partners for the next fifty-plus years. Stanton would be the intellect and writer of the team and Anthony would be the energetic and incomparable organizer and speaker, making seventy-five to one hundred speeches a year. Whenever the situation arose, Anthony would always step back and let Stanton take the lead. At this time she was also working with Harriet Tubman and the Underground Railroad, and as an agent for the American Anti-Slavery Society would conduct lectures, with the meetings often disrupted by egg-throwing and her being threatened. She was hung in effigy and her image dragged through the streets, and she sometimes had to be escorted by police.

The 1860 New York State Married Women's Property Bill became law due larely to her efforts, and changed how women could control their own property, wages and custody of children. In 1863 they formed the Women's Loyal National League and three years later the American Equal Rights Association, whose purpose to gain equal rights for all citizens, including African Americans and women. Susan B. Anthony had been the chief campaigner for the thirteenth amendment, basically abolishing slavery. Both women opposed the fifteenth amendment, however, because, although it guaranteed all rights to all men, it ignored the women. She became a lecturer extraordinaire and a fundraiser at this time to further her goals. 1868 saw the arrival of The Revolution, the newspaper that they published to further their ends. The motto: "Men, their rights and nothing more: women, their rights and nothing less."

For a number of years there was a split in the women's movement with Susan B. Anthony and Elizabeth Cady Stanton demanding no let-up in the suffrage fight, while Lucy Stone and Julia Ward Howe wanted to wait until abolition was achieved. The groups merged finally reunited in 1890 with Stanton as president and Anthony as secretary. She assumed the presidency in 1892.

In 1870 she organized the Workingwomen's Central Association hoping to improve and open up working and educational opportunities for women. In 1872, Susan B. Anthony attempted to vote in Rochester, but was turned away and fined. She refused to pay, and nothing was done. The judge refused to follow through because that would give Anthony the means to challenge her trial in the Supreme Court, and he did not want to give her that option. Her co-authored six-volume, fifty-seven hundred page History of Woman Suffrage was published in 1876. Two years later Anthony and Stanton arranged for Congress to be presented with an amendment proposal for women's suffrage. It was something, however, that would not be accomplished until 1920.

In 1883 Anthony spent nine months in Europe and met with many like-minded women, leading to the founding of the International Council of Women. They had prominent spots at the 1893 Chicago World's Fair, in 1899 in London, a meeting with Queen Victoria, and in 1904 in Berlin, received by the German empress.

On her seventieth birthday there was a national event in Washington, D.C., attended by a number of senators and representatives. On her eightieth birthday, she was invited by President William McKinley to the White House. And in that same year, after a bit of a Susan B. Anthony battle, the University of Rochester began admitting women. Back in 1890 that newly formed National American Women's Suffrage Association was formed. When the nineteenth amendment, also known as the "Anthony" amendment, was finally passed, this organization became the League of Women Voters, still active and relevant today. She appeared before every session of Congress from 1869 to 1906 to push for the vote. She always remained active, even to the point of visiting Yosemite Park, riding on a mule, at age seventy-five.

She died on March 13, 1906 in Rochester of pneumonia and heart failure. The many and varied associations and councils she rallied were all the grandmother of the National Organization for Women (NOW). Since 1970 the New York City NOW chapter grants a Susan B. Anthony Award to worthy recipients. In the Capitol Rotunda is a 1921 statue of Susan B. Anthony and her two colleagues, Elizabeth Cady Stanton and Lucretia Mott. In the Cathedral of St. John the Divine in New York City there is a statue of Susan B. Anthony in the company of Albert Einstein, Mohandas Gandhi and Martin Luther King, Jr. Both in 1936 and again in 1958 postage stamps were issued in her honor. In 1979 the Susan B. Anthony dollar was issued, and in the near future the ten dollar bill will feature Anthony, as well as Stanton, Sojourner Truth, Lucretia Mott and Alice Paul. Ken Burns' documentary Not For Ourselves Alone: The Story of Elizabeth Cady Stanton and Susan B. Anthony aired in 1999.

She is in the National Women's Hall of Fame and the Hall of Fame of Great Americans due to her fearless, aggressive, passionate, determined and zealous fight for all things right, the right to vote, the right to work, the right to own property and so much more. A new tradition has come about around Anthony's headstone in Mount Hope Cemetery in Rochester, New York. All around election days, women place "I Voted" stickers on her headstone. And even the cemetery allows this, staying open late on election days. February 15 is Susan B. Anthony Day. Her home in Rochester has been designated a National Historic Landmark and her birth home in Adams, Massachusetts and childhood one in Battenville, New York are on the Register of Historic Places.

#7B- Elizabeth Cady Stanton (1815-1902)

Seneca Falls, 1848

Elizabeth Cady Stanton, the truest symbol of the women's movement in America, was born in Johnstown, New York, on November 12, 1815. She was what every woman can be. She was the daughter of Margaret and Daniel Cady, an eventual New York Supreme Court judge and former congressman. In this judicial environment she saw discrimination based on gender and race. She was well-educated, having attended Johnstown Academy and Troy Female Seminary, and studied the law under her father's guidance, but because she was a woman she was denied admission to the bar. In 1840 she married Henry Brewster Stanton, a lawyer and co-founder of the Republican party. She had the phrase "promise to obey" removed from the ceremony. On their honeymoon they attended an anti-slavery convention in London. There she met Lucretia Mott, and both were refused admission because women were not allowed. Needless to say, both women were upset, and this eventually led to the 1848 Seneca Falls Women's Rights Convention. The Stanton's had been living first in Johnstown, then in in Boston, but in 1847 had moved to Seneca Falls, New York, on Cayuga Lake, one of the Finger Lakes. While in Boston, Elizabeth Cady Stanton had become acquainted with and friends with the likes of Louisa May Alcott, Ralph Waldo Emerson, William Lloyd Garrison and Frederick Douglass.

This convention, attended by three hundred, was the beginning of that long hard-fought battle to improve the place of women in American society. In her opening statement in the "Declaration of Sentiments," Stanton said that "we hold these truths to be self-evident... That all men and women are created equal." She also added the "history of mankind is a history of repeated injuries on the part of man toward woman." Not everyone, including Mott, agreed with everything for which Stanton stood, but with the aid of the eloquence of Frederick Douglass, she not only won the day, but was now considered a radical. A second convention later that year in Rochester, New York sealed her reputation. A few years later Stanton formed a partnership with Susan B. Anthony, first in the temperance movement, presiding over the short-lived Woman's State Temperance Society, and then for the next fifty years they struggled together for the cause of women's rights, a goal that neither would live to see totally accomplished, with Stanton the writer and Anthony the speaker.

With Anthony she formed the Women's Loyal League to unite women to support the abolitionist and union cause during the Civil War. They also co-edited The Revolution, a periodical of the women's suffrage movement. Stanton became the first president of the National Women Suffrage Association. At about the same time Stanton joined the Lyceum Circuit, a movement that sponsored, among other things, adult education, and she gave lectures. But like many great causes, sometimes splintering occurs. The biggest problem was that Stanton did not want the fourteenth and fifthteenth amendments passed because they would afford legal protections to men of color, but no such protection was to be given to women of any color. Some felt Stanton was too adamant in her stand on this issue.

Eventually they made peace. She took part the in 1888 calling for the first International Council of Women, with the result that her association merged with the American Woman Suffrage Association. Joined, they were the National American Woman Suffrage Association, with Stanton as president. In 1892 Stanton, Anthony, Lucy Stone and others appeared before the United States Committee on the Judiciary. Her speech here was the basis for The Solitude of Self.

Not only did social activist Elizabeth Cady Stanton wage an unending struggle against gender discrimination and for suffrage, and did this by now actually speaking all around the country, and assisting in creating the multi-volume History of Woman Suffrage. Anthony and Stanton were quite a pair. Anthony was the unmarried fighter. Stanton was the humorous, charming, intelligent mother of seven, whose eloquence and enthusiasm jump-started the movement into the realm of possibility. It must also be understood that Stanton's life was not just about the right to vote. It was about women and property, employment, income control, divorce, parental custody. and even birth control. Among her writings are The Women's Bible (her feminist understanding of it), The Solitude of Self, and her autobiography, Eighty Years and More. Stanton was more controversial than Anthony, and her Bible was one of the reasons. Over the years, as a result, more people remembered Anthony rather than her.

Her home in Seneca Falls is registered as a National Historic Landmark. Her summer home in Shoreham on Long Island, New York has a plaque place there by local officials. In the United States Capitol Rotunda sits Adelaide Johnson's wonderful statue of Stanton, Anthony and Lucretia Mott. Stanton, along with Amelia Bloomer, Sojourner Truth and Harriet Tubman are commemorated on the Episcopal Calendar of Saints on July 20. In 1999 documentarian Ken Burns presented Not For Ourselves Alone: The Story of Elizabeth Cady Stanton and Susan B. Anthony. By 2020 there will be changes in the United States currency, and the present plan is to have Stanton, Anthony, Mott, Sojourner Truth and Alice Paul all on the ten dollar bill. A 1948 postage stamp honored the Seneca Falls convention with her likeness and that of Lucretia Mott and Carrie Chapman Catt.

Stanton died of heart failure in New York City on October 26, 1902, and is buried in Woodlawn Cemetery in the Bronx. She is, of course, in the National Women's Hall of Fame.

#8- *Virginia Apgar (1909-1974)*

Is My Baby All Right?

Dr. Virginia Apgar, daughter of Charles and Helen Apgar, was born in Westfield, New Jersey on June 7, 1909, and was quite an accomplished violinist and cellist. She went on to get her zoology degree from Mount Holyoke College in 1929 and then on to Columbia University College of Physicians and Surgeons with a medical degree in 1933. This was a time during the Depression and Apgar had to work as a waitress and librarian to make ends meet while studying. Apgar was encouraged by to go into the needed field of anesthesiology, and, so then studied at the University of Wisconsin/Madison and at New York City's Bellevue Hospital. Her area of expertise became obstetrical anesthesiology, dealing with newborns. Eventually she became a pioneer in the field of neontology and teratology, which deals with abnormalities of physiological development. In 1949 she was the first woman to become a full professor at Columbia University College of Physicians and Surgeons, remaining there until 1959.

In the early 1950s she developed the revolutionary "Apgar score". The Apgar Newborn Scoring System, became more commonly known as the "Apgar score" was the first standardized method of evaluating a newborn's health. It was a breakthrough, a way to determine the effects of anesthesia given to a mother during labor. There were five areas of concern: heart rate, respiratory effort, muscle tone, reflex response, and color. It predicted the neonatal chances of survival and neurological development. The test was given one minute after birth, and the again five minutes after birth. An additional benefit of the test was that now doctors would pay as much attention to the baby as to the mother. It is now an accepted procedure everywhere. The New England Journal of Medicine has declared that the "Apgar score" is still the best predictor of infant health. She became a professor at Cornell University School of Medicine in the 1970s, as well as teaching at the Johns Hopkins School of Public Health.

For close to twenty years, Dr. Apgar worked for the March of Dimes organization, initially as a vice president in charge of research on the prevention of birth defects and premature births. After that she became their director of research. During the 1960s rubella outbreak, she was an advocate for vaccination, especially in the case of transmission from mother to child, which could result in miscarriages, deafness, blindness, mental retardation and other ailments. In 1972 came Apgar's well received Is My Baby All Right? It is an essential guide to help women improve their chances of having a healthy baby. It explores the causes, as well as the treatments, of numerous birth defects. It is both a diagnostic and therapeutic.

Dr. Virginia Apgar has received honorary doctorates from Mount Holyoke College, the Women's College of Pennsylvania, and the New Jersey College of Medicine and Dentistry. She has received the Elizabeth Blackwell Award from the American Medical Women's Association, the Distinguished Service Award and the Ralph M. Waters Award from the American Society of Anesthesiologists, and the Alumni Gold Medal for Distinguished Achievement from the Columbia University College of Physicians and Surgeons. She became a fellow of the American Public Health Association, the New York Academy of Science and the New York Academy of Medicine. And along with all this hard and productive work, she managed to be quite the accomplished violinist, and a golfer, fly fisher, photographer and gardener. And she actually made violins, violas and cellos.

After suffering from liver disease, Virginia Apgar passed away due to liver failure in New York City on August 7, 1974. She had been Ladies Home Journal Woman of the Year in Science, and has been inducted into the National Women's Hall of Fame. In 1994 a United States commemorative stamp was issued in her honor. There is an Annual Virginia Apgar Seminar which encourages discussion on recent advances in obstetrical anesthesiology, and a Virginia Apgar Award in Neonatal and Perinatal Medicine, granted from the American Academy of Pediatrics.

Group Two

Alice Ball - Frances Burnett

#9- Alice Ball (1892-1916)

Leprosy

Chemist Alice August Ball was born on July 24, 1892 in Seattle, Washington to newspaper editor/photographer James, Jr. and Laura Ball. Her grandfather was a famous and prize-winning daguerrotype photographer JP Ball. This was an early photographic process. Supposedly he was so well-known that he managed to photograph such personalities as Queen Victoria, Charles Dickens, Frederick Douglass and singer Jenny Lind. He moved with the entire family to Hawaii in 1903 to alleviate his rheumatism, but died a year later, and the family moved back to Washington in 1905.

His granddaughter Alice graduated high school in 1910 and attended the University of Washington, earning degrees both in pharmaceutical chemistry in 1912 and pharmacy in 1914. She was brilliant enough to have an article, with the assistance of one of her professors, published in the Journal of the American Chemical Society. She was offered graduate scholarships to both the University of California at Berleley and the College of Hawaii (later University of Hawaii). She chose to go back to Hawaii.

In 1914 and 1915 she taught chemistry at the college, and In 1915 was the first woman and the first African American to earn a master's degree from the University of Hawaii. Her graduate chemistry thesis on the kava plant was so impressive that a surgeon from United States Public Health Office, Dr. Harry T. Hollmann, working at Kalihi Hospital, asked for her help. Hansen's Disease, also known as leprosy, was deemed not only hopelessly incurable, but painful. Patients were deemed contagious and placed in leper colonies, under strict quarantine. They were practically considered dead by society. For centuries the medical personnel of India and China had made some use of the oil of the chaulmoogra tree, but only with limited success. It was sometimes rubbed on the body for temporary relief. And it tasted bitter when ingested and led to vomiting and stomach problems.

Even though she was teaching during the day, in the evenings and at every opportunity, Alice worked for some sort of solution. What Alice Ball did was a groundbreaking development of a treatment for the suffering, a method to isolate the active chemical compounds of the chaulmoogra oil. She wound up isolating the ethyl esters in the chaulmoogra oil and the hydnocarpic acid, creating an oil extract water soluble treatment that could now be injected. Not only did it work, but it became the accepted treatment of leprosy until a cure was found in the 1940s. Due to Alice Ball's work, lepers found a treatment that permitted them to return to their homes, painless and non-contagious.

Unfortunately, while working in the laboratory, Ball inhaled deadly chlorine. At first it was thought she contracted tuberculosis. She returned home for treatment to Washington where, at the young age of twenty-four, she unexpectedly died from the chlorine poisoning. Arthur L. Dean, University of Hawaii president, put the work together, published it and tried to take the credit, referring to it as the "Dean Method." However that same Dr. Harry T. Hollmann corrected that claim, making sure Alice Ball got the credit, with the procedure called the "Ball Method." The success of this "Ball Method" was acknowledged in 1918 in the Journal of the American Medical Association. In 2000 the University of Hawaii finally honored Alice Ball with a plaque placed by the university's only chaulmoogra tree, and February 29, 2000 the first Alice Ball Day was celebrated, and is done so every four years. In addition, she was posthumously awarded the University of Hawaii Medal of Distinction in 2007.

#10- *Lucille Ball (1911-1989)*

"Lucy"

The world of television, especially comedy, would be so much poorer if it had it not been for actress and comedienne Lucille Ball and her "I Love Lucy" show and its various spin-offs. This most beloved of comediennes was born Lucille Desiree Ball in Jamestown, New York on August 6, 1911 to her parents, Henry and Desiree (De De) Ball. Due to her father's work they moved to Montana, New Jersey and Michigan. At the age of three, her father died and they moved back to Jamestown. However, when her mother remarried she was sent to live with her stepfather's parents in nearby Celeron on Lake Chautaugua. She was raised by these rather strict folks, but they urged her to join a chorus line as part of an entertainment by an organization favored by these people. She loved it and that was the beginning.

She attended drama school in New York City as a teen, but was discouraged. She made it as a model from 1928 and did some minor Broadway work as Dianne Belmont, but in the 1930s she was in Hollywood, mostly in minor rolls, and in the 1940s she was mostly in "B" films. In fact, she became known as "Queen of the Bs." A few of her better known films of this time were: DuBarry Was a Lady, Stage Door, Room Service (with the Marx Brothers), Dance Girl Dance, The Next Time I Marry, and Five Came Back. She met her husband, Cuban band leader Desi Arnaz in 1940, while they were both in the film, Too Many Girls. Soon after that they eloped.

In 1948 they were on the radio with My Favorite Husband, but when Lucille Ball and Desi Arnaz early on tried to convince the television producers that an American girl/Cuban band leader romantic comedy would be a success also on television, they failed. They took their show on the road, and it was a great hit. In the 1950s they created one of the most iconic and beloved programs in television history: nutty Lucy trying to be a star in her own right, despite the misgivings of her bandleader husband, along with her landlady/friend/unwilling accomplice Ethel, and her husband, grumpy Fred. Lucille Ball will always be best remembered for her I Love Lucy, and the ones that followed: The Lucy-Desi Comedy Hour, The Lucy Show, Here's Lucy and Life with Lucy. Some of the episodes created such hilarity that they will always be remembered by those who saw them: Lucy and Ethel stomping grapes, Lucy trying to do an advertisement for "vitameatavegamin," Lucy and Ethel trying to wrap candy from a conveyor belt, and Lucy dancing with eggs. Ball's full name in the show was "Lucille Esmerelda McGillicuddy Ricardo", and Arnaz was "Enrique Alberto Fernando de Acha Ricardo lll". I Love Lucy is still syndicated in dozens of languages. When the show left the air they were still on the top of the ratings. The couple also made the films, The Long, Long Trailer and Forever, Darling during this time. Later, without Arnaz she appeared in the original Yours, Mine, and Ours, and then Mame (for which she was nominated for a Golden Globe award.

In the process they had formed Desilu Productions. In many ways it was an innovative company. It was the first to use multiple cameras in shooting, using a live audience, and was the first to show a pregnant woman on television. In fact, the episode where Lucy gives birth to "little Ricky," it garnered more viewers than the inauguration of President Dwight D. Eisenhower. The Desilu Company was not only noted for its "Lucy" shows, but was also behind many other well-known successful programs, including Star Trek, The Dick Van Dyke Show, Mission Impossible, Our Miss Brooks, The Untouchables, Make Room For Daddy, and others.

The list of nominations and awards Lucille ball received is staggering. She actually earned five Emmy awards from the Academy of Television Arts and Sciences, including the 1989 Governor's Award, as well as numerous Golden Globe nominations. In 1971 she was the first woman awarded a gold medal from the International Radio and Television Society, in 1977 the Women in Film Crystal Award, and in 1979 the Golden Globe Cecil B. DeMille Award. She was given the Lifetime Achievement by the American Comedy Awards in 1987. In addition she was inducted into the Television Hall of Fame in 1984, and was an honoree at the Kennedy Center Honors in 1989, and postumously the Presidential Medal of Honor. Time magazine listed her as one of the "100 Most Important People of the Twentieth Century." TV Guide named her the "Greatest TV Star of All Time." In fact, Lucille Ball graced the cover of TV Guide thirty-nine times, more than any other star in the history of that magazine. Later I Love Lucy was judged to be the second best television program in history, following Seinfeld, although in 2012 People Magazine and ABC News rated it the "Best TV Show of All Time." And in a poll, she came in second to Johnny Carson as one of the "50 Greatest TV Icons." She was also given the "Legacy of Laughter" award by TVLand in 2007. In 2001 the postal service issued a postage stamp in her likeness. She, of course, has her star on the Hollywood Walk of Fame, and was inducted into the National Women's Hall of Fame.

After Lucille Ball's divorce from Desi Arnaz in 1960, she bought out his interest in Desilu, and became the first woman executive and producer, and manager of a major television studio. In 1967 it merged with Paramount Pictures. She later married comedian Gary Morton. In 1988 she had a mild heart attack. Lucille Ball passed away in Beverly Hills, California on April 26, 1989 of an abdominal aortic dissection, whereby a tear occurs inside the wall of the aorta, stopping the flow of blood to the heart. In 2009 a rather weird statue of her erected in Celeron was dubbed the "Scary Lucy" statue. It was replaced in 2016 with a more appropriate one. In Jamestown there is the Lucille Ball-Desi Arnaz Center and the Lucille Ball Little Theatre. She is buried in Jamestown.

#11- *Clara Barton (1821-1912)*

Red Cross

Captain Stephen and Sarah Barton's daughter, Clarissa Harlowe Barton, who would grow up to be founder of the American Red Cross, was born in North Oxford, Massachusetts on December 25, 1821. In 1833 her brother was seriously hurt in a fall from his barn roof, and she spent two years nursing him back to health. But the medical field did not seem a part of her future at that time. At fifteen Clara (as she preferred to be called) began a career in teaching in Massachusetts and Georgia. In 1850 she decided to enhance her education by taking up the study of writing and languages at the Clinton Liberal Institute in New York. In 1852, even though she was asked to set up the school system of Bordentown, New Jersey, when it successfully done, they passed her over for the position of principal for a male. She tolerated this miscarriage for a while, but had to give up teaching due to health problems. In 1854 she became the first female federal governmental employee when she began work in the Department of the Interior's patent office until 1861.

When the Civil War broke out she tried to be a nurse, but at age forty, she was told she was too old. But she was determined to help in some way, and just stated to care for the wounded in any manner that was helpful, including applying dressings and cleaning hospitals, and brought them clothing, bandages, and things to eat. In the battles of Cedar Mountain, Second Bull Run, Antietam and Fredericksburg, she began going out on to the battleground to the wounded. She continued this daring and dangerous work throughout the war. After a while she was called "The Angel of the Battlefield" and was assigned fifty men to aid her in her work, as the "Lady in Charge" of hospitals on the front lines. Clara Barton went as far as leading a relief expedition to South Carolina. And she became a national hero! Toward the end of the war, assisting President Abraham Lincoln, she created the "Office of Missing Soldiers," and made it a mission to find those missing soldiers, and she did, well over twenty thousand.

From 1865 to 1868 she lectured all around the country and found herself exhausted and in poor health, and sojourned in Europe to recuperate. While in Geneva, Switzerland she became acquainted with the International Red Cross, and assisted them during the Franco-Prussian War. She was awarded the Iron Cross. On returning home she sought how America might be involved and affiliated with that organization.

By 1881 she had formed the American Association of the Red Cross, and was its first president, remaining as such until 1904. During the 1880s they responded to floods on the Ohio River, a famine in Texas, a tornado in Illinois, yellow fever in Florida and the Johnstown Flood of 1889. Her own last relief trip was helping out with the effects of the 1900 Galveston hurricane. In 1904 she was rather unceremoniously removed by males who felt her humanitarian outlook had to be replaced by a more scientific approach. Her American Red Cross had brought relief aid not only to battleground, but also to those impacted by disasters, including earthquakes and forest fires, as well. However, she did go on to found the National First Aid Society.

Clara Barton herself had gone on and led many a relief trip including those to Turkey and Cuba, this last one when she was seventy-seven years old.This woman, who almost all by herself founded the American Red Cross, died on April 12, 1912 in her home in Glen Echo, Maryland, which is listed as the Clara Barton National Site. She is buried near her childhood home, which is now a museum, in Massachusetts. She had published her Story of the Red Cross. She also published The Story of My Childhood, Red Cross in Peace and War and The Red Cross -Glimpses of Field Work. In her honor throughout this country there is the Barton Center for Diabetes Education in Massachusetts, the Clara Barton Hospital and Clinics in Kansas, Clara Barton Woods in New York, and Lake Barton in Virginia. Elementary, junior high and high schools in at least a dozen states are named in her honor. In 1948 a postage stamp was issued in her likeness. She has also been inducted into the Hall of Fame of Great Americans and the National Women's Hall of Fame.

#12- *Ruth F. Benedict (1887-1948)*

Patterns of Culture

Ruth Fulton Benedict, one of America's first female and outstanding anthropologists and folklorists, was born in New York City on June 5, 1887. Her parents, Frederick and Beatrice Fulton, moved the family to upstate Norwich, New York to her grandparents farm because of her father's poor health. He died while she was still young, but she remained on the farm. Having contracted measles as an infant she became deaf in one ear.

In 1909 she graduated from Vassar College with a degree in English literature. A wealthy college trustee took her and two other young women on an all-expense paid tour of Europe, where she visited England, Italy, France, Germany and Switzerland. She then began teaching in California and worked for the Charity Organization Society doing social work, but returned to the upstate New York farm where she met Stanley R. Benedict. They wed in 1914 and moved to New York City. In 1922 she received her doctorate from Columbia University, went to work for a year at Barnard College, and then returned to Columbia and began a long and successful association with Columbia University.

In 1927 she was elected president of the American Ethnological Association, and in 1934 her groundbreaking Patterns of Culture was published. This book has become a classic. It had been translated into at least fourteen languages in her lifetime. Ruth Benedict researched the primitive people from around the world and how they are the same and how they are different, how the role of culture shapes life. The Zuni and Pueblo of New Mexico, the Kwakiutl of western Canada, the Dobu of New Guinea. She found that human beings in advanced civilizations demonstrate some of the same peculiarities: sometimes cooperative, sometimes treacherous, sometimes competitive, sometimes traditional, sometimes hostile. Most importantly, to Benedict, was the concept that it is wrong to disparage or criticize the values of cultures other than one's own and that there is a value in diversity. She was made a fellow of the New York Academy of Science. Stanley Benedict died in 1936. Ruth Benedict had become president of the American Anthropologist Association, and a member of the American Folklore Society and editor of the Journal of American Folklore.

She also wrote Tales of the Cochiti Indians, Zuni Mythology, The Chrysanthemum and the Sword: Patterns of Japanese Culture, Race: Science and Politics, and The Concept of the Guardian Spirit in North America (which was her Columbia dissertation). During World War ll she was recruited for the Office of Information, and afterwards was made a fellow of the Washington School of Psychiatry, as well as a fellow of the American Academy of Arts and Sciences, elected vice president of the American Psychopathological Association, and presented with the American Association of University Women Achievement Award. She has also been inducted into the National Women's Hall of Fame. Benedict College of Stony Brook University is named in her honor. A 1995 postage stamp was issued in her likeness.

Ruth F. Benedict was working on an anthropological study of contemporary European and Asian cultures when she died on September 17, 1948 of a coronary thrombosis, shortly after a trip from Europe. Margaret Mead was close, and one of her students, and worked to keep the legacy alive.

She was not only a brilliant scientist, but a talented writer. In her youth she had begun (but never finished) biographies of outstanding women, and was somewhat of a poet whose poetic pen names were Anne Singleton, Ruth Stanhope and Edgar Stanhope.

#13- *Mary McLeod Bethune (1875-1955)*

First Lady of the Struggle

Mary Jane McLeod Bethune was the fifteenth of seventeen children of Sam and Patsy McLeod, former slaves, born in Mayesville, South Carolina, on July 10, 1875. She grew up poor and uneducated on a farm. In time she would come to be regarded as an educator, humanitarian, civil rights activist, stateswoman, publisher, business woman and philanthropist. In 1883 the Presbyterian Board of Home Missions opened the Trinity Mission School about five miles from Mayesville, and she walked it every day.

Eventually she obtained a scholarship to the Scotia Seminary in North Carolina. Here she decided to become a missionary, and went on to the Moody Bible School in Chicago where she was the only African-American. When she completed her training, it was found that she was too young to be a missionary, and so, temporarily, she thought, she took a teaching position at Haines Institute, a training school in Augusta, Georgia. After a while she decided that southern African Americans needed her teaching skills more than Africans needed her missionary skills. She went on to the Kendell Institute in South Carolina, and there met Albertus Bethune. They were married in 1899.

The Bethunes moved to Savannah, Georgia, and then to Palatka, Florida to teach. Upon learning of the horrible conditions of the African American workers' families on the Florida East Coast Railroad, Mary McLeod Bethune now moved to Daytona Beach and founded the Daytona Literary and Industrial School for Girls. The enrollment climbed from a handful of students to two hundred and fifty in two years.

She and the students would bake sweet potato pies to raise funds for the school, and knowing that Daytona Beach was a draw for wealthy vacationers, she would approach them alone, or surrounded by the school's chorus to make a good impression, garnering generous donations from such distinguished folks as John D. Rockefeller (who eventually gave sixty-two thousand dollars), Andrew Carnegie, Henry J. Kaiser, James N. Gamble (of Proctor & Gamble) and Thomas H. White. The latter, a sewing machine manufacturer, left sixty-seven thousand dollars to the school, and Gamble became president of the trustees.

Four-storey Faith Hall was built in 1907, and Carnegie assisted in erecting McLeod Hospital in 1911. In 1918 Thomas White's bequest was responsible for an auditorium to be built, and in that same year Albertus Bethune died. The vice president of the United States and the governor of Florida were guest speakers at the opening. During World War 1 she worked at raising money for the Red Cross. In 1923 her school merged with Cookman College, becoming Bethune-Cookman College, with Mary McLeod Bethune as president until 1942, and again in 1946 and 1947.

She had become the most famous African American woman in America and became an executive board member of the National Urban League, and later became president of the National Association of Colored Women's Clubs. In the early 1930s she became a White House consultant to President Herbert Hoover, and in 1935, she helped form the National Council of Negro Women, now more than four million strong. That same year she was awarded the Springarn Medal of the N.A.A.C.P. (National Association for the Advancement of Colored People). In 1936 she was awarded the Francis A. Drexel Award, and selected by President Franklin D. Roosevelt to be the director of the Division of Negro Affairs of the National Youth Administration, and a part of his "Black Cabinet." This was the first heading of a federal office by an African American woman. Mary McLeod Bethune remained in this position until 1943, helping six hundred thousand African Americans remain in school. If all this was not enough, she also became an assistant director of the Women's Army Corps, operated a publishing concern, and was presented the Thomas Jefferson Award of the Southern Conference of Humane Welfare. When President Roosevelt died, she was chosen as one of the specially-seated people at his funeral. His successor, Harry Truman, then selected her to work with her friend Eleanor Roosevelt on the United Nation's Commission on Human Rights. In 1949 she was awarded the Haitian Medal of Honor and Merit, and in the same year an honorary degree from Rollins College. Soon after this, she retired. She also was the United States emissary at the inauguration of President William V. S. Tubman of Liberia.

On May 18, 1955 Mary McLeod Bethune passed away from a heart attack in Daytona Beach, and was buried on the college grounds. She had not only been an advisor to presidents, but also was a director of the Commission on Interracial Cooperation, president of both the Florida State Teachers Association and the National Association of Teachers in Colored Schools. Columnist Louis Martin stated "she gave out faith and hope as if they were pills and she was some sort of doctor." Ida Tarbell chose her as number ten of the fifty women who contributed "most to the enrichment of American life." Ebony magazine named her "one of the fifty most important figures in Black history." Schools in dozens of cities have been named in her honor.

In 1960 Congress ordered a monument in her honor erected in Lincoln Park in Washington, D. C. On it was engraved her words:

"I leave you love. I leave you hope. I leave you the challenge of developing confidence in one another. I leave you a thirst for education. I leave you a respect for the use of power. I leave you faith. I leave you racial dignity. I leave you a desire to live harmoniously with your fellow men. I leave you, finally, a responsibility to our young people."

Mary McLeod Bethune had, indeed, become "First Lady of the Struggle." Her home in Washington has been designated a National Historic Site, and her home in Daytona Beach a

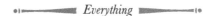

National Historic Landmark. She has been inducted into the National Women's Hall of Fame. In 1985 a postage stamp was issued in her likeness.

#14- Antoinette Brown Blackwell (1825-1921)

The Minister

Antoinette Louisa Brown was born in Henrietta, New York on May 20, 1825 to Joseph and Abigail Brown. The family attended the Congregational Church in nearby Rochester, and Antoinette was preaching there by age nine. She attended Monroe County Academy and then taught school for a few years to save money so she could attend Oberlin College in Ohio. She did not wish to teach; she wanted to be a minister and to preach.

She met future reformer Lucy Stone, her future sister-in-law, at Oberlin. Although they got along, Stone thought Brown too caught up in orthodoxy, that is, sticking to tradition. Brown graduated in 1847 and had her degree, but not her theological degree, and so she attempted to gain admission to the college's theological courses so that she might become a Congregation minister. She was rejected because they felt there was no place for female ministers and she was very controversial. But after putting on constant pressure, the college accepted Brown on the condition that she would not be formally recognized, and would be a "resident graduate student." She reluctantly agreed.

She became quite the public speaker, using religious faith to expand women's rights. It was feminist theology and she used the Bible to prove her point. She refuted St. Paul with St. Peter and Joel from the Bible. She felt those statements in the Bible about women were for the past, but not in her time. But she also spoke on abolition in Ohio and in New York, and did some writing for Frederick Douglass' The North Star newspaper.

In 1850 she attended and spoke at the Women's Rights Convention in Worcester, Massachusetts. She was well-received and it became a launching pad for her. The next year she was granted a license to preach by the Congregationalist Church and became an independent speaker throughout New England, New York, Pennsylvania, and Ohio on her favorite subjects: women's rights and education, abolition and temperance.

In 1852 she was offered an invitation to become the minister of the Congregationalist Church in South Butler, New York. She accepted and was ordained a Congregationalist minister on September 15, 1853, thereby becoming the first woman ordained in a Protestant denomination in the United States. Soon after this she attended and attempted to speak at the World's

Temperance Convention, but they would not allow women to be speakers. Due to this, and her growing doubt and discomfort with religious orthodoxy, Brown resigned the short-lived ministry in 1854.

In 1856 she married Samuel Charles Blackwell in her hometown of Henrietta. Not only was his sister the first woman medical doctor in the United States, Elizabeth Blackwell, but his brother Henry was married to Lucy Stone. Antoinette and Samuel had seven children, five living to adulthood. Domestic life prevented Antoinette Blackwell from doing much traveling and preaching. She turned to writing, encouraging women to seek employment that were sometimes considered men's work, and also encouraging men to share in domestic duties. They eventually moved to New Jersey where she spent most of the rest of her life.

Althouigh active in the feminist movement, in 1869, along with Lucy Stone, she broke ranks with her friends Susan B. Anthony and Elizabeth Cady Stanton. Anthony and Stanton were opposed to passage of the fourteenth amendment which granted voting rights to African American men, but did nothing for women of any race. Stone and Blackwell felt it was important to support such an important step. It led to a breach in the women's rights movement for over thirty years. Stanton and Blackwell also very much disagreed on the topic of divorce.

In 1873 she founded the Association for the Advancement of Women, became president of the New Jersey Suffrage Association, and in 1891 help found the American Purity Association. In 1869 she wrote Studies in General Science in which she demonstrated the relationship of mind and matter, reconciling nature with revealed religion, and uniting the physical and the mental, all leading to harmony. She was somewhat influenced by Charles Darwin. She also eventually wrote The Sexes Through Nature (different, but equal), The Physical Basis of Immortality, The Philosophy of Individuality, The Making of the Universe, and The Social Side of Mind and Matter. She also wrote a novel. The Island Neighbors and poetry, Sea Drift.

In 1878 she decided to return to organized religion, and Oberlin College finally gave her a master's degree, and then later a doctorate. In 1908 she was made Minister Emeritus of the Unitarian All Souls Church in Elizabeth, New Jersey. She had help found the Unitarian Society of New Jersey.

Antoinette Brown Blackwell died at age ninety-six in Elizabeth, New Jersey on November 5, 1921, the only survivor of that 1850 convention, to see the passage of the nineteenth amendment, giving women the right to vote. And she had voted in the presidential election of 1920 for Warren G. Harding.

Her childhood home is on the National Register of Historic Places, and she has been inducted into the National Women's Hall of Fame. Since 1975 the Unitarian Church of Christ, using her as a model and example, grants the Antoinette Brown Award to ordained women "who exemplify the contributions that women can make through ordained ministry..."

#15- *Elizabeth Blackwell (1821-1910)*

Medicine Woman

Sugar refiner Samuel and Hannah Blackwell's daughter, Elizabeth, was born on February 3, 1821 in Bristol, England, but in 1832 the family emigrated to the United States, first to New York City, and eventually in 1838 to Cincinnati. Her father was very liberal in the education of all his children. She not only had a governess, but private tutors, as well. It created an atmosphere in which she was socially isolated. This might be the reason why she had a lifetime problem getting along with people. Her father died soon after, and in 1844 Elizabeth spent some time teaching in nearby Kentucky. But due to her anti-slavery view, she was not very popular there, and did not care for it. Then she taught in North Carolina, staying with the Reverend John Dickson, who had been a doctor. He allowed her to use his medical library. Then briefly to South Carolina and then to Philadelphia looking for medical schools.

So, now determined to get into the medical field, she really began studying the fundamentals of anatomy, chemistry and physics with Dr. William Elder and Dr. Jonathan Allen in Philadelphia. She started applying to medical schools all across America, receiving many, many rejections. Then in 1847 little, and little-known, Geneva Medical School accepted her, the first woman in American history admitted to a medical school. The admission was somewhat of an oddity. The institution thought it was a good idea to present this to the student body for a decision. They thought it was some kind of trick or joke, and agreed, thinking nothing really was going to happen. But Elizabeth Blackwell was well-accepted and went on to graduate, on January 23, 1849, with highest honors as a physician, and thus changed the medical profession, becoming the first woman to achieve a medical degree in the United States. Her thesis was The Cause and Treatment of Typhus. During her summer breaks she worked aiding the poor at the Blockley Almshouse, which gave her some needed experience.

She went on to further her studies in London and Paris where, at La Maternite she became blinded in her left eye while treating an infant with ophthalmia neonatrum, inadvertantly infecting her own eye with contaminated fluid. The eye had to be removed, meaning she now could never become a surgeon. She went to St. Bartholemew's Hospital in London and returned to America in New York City in 1851. Here she found herself unable to make headway attracting patients or even achieve a position at a hospital. She was looked upon as something strange, a female doctor, usually only an abortionist. So with the help of the New York Tribune and Quaker friends, she was able to open her own dispensary. The first year she only had three hundred patients, but by 1854 she had three thousand. Marie Zackryewska and Blackwell's sister Emily, now the third female American doctor, also joined the dispensary and were treating six thousand. This dispensary went on to become the New York Infirmary for Indigent Women and Children, which in 1868 became the Women's Medical College of New York Infirmary.

During the Civil War she was ignored by the physicians of the United States Sanitary Commission. She then formed the Woman's Central Relief Association and worked with health reformer Dorothea Dix. This garnered a great deal of respect for women in the medical profession. Dr. Elizabeth Blackwell did not stop at only practicing medicine, but began giving lectures, and had the lectures printed as The Laws of Life with Special Reference to the Physical Education of Girls. She was also always promoting education for women in medicine. Her brother Samuel married minister Antoinette Brown and her brother Henry married women's rights activist Lucy Stone. Following this she went to England and helped found the London School of Medicine for Women, and even taught midwifery/gynocology there. Back in America she co-founded the National Health Society. Throughout the 1880s and 1890s she took interest in and was involved in many different movements.

However, Elizabeth Blackwell had a rather aggressive and acerbic personality, and over the years some of her colleagues broke away from her, including her own sister and Florence Nightingale, but she did manage to stay friends with women's rights pioneer Elizabeth Cady Stanton. It seems if she were not in charge, she did not care for the organization. She never married because she felt her independence was too important. She left the Infirmary and retired, traveling throughout Europe until 1877. Other writings by Elizabeth Blackwell were The Influence of Women in Medicine, Counsel on the Moral Education of Their Children, and Pioneer Work in Opening the Medical Profession to Women. In 1907, while vacationing in Scotland, she fell down a flight of stairs and was never the same after that, very disabled. She died in Hastings, England on May 31, 1910 and was buried in Scotland. Geneva College later became Hobart College, and that was assimilated into part of Syracuse University. Since 1949 Syracuse University has awarded the American Medical Women's Association Elizabeth Blackwell Medal to an outstanding woman in the medical profession. A 1974 postage stamp was issued in her likeness. She has been inducted into both the Ohio and National Women's Hall of Fame.

#16- *Amelia Bloomer* (1818-1894)

Bloomers and Beyond

Clothier Ananias Jenks and his wife Amelia had a daughter Amelia, who was born in upstate Homer, New York on May 27, 1818. She just may be the most responsible for bringing publicity to the feminist and temperance movements in the United States. For a while she was a teacher and a live-in tutor/governess. In 1840 she married newspaper man Dexter C. Bloomer, and at his suggestion she began working at his Seneca Falls County Courier.

Both Bloomers attended that initial 1848 women's convention in Seneca Falls, New York. The very next year Amelia Bloomer became the first woman journalist and editor/publisher/ owner/operator in the United States with The Lily from 1849 to 1853. It began as a temperance reform newspaper (the full title was The Lily: A Ladies Journal, Devoted to Temperance Literature). Early nineteenth century immigration patterns brought many Germans and Irish to the United States, with a hearty influence of beer and liquor. When Elizabeth Cady Stanton and Susan B. Anthony became columnists, The Lily took on the full gamut of discrimination against women, including divorce, property, and even the Bible. In fact, one of Bloomer's greatest feats was introducing Elizabeth Cady Stanton to Susan B. Anthony, causing one of the great partnerships in history. She felt women publicly lecturing or speaking was unlady-like, and that writing was the proper avenue to follow, and her newspaper "spread about the truth of a new gospel to women.".

1851 is when Amelia Bloomer really made a name for herself. Temperance activist Elizabeth Smith Miller, a cousin to Elizabeth Cady Stanton, started wearing an outfit copied from the women of the Middle East and Central Asia. It was a short skirt with loose trousers underneath, gathered at the ankle. Amelia Bloomer started wearing these that she felt were more sensible clothing. They began to be called "bloomers" after her. The feminist movement went with it, with Susan B. Anthony, Lucretia Mott and Elizabeth Cady Stanton and others wearing them. The bloomers came to be the symbol of the women's movement. Periodicals got caught up in it, as well, sometimes in a mocking way, but wound up giving not only the garment publicity, but the whole feminist movement, as well. But even "The Bloomer Polka" could not keep them in fashion. It seemed that not all women found bloomers to be complimentary, and after about a decade they were out of style.

For just a bit, in the 1890s, they did make a brief comeback. The Bloomers moved to Mount Vernon, Ohio in 1853 where Amelia started up The Lily again, but also was associate editor of her husband's Western Home Journal. The area was rather conservative and they did not stay long. However, Amelia Bloomer had to have her say in print: "To woman equally with man has been given the right to labor, the right to employment for both mind and body; and such employment is as necessary to her health and happiness, to her mental and physical development as to his....the public mind is undergoing a rapid change in its opinion of women and is beginning to regard her sphere, rights and duties, in altogether a different light from that which she has been viewed in past ages."

In 1855 they moved again, this time to Council Bluffs, Iowa where from 1871 to 1873 she was president of the Iowa Woman Suffrage Association. After this Amelia Bloomer lived basically and privately in retirement in Iowa until her death on December 30, 1894 of a heart attack. She has been inducted into both the Iowa and the National Women's Halls of Fame. Her home in Seneca Falls, New York is on the National Register of Historic Places. She is listed, along with many others, in the Calendar of Saints of the Episcopal Church. Dexter C. Bloomer, her husband, wrote Life and Writings of Amelia Bloomer in 1895. The American Library Association's Social Responsibilities Round Table presents the Amelia Bloomer Project, a list of children's book with feminine themes.

#17- *Nellie Bly* (1864-1922)

Around the World

Nellie Bly, born Elizabeth Jane Cochran on May 5, 1864, in Cochran's Mills in Burrell Township, Pennsylvania, a daughter to Irish immigrant Michael, a mill owner and justice, and Mary Jane Cochran, became among the most famous of American newspaper reporters. Her father died when she was young, leaving her mother in some desperate straights and they moved to Pittsburgh. She briefly attended Indiana Normal School, intending to be a teacher, but she could not afford it for too long. Along the way she added an "e" to her surname, thinking it was more sophisticated, now Cochrane, and, when she got her reporter's job, adopted the pen name, Nellie Bly. It was a common practice for women reporters to use pen names.

Her initiation into journalism, came under the name of Lonely Orphan Girl, when she responded to a newspaper column in the Pittsburgh Dispatch dispaging women, "What Girls Are Good For," calling upon them to restrict their duties to domestic chores. The editor was impressed with her response that he offered her a job. She did manage to write some pieces about working girls, factory conditions and slum life, but for the most part her assignments were fluff pieces in the ladies section of the paper, and not satisfactory to her, so she traveled to Mexico to become a foreign correspondent. Her reports came out in book form as Six Months in Mexico. She reported on the jailing of reporters who criticized dictator Porfirio Diaz and his suppression of the people, and on the corruption and poverty. Bly had to leave the country for fear of being arrested, but she let everyone know about Diaz. This was the beginning of her brand of investigative reporting.

After still not getting the kind of assignments she wanted, in 1887 she came to New York City and managed to get a job with the New York World. Her next big break was going undercover, as an insane woman for ten days in the Women's Lunatic Asylum on Blackwell's Island in New York City's East River. This island was later called Welfare Island, and is now known as Roosevelt Island. She put on an act that she was deranged and had amnesia. The doctors believed her. Newspapers believed her. She was taken to court where it was determined she was insane and hopeless. She endured spoiled food, cold and dirty water, lack of any kind of care, and sometimes cruel treatment, not to mention rat infestation. She learned many of the "patients" were very sane, indeed, and being driven somewhat mad by the abuse and beatings. She condemned the prescribing doctors and the attending nurses. Ten Days in a Mad-House brought about changes, and gave her great acclaim and name recognition. Her investigation is dramatized at the Newseum in Washington, D.C., as well as in the film 10 Days in a Madhouse in 2015.

But what made her most famous was her suggestion and follow-through to take a trip around the world, based on Jules Verne's fictional Phileas Fogg and his Around the World in Eighty Days. On November 14, 1889, sponsored by the New York World, she started her trek on the steamer "Augusta Victoria" from Hoboken, New Jersey to begin her 24,899-mile journey. Another female reporter hired by Cosmopolitan took the same journey, but going in the opposite direction. Bly beat her by over four days, completing the trip in just over seventy-two days, a record at the time. Newspapers sponsored contests on Bly's eventual arrival time. She traveled by ship, train, on animals, to England, Europe, the Suez Canal, Singapore, Hong Kong, China, Japan, and America. The last leg of the trip was on the newspaper owner's private train to Jersey City, New Jersey. Nellie Bly's Book: Around the World in Seventy-two Days came out soon after.

In 1895 Elizabeth Cochrane married Robert Seaman, forty-two years her senior, and he died only nine years later. She had retired from the newspaper business, and entered the barrel business, becoming president of the Iron Clad Manufacturing Company which made milk cans. They also created a fifty-five gallon steel oil drum, still used today. She had become one of the most prominent women industrialists in America. She did very well for a while, but employee problems and costs proved to be too much.

Nelly Bly was then back to newspaper reporting, particularly on World War 1 in Austria, and on suffrage events. And she had become a first-rate interviewer with such notables over the years as Jules Verne, Eugerne Debs and Belva Lockwood. Elizabeth Cochrane passed away from pneumonia on January 27, 1922 in St. Mark's Hospital in New York City, and is buried in Woodlawn Cemetery in The Bronx, New York City. In 2002 she was honored with a postage stamp. She is, of course, in the National Women's Hall of Fame.

There was a 1946 short-lived play, Nellie Bly, on Broadway and a 1998 one-woman touring show Did You Lie, Nellie Bly? In 1981 was a television movie, The Adventures of Nellie Bly. For years there was a Nellie Bly Amusement Park in Brooklyn whose theme was about going around the world, and there was once a board game, "Round the World with Nellie Bly." There are countless versions of Nellie Bly's life and adventures in books, television and on film. The New York Press Club gives out the "Nellie Bly Cub Reporter" award to an outstanding individual with three years or less experience.

#18- *Evangeline Booth (1865-1950)*

The General

Evelyne Cory Booth, the seventh child of Catherine and William Booth, was born on Christmas Day, 1865 in South Hackney, London, England. William, who had been a Methodist minister, retired in order to found the Christian Mission, which became the Salvation Army. He referred to it as army because it was to be a "fighting force at war with the powers of evil." She worked in her father's organization from childhood, and at the age of fifteen became a sergeant working in the slums of East London, at seventeen a captain, working some very difficult areas and slums of London. By age twenty-one, and in the 1880s, tall and thin Evangeline took charge as director of field operations throughout all of Great Britain, having gained the reputation as a problem solver. Her reputation called out, "If there's a problem, call Eva."
In 1891 she was named in charge of the International Training College. However, in 1896, her brother, Ballington Booth, broke from the organization and founded the Volunteers of America, also attempting to take over the Salvation Army. To prevent him from succeeding, Evangeline Booth came to America. She was locked out of the New York City headquarters, but she climbed in a back window, wrapped herself in an American flag, and dared her opposition to attack. They backed down; the rebellion was quelled, and she rallied the Salvation Army back to success.

Evangeline Booth first became temporary Territorial Commander of the United States, then temporary Territorial Commander of Canada. This was done due to her sister Emma and her husband, who had held this post, being killed in a train accident. In 1904, in recognition of her great work up to this time, she was again named Commander of the Salvation Army in the United States, a post she held until 1934. At about this time she changed her name to "Evangeline" at the suggestion of friends, because it sounded more sacred. National headquarters was in New York City, and Evangeline Booth made it the most outstanding and prosperous social service agency in the United States, building hospitals, soup kitchens, emergency shelters, homes for the aged, and provided employment services, and getting the organization respect.. In 1906 she raised thousands of dollars to aid the earthquake victims of San Francisco. After this, disaster relief was an integral part of the Salvation Army, as well as services to the homeless, alcoholics, an unwed mothers.

During World War I she assisted the American Expeditionary Forces with fundraising and offering supplies such as canteens, among other things, including Salvation Army volunteers going overseas to comfort the troops. She was honored with a Distinguished Service Medal. In 1934, she was again honored by becoming the first woman general. Not long after this she became a citizen of the United States.

She traveled widely to promote her work, to India, Australia, New Zealand, Hawaii, Norway, Sweden and France. Even though she became an American citizen, the international headquarters was in London, and she worked from there until she retired in 1939. Under this great public servant's leadership The Salvation Army spread its work to the less fortunate in such places as the Philippines, Egypt, Malaysia, Singapore, Algeria and Mexico, about eighty countries. At her father's strong suggestion, Evangeline Booth never married. He felt her strong personality would have been a problem. She did, however, adopt four children.

She returned and stayed in America until her death of arteriosclerosis on July 17, 1950 in Hartsdale, New York, and is buried in White Plains. She wrote Love Is All, Songs of the Evangel, Towards a Better World, and Woman. The Salvation Army Evangeline Booth College in Georgia is named for her, as is the Evangeline Booth Lodge in Chicago, catering to the homeless. Her New York home is on the National Register of Historic Places.

#19- *Gwendolyn Brooks* (1917-2000)

Poet Laureate

David and Keziah Brooks' daughter, Gwendolyn Elizabeth Brooks, was born on June 17, 1917 in Topeka, Kansas, but was brought to Chicago as a baby, growing up there, and spending most of her life there. It was in the segregated Bronzeville community on the southside of Chicago that influenced much of her writing and teaching. American Childhood magazine published her poem, "Eventide," when she was just thirteen. Within a few years she had contributed many poems to the "Lights and Shadows" poetry column of the The Defender, Chicago's African American newspaper. By the end of the 1930s she had graduated from Wilson Junior College, had become publicity director for the National Association for the Advancement of Colored People (N.A.A.C.P.), and had married Henry L. Blakely.

By the 1940s Gwendolyn Brooks poems began appearing in such periodicals as Poetry, the Yale Review, and The Saturday Review of Literature. Her A Street in Bronzeville was published in 1945, including "Kitchenette Building" and "Of DeWitt Williams on His Way to the Lincoln Cemetery." It was given immediate praise and given awards from the American Academy of Arts and Letters and from Mademoiselle magazine, and she was chosen as one of the ten most outstanding young women of the year. She had already won the Poetry Workshop Award from the Midwestern Writers Conference. Over the next two years she was given Guggenheim Fellowships. Over her lifetime she was given the Shelley Memorial Award, a Lifetime Achievement Award from the National Endowment for the Arts, and the National Book Foundation Medal for Distinguished Contributions to American Letters.

As if she was not successful and appreciated enough, her 1949 Annie Allen, which included such poems as "The Anniad" and "Manicure" made her place in American literature one of great success. Not only did this volume garner her the Eunice Tietjens Memorial Prize from Poetry, but also got her the prestigious Pulitzer Prize, the first African American to do so. Her poetry used such unusual images and descriptive terms. The popular urban childhood-themed thirty-six poem Bronzeville Boys and Girls followed her novella, Maud Martha, in 1953. All this led to her more militant, more controversial The Bean Eaters in 1960. There is "The Ghost at the Quincy Club," "The Last Quatrain of the Ballad of Emmett Till" and "We Real Cool".

Selected Poems of 1963 got her the Friends Literature Award for Poetry. And now she began to conduct writers workshops and getting involved with the publishing of more African American writers. She wrote with beauty about triumphs and the struggles of African Americans. In 1968, following the death of Carl Sandburg, Gwendolyn Brooks became the poet laureate of Illinois. But her poetry was still growing in its militancy, as reflected in both Riots and In the Mecca, the latter dealing with the search of a mother for her lost son.

In 1970 the Negro Digest started, because of her, an award for African American poets and poetry. Her next volumes were Family Pictures, Aloneness and Beckonings. 1972's Report From One Part was autobiographical in nature. Report From Part Two was published in 1995.

Gwendolyn Brooks was given an award from the National Institute of Arts, and given membership. Also bestowed on her was the Thormon Monsen Award. Throughout her lifetime she was granted many additional honors: the Robert Frost Medal; and the Aichen Taylor Award from Sewanee Review among others.

She died in on December 3, 2000 in Chicago. In 2002 she was declared to be among the 100 greatest African Americans. Especially prestigious was her being named Poet Laureate Consultant to the Library of Congress, given the Order of Lincoln, the highest honor by the State of Illinois, and the National Endowment for the Humanities' Jefferson Lecturer award, one of the highest honors given by the federal government. In 2012 a postage stamp was issued in her likeness. And she has, of course, been inducted into the National Women's Hall of Fame. There is a Gwendolyn Brooks Cultural Center as part of Western Illinois State University and a Gwendolyn Brooks Center for Black Literature at Chicago State University. In addition there are many schools, academies and libraries named in her honor. She was one of America's greatest poets.

#20- *Pearl Buck (1892-1973)*

The Good Earth

Pearl Sydenstricker Buck was born in June 26, 1892 in Hillsboro, West Virginia, and at five months was brought to Chinkiang, China by her Presbyterian missionary parents, Absalom and Caroline Sydenstricker, first in Huaian, then to Nanking. She actually spoke Chinese before English, and was educated in Shanghai. Her Chinese name was Sai Zhengzhu. As a teen she had short stories printed in the Shanghai Mercury.

Back in America she attended and graduated Phi Beta Kappa as class president from Virginia's Randolph-Macon College in 1914. However, she returned as a missionary to China, marrying agricultural missionary John L. Buck. In 1921 she began teaching English at the University of Nanking, Ginling College and the National Central University, living on the campus grounds, off and on to 1933. They briefly returned to America in 1924 where she earned her master's degree from Cornell University. In 1927 they went into hiding with the help of some poor Chinese, and eventually rescued by American gunboats. They then fled China due to the violence there and spent a year in Japan.

In 1929 Pearl Buck returned to the United States to get needed care for her daughter Carol, who suffered from phenylketonuria, which could lead to seizures, mental disorders and disability and behavior problems.

She had stories appearing in the Atlantic Monthly and other magazines. Pearl Buck published her first novel, East Wind, West Wind, in 1930. While teaching, she also wrote her most well-known work, The Good Earth, published in 1931. This garnered her the Pulitzer Prize, and in 1935 the William Dean Howell Medal from the American Academy of Arts and Letters. In 1938 she became the first American woman Nobel Prize for Literature winner, and it included her The Exile and The Fighting Angel, and biographies of her parents. In 1933 she received the O. Henry Memorial Award for her short story, "The Frill."

Over the next few years she resigned from the Presbyterian Board of Foreign Missions because she felt they really did not understand the Chinese culture, returned to America, divorced her husband, and married her publisher, Richard J. Walsh. Following this came The House of Earth, which in reality was The Good Earth and two sequels. The Good Earth was made into a play, and in 1937 the film version won the Oscar for best picture.

All in all Pearl Buck wrote eighty-five novels, and had been awarded the Brotherhood Award for Distinguished Service to Humanity. She became an advocate for women's rights, especially of minorities, and particularly Asian. In 1949 she co-founded Welcome House, an interracial adoption agency. In 1964 she founded the Pearl S. Buck Foundation dedicated to halt discrimination faced by Asian children, and in the same year founded Opportunity Center and Orphanage in South Korea. The "Opportunity" centers also were begun in Vietnam, the Philippines and Thailand. Her philanthropic and social generosity also spread to the issues of women's rights, immigration, and missionary work. After 1949 with the success of communism in China, she could not go back. During the Chinese Cultural Revolution she again was not allowed back in. Her 1962 Satan Never Sleeps condemned communist tyranny in China. Other noteworthy novels were: The Mother, Dragon Seed, The Big Wave, Letter From Peking, China Sky, Peony, All Men Are Brothers, Kinfolk, The Living Reed, The Long Love, Imperial Woman, and Come, My Beloved. In 1950 The Child Who Never Grew, about her daughter Carol born with that phenylketonuria, was published. My Several Worlds and A Bridge For Passing were autobiographies she wrote later in her life.

In 1973, All Under Heaven, about a couple returning to America after twenty-five years, was published. Pearl Buck died of lung cancer on March 6, 1973 in Danby, Vermont, and is buried near the home she shared with Walsh in Perkasie, Pennsylvania. He had died in 1960. In 1983 a United States postage stamp was issued in her honor. Her birth home in West Virginia, Stulting House, is now a historic site, and she has been inducted into the National Women's Hall of Fame. President George H.W. Bush visited China and commented on how he shared Pearl Buck's appreciation of China. In 1999 Buck was Women's History Month Honoree, sponsored by the National Women's History Project.

#21- Frances Burnett (1849-1924)

Little Lord Fauntleroy and The Secret Garden

Frances Burnett was born Frances Eliza Hodgson, daughter of Edwin, an ironmonger, and Eliza, in Manchester, England, on November 24, 1849. She attended the Select Seminary for Young Ladies and Gentlemen. When her father died when Frances was four years old, the family was reduced to financial hard times. In 1865 they moved near Knoxville, Tennessee, to be near an uncle who had a successful business. However, following the Civil War his business slumped, and Frances and her family were forced to live in a nearby log cabin. At nineteen years of age, Frances began writing stories for Scribner's, Harper's Bazaar, Peterson's Magazine and Godey's Lady's Book.

In her early twenties she married Swan M. Burnett, a Knoxville neighbor. They lived for a while in Paris, and then in Washington, D.C. Frances Burnett lived quite a lavish lifestyle there, and even though she made money writing, she spent much on clothing. To help with expenses she started making and designing clothes for her two sons, including velvet suits, lace collars and frills. She also hosted a literary salon on Tuesdays in her home, with writers and politicians often present. In 1877 her first of some forty novels was published. That Lass o'Lowrie's was about the life of the coal miners in Lancashire, and was a success. In the early 1880s she began submitting short works to St. Nicholas Magazine, and her play, Esmerelda, in 1881, went on to become the longest running Broadway play in the nineteenth century. In 1886 one of her most spectacular and well-known works, Little Lord Fauntleroy, was published. It is the tale of an American lad, Cedric, who becomes heir to an English dukedom. It had been translated into twelve languages. In it the clothing she had designed for her sons was included, and a fashion in boys' clothing was ushered in. Mothers thought it all wonderful while their sons hated the style. It was a favorite of Helen Keller. Little Lord Fauntleroy also went on to become a successful play, and also both a film and a television movie.

Other of Burnett's novels were dramatized, as well. 1888's Sara Crewe or What Happened at Miss Minchin's became the play, The Little Princess in 1905, and later into a film. In 1893 she wrote This One I Knew Best of All: A Memory of the Mind of a Child, dealing with the death of her older son, Lionel, from tuberculosis. In 1896 came The Lady of Quality, and in 1909, The Secret Garden. This last one, probably her most beloved and best remembered book, was also made into a film. In New York City's Central Park Conservatory Garden there is a memorial sculpture of the two main characters, Mary and Dickon, from The Secret Garden. Of the many books Frances Burnett wrote, it seems as if the ones that dealt with children were the best received and most memorable, which included The Little Pilgrims' Progress and Little Saint Elizabeth. However The Shuttle, T. Timbarom, and The Head of the House of Coombe were all very popular and big sellers. Other Burnett books are Lost Prince, Haworth, The Making of a Marchioness, Louisiana, A Fair Barbarian, In Connection with the DeWilloughby Claim, Through One Administration, The Methods of Lady Walderhurst, Robin, The Dawn of Tomorrow, and The Fortunes of Phillippa Fairfax. In her later years, at the urging of her son Vivian, now a publisher, she became an editor of Children's Magazine.

Her two most popular books were both highly successful, but while Little Lord Fauntleroy has faded somewhat, The Secret Garden is still quite popular.

Frances and Swan Burnett divorced in the late 1890s, but she was found to have been in somewhat of a scandalous situation with actor Stephen Townsend. After her divorce from Swan Burnett, she married the neer-do-well actor, which turned out to be a disaster. In 1902 Frances Burnett collapsed and entered herself into a sanitorium to recover, and divorced the unscrupulous Townsend. Throughout her life, Frances Burnett traveled extensively, and even lived for a while in England, France, Italy, Germany, Bermuda and the United States, of which she became a citizen in 1905. She died at her home in Plandome Manor, Long Island, New York on October 29, 1924. Her son Vivian also wrote her biography, The Romantick Lady. He is buried in Roslyn Cemetery on Long Island, near his mother, with a statue of her son Lionel nearby.

Group Three

"Mother" Cabrini-
Susan Ahn Cuddy

#22- Frances X. (Mother) Cabrini (1850-1917)

First American Saint

Maria Francesca Cabrini was born in the northern Italian village of Sant'Angelo di Lodi, near Milan, which then was part of the Austrian Empire, on July 15, 1850, the youngest of thirteen children of cherry farmers Agostino and Stella. She graduated cum laude in a school run by the Daughters of the Sacred Heart. She always felt she had the calling to be a missionary to India and China, but was rejected by those same Daughters due to her delicate health. So she settled on teaching in her village and those nearby.

A neighboring priest of Codogno asked if she would help at the House of Providence orphanage there, and though frail, she did, and, as headmistress, made it successful, even opening a school of nursing. In 1877 she took her vows as a nun, adding "Seviero" (Xavier) to her name, and she formed the Institute of Missionary Sisters of the Sacred Heart of Jesus in 1880, remaining superior general for the rest of her life, and resumed her orphanage work again, which had been disrupted by financial problems. By the early 1880s, she had a school in Milan. In 1887 she was in Rome where she founded another orphanage, and a kindergarten, and those worthy efforts gained the attention of Pope Leo XlII.

Cabrini tried desperately to have the Pope send her and her missionary sisters to China, but he convinced her to go to the United States, saying "Not to the East, but to the West." She arrived in America in New York City in 1889 to many problems, including Archbishop Michael Corrigan wanting her to go back to Italy. She managed to get lodging with the Sisters of Charity, and soon began teaching classes for Italian immigrants, and then, against all odds successfully started establishing schools, orphanages and hospitals. She concentrated on the big cities, principally New York, Denver, Chicago, New Orleans, Los Angeles, Philadelphia and Seattle. Among those most helped by Mother Cabrini were the poor Italian immigrants. During this time she also decided to become an American citizen, in 1909. She continued her work even outside of the urban areas, helping prisoners in Sing Sing prison in New York and to Colorado miners, and even in Central and South America.

Mother Cabrini died in Chicago from dysentary complications on December 22, 1917, while preparing Christmas for children. At the time of her death there were at least five thousand students in schools she started. Now there are many, many more. There were sixty-seven institutions she founded at the time of her passing. There are many streets, churches and hospitals that have been dedicated in her honor in at least 13 states. The Mother Cabrini Shrine in Golden, Colorado and the National Shrine of St. Frances Xavier Cabrini in

Lincoln Park, Chicago are among the most notable shrines in her honor. There are others. The Saint Frances Cabrini Church in New Orleans was destroyed by Hurricane Katrina in 2005. Cabrini College in Pennsylvania is named for her, as are countless schools on all levels throughout the United States, Puerto Rico and around the world.

In 1938 she was beatified and in 1946 Pope Pius Xll had her canonized as a saint. She is the first American citizen so honored. Her feast day is November 13, and is the patron saint of immigrants and hospital administrators. One hundred twenty thousand people attended a Mass of Thanksgiving at Soldier Field in Chicago on her canonization.

Francesca Severio Cabrini, Americanized Frances Xavier Cabrini, has also been inducted into the National Women's Hall of Fame. Her Missionaries of the Sacred Heart of Jesus, along with its volunteers supply teachers, nurses, social workers and administrators on six continents and in fifteen countries. The Cabrini Mission Foundation, also, carries on her work.

#23- *Rachel Carson* (1907-1964)

The Silent Spring

Robert and Maria Carson's daughter, Rachel Louise Carson, was born on May 27, 1907 in Springdale, Pennsylvania, not far from Pittsburgh. She graduated from the Pennsylvania College for Women, and received her master's degree in biology from Johns Hopkins University. She did further study at the Marine Biological Laboratory at Wood's Hole, Massachusetts, on her way to becoming one of history's greatest conservationists and marine biologists. They have erected a statue of her there.

From 1936 until 1952 she was a biologist for the United States Fish and Wildlife Service. Rachel Carson took this job supposedly only temporarily for the immediate needed income to care for her mother after her father had died. But she also became the editor-in-chief of its publications, and published her own book, Under the Sea Wind.

In 1951 The Sea Around Us was a deep study of the oceans from its origins, leading up to the most recent scientific findings. It is a great book and almost immediately hailed as a classic, and received the National Book Award for non-fiction, spending eighty-six weeks on the New York Times Best Seller List. It was followed in 1953 by The Edge of the Sea. This was made into an Academy Award winning documentary, but Carson was not pleased with it. At this time she moved to Maine and had enough financial security to write full time.

With its dedication to Albert Schweitzer, Rachel Carson's 1962 classic The Silent Spring wanted the world to be more cautious and accused mankind of gross misuse and irresponsibility due to careless overuse and indiscriminate use and disposal of chemicals and other pollutants. This was stated in an understandable and very clear way. It first was serialized in New Yorker magazine and was released as a novel in September of that year. This truly was the beginning of the worldwide controversy/debate over the use of pesticides. She pointed out factually the causes of harm to humans and wildlife, and issued a dire warning about the future. She wanted transparency of details, research and controls. It is still relevant today! It was a best seller and garnered for Carson the Conservation Award for 1962, and the Albert Einstein College of Medicine Achievement Award. In addition, awards and praise poured in from all over. This book, in some ways, was a horror story, but was milestone book of the twentieth century.

Although Carson felt tremendous opposition from many businesses and politicians, she did, indeed, advance the environmental movement, and led not only to the banning of DDT and other harmful chemicals, but also led to the formation of the United States Environmental Protection Agency. Many laws were already on the books, but disregarded, mainly because chemical big business knew you wanted the grass even greener and all the bugs dead, and the politicians closed their eyes! She was given the National Outdoor Writers Award for Distinguished Service, the Isaak Walton League's Annual Founders Award, the Constance Lindsay Skinner Achievement Award, the Schweitzer Medal, as well as praise from former Secretary of the Interior Stewart Udall. In a 1994 reprint of The Silent Spring Vice president Al Gore wrote the introduction. The impact of the book was enormous and timely, but led to many industry attacks on Carson.

Rachel Carson did not live too long to bathe in the praise. She was diagnosed with cancer in 1960 and died on April 14, 1964 in Silver Spring, Maryland. Unfortunately, many of the issues still exist.

In Maine there is now a Rachel Carson National Wild Life Refuge, schools named after her in Maryland, Washington, Oregon, Virginia and even Brooklyn, New York, and a Rachel Carson College at the University of California at Santa Cruz. In Pittsburgh they named a bridge in her honor and the Pennsylvania Department of Environmental Protection did the same with their headquarters. Her home in Springdale has been preserved and placed on the National Register of Historic Places and the same with the one in Silver Spring.

Over her lifetime she was also awarded the Audubon Medal, the Burroughs Medal, the Cullen Geographic Medal, inducted into the American Academy of Arts and Sciences, had a postage stamp issued in her honor, and became a member of both the Maryland and National Womens Hall of Fame, and postumously granted the Presidential Medal of Freedom in 1980 from Jimmy Carter.

#24- Mary Cassatt (1844-1926)

American Impressionist

One of America's truly outstanding artists was Mary Stevenson Cassatt, born of well-to-do parents, stockbroker Robert and Katherine, in Allegheny City, Pennsylvania, now a part of Pittsburgh, on May 22, 1844. Her father's French family dated back to New Amsterdam in 1622. Her family moved to Lancaster, but then settled in Philadelphia when she was young.

But as was proper for young wealthy girls, she traveled for a number of years to England, Italy, Spain, Holland, Belgium, Germany and France as a child, becoming fluent in both French and German. For the first time she witnessed the works of Edgar Degas and Camille Pissarro in Paris in 1855. Her interest in art was resisted by her father, but she did attend the Pennsylvania Academy of Fine Arts, and managed again to go to Paris as an aspiring artist, with her mother as chaperone, in 1866. Her first real success was the romantic "A Mandolin Player." But she soon was influenced by and became friends with Impressionist Degas. She also became friends with Claude Monet and Pissarro, both of the Impressionist world.

In 1870, she returned to America, to Altoona, Pennsylvania. The Bishop of Pittsburgh heard of her abilities, and requested, expenses paid, for her to go to Parma, Italy and make copies of Antonio da Correggio paintings there. She went, completed her commission, and remained in Europe. Her concentration was on images of the private occasions of women, particularly of mothers and children. In 1877 she received an invitation from Degas, and from 1879 to 1888 she began showing her work with the Impressionists and had great success in her own first show in 1891. She had gone from an "indoor" artist to an "outdoor" one.

Two years later she was commissioned to work on the Women's Building at the Columbian Exposition in Chicago. This work showed her "Modern Woman" as representing women as accomplished people in their own right. The theme of the work was a young woman plucking the fruits of knowledge, surrounded by young girls pursuing fame, and by art, music and dance. Unfortunately it was lost when the building was razed. It was the first artistic public appointment for a woman. Cassatt was now becoming a role model for aspiring female artists.

She established a studio in Paris and became known particularly for those themes on maternal subjects. Children were depicted with a greatness of originality, truthful without being pretty. She was one of the main forces bringing acceptance of Impressionistic art in America. Some of her best works are, "Maternity," "Mother and Child," and "The Young Mother." Her "In the Box" has been sold for over four million dollars.

Among her other more well-known works were: "The Boating Party," "Pearl Necklace," "Little Girl in a Blue Armchair," "Young Woman in a Black and Green Bonnet," "Spanish Dancer Wearing a Lace Mantilla," "Summertime," "Woman Standing Holding a Fan," "Lilacs in the Window," "Woman in a Loge," "The Bath," "Two Women Throwing Flowers During Carnival," "Portrait of the Artist's Mother," "Portrait of Alexander Cassatt and His Son Robert Kelso," "Self-portrait," "Tea," "Girl Arranging Her Hair," "At the Theater," "Under a Horse Chestnut Tree," "At the Opera," "After the Bullfight." and "Mother and Child Before a Pool." Starting 1886 she started showing her work in New York City galleries, and had two of her paintings as part of the first Impressionist exposition there. The 1890s were here most successful period, and she even became enthralled with "japonism," the simple, but clear Japanese design.

She was most responsible for promoting Impressionism, and particularly Degas, in America. In 1915 she put on a joint exposition with Degas to promote and support women's suffrage. Cassatt also urged making donations to American art museums. She began going blind in 1914, and also suffered from diabetes and rheumatism. Mary Cassatt died in France on June 19, 1926.

The television series, The Originals: Women in Art, opened with the story of Mary Cassatt. An award-winning string group, the Cassatt Quartet, was named in her honor. She had been awarded the French Legion of Honor and is inducted into the National Women's Hall of Fame. In 1943 the liberty ship, the SS Mary Cassatt, was launched. Not only was her "The Boating Party" made into a stamp in 1966, but four of her paintings, "Young Mother," "Children Playing on the Beach," "On a Balcony," and "Child in a Straw Hat" were part of the Great Americans stamp series.

#25- *Willa Cather (1873-1947)*

Prairies and Plains

Real estate businessman Charles and his wife Mary's daughter, (Wilella) Willa Sibert Cather, became one of the greatest of the American regional writers, and considered one of the top writers of the first half of the twentieth century, was born in Gore, near Winchester, Virginia on February 7, 1873. In 1883 the family moved to Nebraska, eventually to Red Cloud. Some of Cather's earliest writing appeared in the Red Cloud Chief and the Nebraska State Journal. In 1895 she graduated from the University of Nebraska, but relocated to Pittsburgh, becoming an editor of the Home Monthly, a women's magazine, and in 1897 of the Daily Leader. Eventually she became its managing editor.

In 1901 she turned to teaching, becoming a department head in 1906, and at the same time had begun writing, with a volume of poetry, April Twilights, appearing in 1903, but garnering little interest. However, in 1905, The Troll Garden, a collection of stories of Nebraska, did gain some notice, especially the stories, "Paul's Case" and "A Wagner Matinee."

In 1906 she was offered a job at New York City's McClure's Magazine, of which she became managing editor from 1908 until 1912. In 1909 she co-authored The Life of Mary Baker Eddy and the History of Christian Science. Her first novel, of Boston life, Alexander's Bridge, was published during this time.

1913, however, with the publishing of O! Pioneers Cather was established as a great novelist. It brought her huge success and a national reputation. It told the story of the hard-working, humble, everyday people who settled the plains. It was also the first part of a trilogy of the plains and prairies. Song of the Lark appeared in 1915, and in 1918, My Antonia. This last novel, probably her most well-known is a story of a frontier girl of the plains, some of it probably based one of her girlhood friends: happy though desperate, taking care of her family, squelching her own artistic longings. It was apparent that Willa Cather knew the ways of the average folks of the Nebraska area. However, her short story collection, Youth and the Bright Medusa, in 1920, also displayed the artistically suffocating prairies.

In 1922 she purchased a summer home on Grand Manon Island in New Brunswick. It is the setting for her classic short story, "Before Breakfast," and in 1923, One of Ours, set in the World War I period, despairs of the loss of the wonderful pioneering spirit. It won the Pulitzer Prize. This was followed by The Lost Lady, showing a dignified and charming woman trying to deal with the same disillusioning theme, as does 1925's The Professor's House.

Finally a change came with Death Comes to the Archbishop in 1927. Cather had converted from Baptist to Episcopalian, but had also become very curious of certain aspects of Catholicism. This interest of hers is reflected here in not her best-selling or most-known work, but just possibly might be her best. Set in the New Mexico it is pessimistic, yet realistic. Shadows on the Rock, set in seventeenth century Quebec, won her the Prix Femina Americaine in 1931, and also displays the interest in Catholicism. Her most accomplished short stories were published in Obscure Destinies in 1932, including "Neighbor Rosicky." 1933 brought the dark Lucy Gayheart, which was also a best seller.

Willa Cather came to believe that many Americans were too materialistic and mercenary. She always admired those pioneers as opposed to what she saw as many shallow people. She was bitter and wanted Americans to know that the rough life of the frontier, though not glamorous or artistic, was more alive and superior to the later development of refinement. She also wrote Not Under Forty, My Mortal Enemy, the very dark Sapphira and the Slave Girl, and The Old Beauty. Willa Cather died on April 24, 1947 of a cerebral hemorrhage in New York City and is buried in Jaffrey, New Hampshire. At the time of her death she was working on Hard

Punishments, set in Avignon, France in the mid-1300s. The core of the novel centers on two youths, one who has his tongue torn out for blasphemy.

She received an honorary degree from Princeton University, a gold medal for fiction from the National Institute of Arts and Letters, and had been elected to the American Academy of Arts and Letters. The United States Mint created a half-ounce gold medallion in her image in 1981. She has been inducted into the Nebraska Hall of Fame (and a University of Nebraska building bears her name), the Virginia Women of History, the National Cowgirl Museum and Hall of Fame, and the New York Writers Hall of Fame, and the National Women's Hall of Fame.

In 1973 a Willa Cather United States Postal Service stamp was issued and in 2005 PBS aired the documentary "Willa Cather: The Road is All." The National Endowment of the Humanities gave a grant to the Willa Cather Foundation to preserve and curate her home in Red Cloud, creating "Catherland."

#26- Carrie Chapman Catt (1859-1947)

Successful Successor

Carrie Clinton Lane Chapman Catt was one of the most important women in the suffrage movement and who successfully completed the work begun by Elizabeth Cady Stanton and Susan B. Anthony. She was born on January 9, 1859 in Ripon, Wisconsin, but was raised in Charles City, Iowa by her parents Lucius and Maria Lane. She graduated as valedictorian from Iowa State Agricultural College in 1880 in Ames, and went on to both study law and teach school, becoming a principal, and in 1883 the district superintendent of the Mason City, Iowa schools, the first woman to hold that position.

In 1884 she married editor Leo Chapman, and when she went to join him in California in 1886, she found he had just died. She remained in San Francisco for a while, becoming that city's first female reporter. In 1887 she was back in Iowa, and at this time became more aware of the suffrage movement, and became active organizing the Iowa Woman Suffrage Association. And in 1890 married engineer George W. Catt.

In 1904 Carrie Chapman Catt became president of the International Suffrage Alliance, until 1923. But prior to this she began to be associated with the National American Woman Suffrage Association, becoming a speaker at their convention in 1890. In 1892 Susan B. Anthony asked Catt to address the Congress of the United States on the proposition of granting women the right to vote. She eventually succeeded Anthony as president in 1900, serving until 1904. She resigned to care for her ailing husband, though he died in 1905. She returned as president to repair a damaged organization from 1915 to 1920. It was through her tireless efforts that she first got the United States congress to back the amendment, and then traveled extensively to get the individual states to grant their approval. She again resigned, but only because the suffrage amendment had passed, and she felt her job there was done.

In 1911 and 1912 she had gone on a worldwide tour promoting women's rights, and with the passage of the nineteenth amendment, Catt founded the National League of Women's Voters, formed to assist women now that they were voters. She remained as honorary president until her death. It was, indeed, due to her efforts toward the end of this struggle that the nineteenth amendment, giving women the right to vote, was passed in 1920. She was really the uncontested leader of the end fight. In 1926 she made the cover of Time magazine and was given the Pictorial Review Award in 1930. She is considered one of the best-known women of the first half of the twentieth century, and on any list of outstanding women, her name is sure to be there. However, to secure success in her long fight for women's suffrage, Catt made many controversial moves, including jumping back and forth on the sides of issues just to gain support, and then reverting back to her previous stand.

In addition to her ardent interest in women's rights, Carrie Chapman Catt fostered the keeping of peace and founded the National Committee on the Cause and Cure of War. She wrote Why Wars Must Cease. To show her displeasure with Hitler, in 1933 she organized the Protest Committee of Non-Jewish Women Against the Persecution of Jews in Germany. She was awarded the American Hebrew Medal.

Carrie Chapman Catt was that last needed connection from those early fighters for women's suffrage to her, with continually speaking, organizing and writing until the goal was achieved, and beyond. When the state of Tennessee gave that last state approval, the basic part of her job was done. Woman Suffrage and Politics: The inner Story of the Suffrage Movement was her summation. In 1919 Carrie Chapman Catt moved to Westchester County, New York, and in 1928 to New Rochelle there. She died of a heart attack in New Rochelle on March 9, 1947. In the 2004 film, Iron-Jawed Angels, Catt was portrayed by Anjelica Histon. She was also a character in the 2014 play, Winter Wheat, about that state vote in Tennessee.

Carrie Chapman Catt has been honored in many ways. There is a Carrie Chapman Catt Girlhood Home in Charles City, Iowa. The Tennessee Suffrage Monument in Centennial Park in Nashville has a sculpture of Catt and four others, and Eleanor Roosevelt presented her the Chi Omega award. She was honored on a postage stamp in 1948, the Iowa Memorial Foundation has named her one of the ten most important women of the century, and has been honored at the Iowa Women of Achievement Bridge in Des Moines, as well as Iowa State University having a Carrie Chapman Catt Center for Women and Politics. She is in the Iowa Women's Hall of Fame and the National Women's Hall of Fame.

#27- *Shirley Chisholm (1924-2005)*

Unbought and Unbossed

Factory worker Charles St. Hill emigrated to the United States from British Guiana and seamstress Ruby St. Hill emigrated from Barbados to Brooklyn, New York. They married and Shirley Anita St. Hill (later Chisholm) was their daughter, born there on November 30, 1924, and would become not only the first African American woman elected to Congress, but also the first African American to seek to be the presidential nomination of a major political party. At the age of five Shirley was sent to stay with her maternal grandmother in Barbados for five years, and forever afterward had that accent. When she came home she eventually attended and graduated with honors from Brooklyn College, where she was a member of the debate club. She had been offered a number of scholarships to other colleges, but her family was so poor that they would not be able even to afford the room and board. She went further acquiring a master's degree in elementary education from Columbia University, and married private investigator Conrad Chisholm in 1949.

From 1953 to 1959 she was a teacher, and then director, of the Hamilton-Madison Child Care Center, and thereafter became a counselor/consultant with the New York City Bureau of Child Welfare, becoming quite the expert on early childhood education and welfare. Chisholm also joined the League of Women Voters and conditions prompted her also to get involved with the local Democratic Party club and in politics. In 1965 she ran and was elected to the New York State Assembly, and remained there until 1968, concentrating on unemployment benefits and remedial education. In 1968 she decided to take a chance and seek the Democratic Party nomination for Congress in her Brooklyn neighborhood. It was a tough three-way primary, but she pulled it off, basically with just her own friends and supporters, and then went on to win the election, defeating famous civil rights activist James Farmer, becoming the first African American woman elected to the United States House of Representatives. She remained there for seven terms.

In Congress she was first put on the Forestry Committee and the Agriculture Committee, and feeling assigned where her constituents would not benefit, she complained. She was still able to get the Special Supplemental Nutritional Program for Women, Infants and Children passed, and managed to eventually get assigned to the Veteran's Affairs Committee and the Education and Labor Committee. Chisholm became a member both of the Congressional Black Caucus and the National Woman's Political Caucus. Her speech, "For the Equal Rights Amendment" is considered one of the greatest speeches of the twentieth century.

"I wish to introduce today a proposal that has been before every Congress for the last 40 years, and sooner or later must become part of the basic law of the land... Existing laws are not adequate to secure equal rights for women. Sufficient proof of this is the concentration of women in low-paying menial, unrewarding jobs..."

In 1970 she wrote her early biography, Unbought and Unbossed. She also decided to make a run for the presidential nomination of the Democratic Party in 1972, the first African American woman to do so. However, she really was too poorly funded, and she felt no one took her seriously, thinking she was just doing this to make a statement, or be a symbol. Although NOW (National Organization for Women) endorsed her and major female spokespersons came out for her, such as Betty Fridan and Gloria Steinem, the campaign did not go well. The best she did in any state primary was seven and one-half percent, and only less than three percent overall. At the convention she came in fourth place. However, it was a fact by the end of the election process she was ranked as one of the ten most admired women in the world.

One of the other candidates was segregationist George Wallace from Alabama, who was shot and severely wounded early on. Even though she and Wallace were on opposite sides in so many ways, she still went to visit him in the hospital. Later on, George Wallace came to bat for Shirley Chisholm, by urging southern representatives to vote for her efforts to have a law passed granting minimum wage to domestic workers. The Good Fight was her take on the election. She would remain in congress, retiring in 1983, always trying for inner-city people and for peace, and opposed to the Vietnam war. She and Conrad Chisholm divorced in 1977, and Shirley married a former New York State assemblyman Arthur Hardwick from Buffalo. He died in 1986.

After her time in politics, Shirley Chisholm remained involved. She became the Purington Chair at Mary Lyon's Mt. Holyoke College, while still being a visiting scholar at Spelman College. She went on lecture tours, speaking at over one hundred and fifty college campuses, mostly on the evil of intolerance. She also helped found the African-American Women for Reproductive Freedom. There are numerous biographies written about her. In 1991 she retired to Florida. In 1993 President Clinton nominated Shirley Chisholm as Ambassador to Jamaica, but she was too ill to accept. Over her retirement years, she suffered a series of strokes. She died in Ormond Beach, Florida on January 1, 2005, and is buried in Buffalo, New York.

She is on the list of One Hundred Greatest African Americans, and has been inducted into the National Women's Hall of Fame. In 2005 Shirley Chisholm '72: Unbought and Unbossed, was a documentary presented at the Sundance Film Festival. It went on to win a Peabody Award, the "Pulitzer Prize of media." There is a Shirley Chisholm Center For Research on Women at Brooklyn College. In 2014 a stamp in her honor was issued, and in 2015 pioneer Shirley Anita Chisholm was awarded the Presidential Medal of Freedom posthumously by President Obama.

#28- Alice Coachman (1923-2014)

First Olympian

Alice Marie Coachman was born in Albany, in southwest Georgia on November 9, 1923 to her parents, plasterer Fred and Evelyn Coachman. Always the tomboy, she was interested in track events, but without access in the segregated South to facilities, training and equipment, she would practice running barefoot and on her own.

While she attended Madison High School, she was entered in the AAU (Amateur Athletic Union) Women's National Championships. Not only did she break the existing high jump record, she dominated high jump for the next ten years. At sixteen Tuskeegee Prepatory School in Macon County, Alabama. offered her a scholarship. She continued on to Tuskeegee Institute itself. Coachman also consistently won the fifty meter dash, the one hundred meter dash and was part of the winning four hundred meter relay team. All in all Alice Coachman won twenty-five AAU titles. She also won three conference championships as a guard on Tuskeegee's women's basketball team, graduating in 1946. Later she went to Albany State College where she got a degree after the Olympics in 1949. She broke records on all levels: high school, college, national and Olympic.

Due to World War ll, the 1940 and 1944 Olympics were cancelled. This was in her athletic prime. But in the 1948 Olympics in London, in the preliminary round she broke the world record. On her first try during the meet she broke the record again. She became the first African-American woman to win an Olympic gold medal, and the first Black from any country. She was given her medal by King George VI. Arriving home she met President Harry Truman and former first lady, Eleanor Roosevelt. There were parades for her in Atlanta and Albany, Georgia. Even the famous (William) Count Basie threw her a party. In her hometown of Albany she was honored in the Albany Municipal Auditorium, on the stage with the mayor, who did not shake her hand, and before a separated segregated audience. She quit running.

Those Olympic games of 1948 were her last competitions. But she had set the bar for others such as Wilma Rudolph and Jackie Joyner-Kersee and others to follow. She went on to become a coach and physical education teacher in elementary and high school, and college, retiring in 1987. Coachman also briefly worked with Job Corps. She had married N. F. Davis, had two children, Rich and Diane, and divorced, and later married Frank A. Davis, who died in 1992. She became the first African-American woman to endorse an international product, Coca Cola. There is a street and a school named after her in her home town.

In 1996, at the Atlanta Olympic games she not only was honored as one of the one hundred greatest Olympians, she was selected to be one of the final twelve Olympic torch bearers. She told The New York Times, "If I had gone to the Games and failed, there wouldn't be anyone to follow in my footsteps." In the same period she was one of the included in Avon's "The Olympic Woman," part of New York's Olympic Arts Festival. In 2002 the National Women's Project made her a Women's History Month Honoree. She herself found the Alice Coachman Track and Field Foundation, which benefits older and retired Olympians.

Alice Coachman has been inducted into the Alabama Sports Hall of Fame, the USA Track and Field Hall of Fame and the United States Olympic Hall of Fame. As a result of a stroke she was placed in a nursing home, but died from breathing problems and cardiac arrest in Albany, Georgia on July 14, 2014.

#29- *Jacqueline Cochran (1906-1980)*

Speed Queen

Bessie Lee Pittman, who later became pioneer aviator Jacqueline Cochran, was born on May 11, 1906 in the now non-existent town of Muscogee, and grew up in De Furiak Springs, on the Florida panhandle, not far from Pensacola. Her parents, millwright Ira and Mary Pittman, were very poor. Bessie had very little formal education, and worked in the mill, but also got a job cleaning up in a local beauty parlor, after a while learning how to style hair. Still a teenager she married Robert (Jack) Cochran, and had a son who died young. Around this time she began calling herself Jacqueline, or Jackie. This is when the name Jacqueline Cochrane came into being, whose marriage only lasted until 1927, and who forever after would say she was adopted and did not reveal anything of her early life.

She became a hairdresser in Pensacola, but eventually left for New York City and a job with Saks Fifth Avenue. She did so well, she would travel with her wealthier clients. On such a trip to Miami in 1932 she met Floyd B. Odium, founder of the Atlas Corporation, and CEO of RKO studios in Hollywood. He was fourteen years older than the very pretty Cochran, and became infatuated with her.

Around the same time she had been taking flying lessons at Roosevelt Field on Long Island, and soon she had a pilot's license. In 1934 she became the only woman to enter the MacRobertson Air Race, from London to Melbourne. In 1935 she entered the Bendix Race, and won it in 1938, and worked with Amelia Earhart to open aviation to women. Jacqueline Cochran went on to set speed, altitude and distance records. She won five Harmon trophies as the most outstanding female pilot, and took on the nickname, "Speed Queen." By the time of her death she had more aviation records in all areas of flight than any pilot, male or female.

Meanwhile, Odium set her up in her own cosmetics line she called Jacqueline Cochran Cosmetics, "Wings." Cochran married Odium in 1936. With her pilot's license, she would fly promotional tours for her cosmetics.

Just prior to America getting into World War II, Cochran went to England to work for "Wings for Britain", transporting American-built aircraft to England, at that time becoming the first woman to fly a bomber, a Lockheed Hudson V, across the Atlantic Ocean. Then she became a flight captain for England's Air Transport Auxiliary. With assistance from Eleanor Roosevelt in 1940 she urged the creation of a women's flying division of the Army Air Force, with women pilots flying domestic jobs in order to free up more men for combat. At first denied, but eventually she got permission from General "Hap" Arnold to train twenty-five women pilots in England to join England's auxiliary. In America in 1943 she headed up the Women's Flying Training Detachment, which then merged with another similar group, which became the Women Air force Service Pilots (WASP), with Cochran as director and trained in Sweetwater, Texas to do those domestic duties. During the war she also became the first woman to take off on an aircraft carrier.

Following the war she wrote for Liberty magazine covering both General Tomoyuki Yamashita surrender, and the Nuremberg trials in Germany. She also joined the United States Air Force Reserve, as a lieutenant-colonel, eventually a full colonel, retiring in 1970.

In 1953 she flew an F-86 Sabre to 652.337 miles per hour, the first woman to break the sound barrier and go "supersonic." As a consultant and test pilot for the Northrop Corporation in 1961 she got an aircraft up to 56,072. 83 feet. In 1964 she flew at a rate of speed 1429 miles per hour. If that was not all, she even flew the Goodyear Blimp. Early on she was in favor of female astronauts, but when it became apparent that the requirements would have eliminated her from contention, she let it go. Cochran also became director at Northwest Airlines. In 1951 the Boston Chamber of Commerce voted her as one of the top twenty-five outstanding women in business. In 1953 and 1954 the Associated Press selected her as "Woman of the Year in Business." With his Hollywood connections, her husband got Marilyn Monroe to endorse "Wings" lipstick. She sold her cosmetics firm in 1963.

She had also become friends with General Dwight D. Eisenhower, and she is partially responsible for getting him to seek the presidency, and worked for that campaign. She tried to run for congress herself in her home district in California, and failed, just barely, getting close to forty-nine percent.

Except for her congressional loss, Jacqueline Cochran was, by all accounts, a winner. She received the gold medal from the Federation Aeronautique Internationale, and later was the president. She is also the recipient of the Legion of Merit, the Distinguished Service Medal, and on three occasions the Distinguished Flying Cross, as well as the American Campaign Medal, World War II Victory Medal, Armed Forces Reserved Medal and the Turkish Diamond Brevet. Her 1954 autobiography was entitled The Stars at Noon.

She has been inducted into the National Aviation Hall of Fame, the International Aviation Hall of Fame, the Motorsports Hall of Fame, the Aerospace Walk of Honor, The Florida Women's Hall of Fame, and the National Women's Hall of fame. A display of Cochran material is on display at the United States Air Force Academy in Colorado. In 1970 she had to have a pacemaker, and that was the end of her flying. She suffered a heart attack and died in her Indio, California home on August 9, 1980, and is buried in nearby Coachilla, California. In 2004 the local airport was renamed the Jacqueline Cochran Regional Airport, where there is a biennial Jacqueline Cochran Air Show. Jacqueline Cochran was not as well-known as her friend Amelia Earhart, but her accomplishments actually were superior.

#30- *Bessie Coleman* (1893-1926)

Queen Bess

(Elizabeth) Bessie Coleman was born in a cabin in Atlanta, Texas on January 26, 1893, and moved to Waxahachie as a youngster, and picked cotton and did laundry. Her mother Susan was African-American and a maid. Her father George was African-American and Native American, and left to return to his Oklahoma reservation when she was still a youngster. She enrolled in Langston Industrial College in Oklahoma, but had to quit due to lack of funds. She moved back to Texas for a while, but then went to live with her relatives in Chicago in 1915, worked as a waitress, and went to the Barnham School of Beauty, becoming a manicurist at the White Sox Barber Shop. Here she heard stories of the World War I returning servicemen talking about flying. Eventually she wound up marrying Claude Glenn, a much older man.

And now all she could think of and read about was flying because she felt it brought respect, but due to facts that she was both a woman, and an African American, she was not accepted to any flying school. So, on the advice and assistance of Robert S. Abbot, a successful newspaper publisher, she saved her money, learned some French, and sailed for France in November, 1920, and was accepted at the Ecole d'Aviation des Freres Caudron there, taking lessons from both French and German aviators. On June 15, 1921 she became the first African American, and first Native American, woman to earn an international pilot's license, from the Federation Aeronautique Internationale. She remained in France for a short while, taking more lessons. She returned to the United States as a media sensation, but tried in vain to earn money, so returned briefly to France, Holland and Germany in 1922, and in this less racist atmosphere was a huge success and big news, as a flying circus performer, doing stunts at air shows, even met Anthony Fokker, the Dutch aircraft designer, who admired her.

Back in America, Queen Bess, as she came to be called, would take people up for rides and would try to encourage a delivery and passenger service. She did the stunts the crowds love to see: loops, flying upside down, flying very low, figure 8s, flying up, up, up and the engine would fail, so she would dive, apparently going to crash, and at the last second, pull up. And to add to her appeal, she always dressed in a flamboyant manner, with a long military-type coat and leather boots. Her first show was at Curtiss Field on Long Island on Labor Day, 1922, billed as "the World's Greatest Female Pilot". She also performed in Columbus and Chicago. And the very well-spoken Bessie Coleman also lectured on flying, hoping to earn enough money to open her own flying school. A film, "Shadow and Sunshine," by the African American Seminole Film Producing Company was to star Bessie Coleman, but she dropped out because she felt she was being racially stereotyped. This alienated many of the black entrepreneurs who put up the backing, and labeled her unreliable.

Barnstorming in Tennessee, Illinois, Florida, New York and Texas, and finally, in 1924, Bessie went to California where she received an endorsement from the Coast Tire & Rubber Company to do promotion work, and she was able to buy her own plane, an old Curtiss JN-4, known as a Jenny for $400. Performing in southern California on February 22, 1923, her plane's engine went dead, she stalled, dove and crashed. She had a broken leg and ribs, some cuts and bruises, and internal injuries that kept her grounded for a year. And the plane was lost. Bessie went back to Chicago, but found no help due to poor weather and some doubting her reliability after the crash. Then it was off to Texas in 1925 and in Houston, Dallas, San Antonio, Fort Worth and smaller cities and towns she found success putting on air shows, giving rides and lecturing with great bluster and a good deal of exaggeration. She really was quite a little beauty, and very vivacious. From there it was off to Savannah, Atlanta and Augusta, Georgia and St. Petersburgh, Tampa, West Palm Beach and Orlando, Florida. In Orlando she became "born again" and her friend the Reverend Hezakiah Hill urged her not to do any more stunts.

Since she no longer owned her own plane, she had to borrow them, and sometimes it limited what she could do. But in 1926 she finally managed to get her own plane, although a very old one, through the generosity of Edwin Beeman, a chewing gum magnate. The plane was in Texas and she arranged for it to be flown to Florida by pilot and mechanic William Wills. It broke down twice in Mississippi on its journey. Robert Abbott, her friend and advisor was in Jacksonville, and he, too, urged her not to fly.

In this instance Wills was to pilot and Bessie was going to parachute down to the crowds. On April 30, 1926, at the Jacksonville Negro Welfare League's Celebration, on an aerial tour of the field before the performance, the plane in which she was a passenger, went up to 3500 feet, accelerated unexpectantly, went into a nose-dive and a tail-spin, and flipped over, with Bessie falling out at about 2000 feet. She was killed. She was not wearing her seat belt because she wanted to lean over to study the field.

There was a service for her in Orlando with 5000 people in attendance. Coleman's body was sent to Chicago. And even though the white press ignored her in life, they also did in her death. But she had overcome the dual handicaps, at the time, of being a woman and being African American. William J. Powell, a service station owner in Chicago admired her so, that he sold his business, went to Los Angeles and with the help of some other admirers, opened the Bessie Coleman Aero Club in 1929.

In Chicago there is a plaque on the home in which she lived and a Bessie Coleman Aviator's Club was started, and a tradition of flying over Bessie Coleman's grave was begun every Memorial Day. It was discontinued for a while, but revived in 1980. In 1990 Mayor Richard M. Daly renamed a street at O'Hare Airport "Bessie Coleman Drive." There's a library there named for her, as well. Oakland, California's airport also has a road named for her, and also in Orlando. In 2012 a plaque was also placed at the Paxon School of Advanced Studies at the Jacksonville airfield. In 1995 a postage stamp was issued with her likeness. She has been inducted into the National Women's Hall of Fame and the National Aviation Hall of Fame, and voted one of the "51 Heroes of Aviation" by Flying Magazine.

#31- Miriam Colon (1936-2017)
The Puerto Rican Traveling Theater

National Medal of Arts winner Mama Montana! No it it is Miriam Colon, born in Ponce, Puerto Rico on August 30, 1936, but moved with her mother when young to a housing project in San Juan. While in high school in Old San Juan she was given the opportunity to sit in on drama classes at the University of Puerto Rico. She made her film debut as Lolita in Los Peloteros (The Baseball Players) and managed a scholarship to the Dramatic Workshop and Technical Institute of Elia Kazan's Acting Studio, which was under the direction of Lee Strasburg.

Over the next fifty years or so she made many movies, many of them westerns. A most notable role was as Mama (Georgina) Montana, the mother of Al Pacino's Tony Montana in 1983's Scarface (even though she was only four years older than him), famously saying, "He was a bum then, and he's a bum now!" Another iconic role was in 2013's Bless Me, Ultima. She was also so good as the legendary madam/gangster/brothel owner Isabel la Negra in The Life of

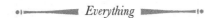

Sin. Along the way she also appeared in two movies with Marlon Brando, One-Eyed Jacks and The Appaloosa, as well as Gloria, Sabrina, Lone Star, Goal! The Dream Begins, I and II and so much more. She also appeared on Broadway in The Summer House, The Innkeeper and The Wrong Way Lightbulb.

Her diverse talents also brought her to television, where not only did she appear in soap operas such as Guiding Light, All My Children and The Edge of Night, she appeared in practically every prime time show made in the 1950s to the twenty-first century: Gunsmoke, Bonanza, Alfred Hitchcock Presents, The Dick Van Dyke Show, Dr. Kildare, The Fugitive, Law and Order, Murder, She Wrote, The Virginian, Bronco, Law and Order SVU, Sanford and Son, Better Call Saul, Highway to Heaven, and countless more. In 1966 she married George Paul Edgar, who died in 1976.

There had existed in New York City a group called El Nuevo Circulo Dramatico (The New Drama Circuit) presenting Hispanic and Puerto Rican theater. It was struggling until they put on a play in 1953, La Carreta, starring a young Miriam Colon. The success jump-started the organization. In 1966 Colon took the English version, The Oxcart, to off-Broadway. It was in this play that she met Fred Valle, who would become her husband in 1987. This play was also a success, but now El Nuevo Circulo Dramatico was dying. The next year she founded the Puerto Rican Traveling Theater, and with assistance from New York City, initially it traveled to Hispanic neighborhoods in the summertime, putting on plays for people who had never seen a play. They finally found a home in the Chelsea neighborhood of Manhattan, but now they are permanently in the Pregones Theater at 304 West 47 Street in the theater district, and thriving.

Actress, director, producer, the revered Miriam Colon spent most of her final years in Albuquerque, New Mexico, but passed away in New York City on March 3, 2017 from complications from a pulmonary infection. In addition to President Obama's presentation of the National Medal of Arts, she was presented with an OBIE Lifetime Achievement in Theater award, and given the HOLA (Hispanic Organization of Actors) Raul Julia Award.

#32- *Mary Colter (1869-1958)*

The Grand Canyon

Mary Elizabeth Jane Colter, daughter of William and Rebecca Colter, one of the few, but probably the best, female architect of the twentieth century, was born on April 4, 1869 in Pittsburgh, Pennsylvania. She is probably one of the least known talented women who should be well known. The family moved about, to Colorado, to Texas, and finally to St. Paul, Minnesota. She went to the California School of Design (now the San Francisco Art Institute) and got an apprenticeship with a local architectural firm. She also spent fifteen years teaching high school and university extension classes.

In 1901, she took a part-job with the Fred Harvey Company, operators of railroad stop restaurants. The whole organization gained fame from the 1946 film, The Harvey Girls. She started out as an interior decorator at their Alvarado Hotel in Albuquerque, New Mexico. By 1910 she was a full-time employee, moving from interior designer to architect, to chief architect, and an architect of great innovation and influence. Mary Colter made the rugged landscape of the southwest appealing and accessible to visitors.

Mary Colter's greatest sphere was in that American southwest and the Grand Canyon. She blended rustic, Native American, Mission style and Spanish Colonial. Her buildings seemed to be the work created in prehistoric times, or by some early travelers across the wild land. 1905's multi-story sandstone Hopi House with its roof terraces in the Grand Canyon was created for the Hopi artisans to sell their crafts and wares. In 1914 came both the Hermit's Rest, created as if it were the home of a rugged mountain man, and the Lookout Watchtower Studio. This had many windows overlooking the Grand Canyon, making it easy for visitors to take photographs. As with many Colter creations, it was one with the landscape, almost appearing to emerge out of the canyon itself. In 1922 she created the Phantom Ranch at the bottom of the Grand Canyon. Since it was extremely difficult to arrange for materials at the canyon's bottom, she made use of what was there: rough-hewn wood and available fieldstone. Nothing like this had ever been done.

In 1923 El Navajo hotel in Gallup, New Mexico was a masterwork, blending Native American inspirations into everything, including rugs and hand-carved furniture. 1925 brought Bright Angel Lodge at the Grand Canyon. All in all she created twenty-one hotels, lodges and other spaces. Her buildings there are now the "Mary Jane Colter National Historic Landmark." In 1930 the huge La Posada Hotel and Resort, in the Spanish hacienda style, was Colter's proudest accomplishment, in Winslow, Arizona. It had lodgings for seventy and had three restaurants, reading alcoves and a ballroom. She did it all: furniture, china and a sunken garden. It eventually was shut down, but remodeled and opened again in 1996, and is the "La Posada Historic District." Many of the elite stayed here: Harry Truman, Clark Gable, Albert Einstein, and others.

The seventy-foot Indian Watchtower at Desert View was erected at the eastern end of the canyon's south rim in 1932. It was inspired by an Anasazi watchtower, but this tower was a rock tower with a steel skeleton. There was a one hundred mile panorama with views from the Colorado River to the Painted Desert to the mountains. It is most impressive. The interior was styled as a Hopi ceremonial chamber.

She renovated the Painted Desert Inn in the late 1940s, making full use of Hopi artists' murals. In 1987 it was placed on the National Register of Historic Places. Much the same was done with La Fonda Hotel in Santa Fe, New Mexico. The entire interior design with Native American motifs and hand-crafted chandeliers. It became known as the "Santa Fe Style." Mary Colter retired to Santa Fe in 1948. In addition, she did design and decorate the El Tovar hotel. She also created her well-known Membreno china. In all, eleven of her buildings are on the Register of Historic Places and five are National Historic Landmarks.

And beyond the southwest, Mary Colter was in demand. She was responsible for Los Angeles' Union Station and also for those in Kansas City, Chicago and St. Louis, as well, with arched ceilings and geometric designs, and cocktail lounges and dining rooms. Horseback riding, chain-smoking Mary Colter died in New Mexico on January 8, 1958 and will always be remembered for her "Pueblo Deco" style of architecture. She donated her collection of Navajo jewelry, baskets, rugs and pottery to the Mesa Verde National Park. She is in the National Cowgirl Hall of Fame.

#33- *Maureen Connolly (1934-1969)*

Little Mo

Maureen Catherine Connolly was born on September 17, 1934 to parents Marty and Jessamine in San Diego, California. As a youngster she took up tennis lessons only because her mother could not afford horseback riding lessons, Maureen's first love. But she was good at it, at the age of fourteen going on to win fifty-six consecutive matches, and becoming the youngest ever to win a girls under-eighteen USA Junior International Grass Court Championship in both 1949 and 1950.

At sixteen years of age, in 1951, she became the youngest player to win the United States Championship (later called the US Open) with speed and a powerful stroke. What is written next will seem too impossible to be true, but yet it is.

In addition to winning the US Open in 1951, "Little Mo," as she started being called, at only five feet, five inches tall, went on to win Wimbledon (British Open) and the US Open again in 1952. In 1953 she won the Australian Open, the French Open, Wimbledon and the US Open. At eighteen she had become the first woman to win all four Grand Slam events in a single calendar year. That is an accomplishment that has never been matched by an American. In that Grand Slam year she only lost one set! In 1954 she again won the French Open and Wimbledon. She had won nine Grand Slam singles championships from 1951 to 1954. In addition she also won the Australian doubles in 1953 and the French doubles in 1954, as well as the French mixed doubles in 1954, and played and never lost on the British/US Wightman Cup series from 1951 to 1954, going 7-0 in singles. Maureen Connolly not only won fifty consecutive singles matches, but ranked the number one female tennis player in the world three times in the four years she played, and selected as Female Athlete of the Year by the Associated Press three times. Oh, and she had won the Italian Championships in 1953 and 1954 as well.

It was said that she had a powerful groundstroke and a quote from the New York Times said she had, "...perfect timing, fluency, balance and confidence."

On July 20, 1954, incomparable nineteen year old Maureen Connolly was doing her favorite thing, horseback riding on her own Colonel Merryboy, when a passing truck frightened the horse, throwing Connolly, and, in the end, causing a breaking of her leg, crushing of her tendons and muscles, and causing a compound fracture of her right fibula. Her astronomical tennis career was over before she even made it to twenty years of age. She officially retired the next year. What she had accomplished in four years would have been marvelous even if it had taken twenty years to do. There are those who say she could have been the greatest tennis player ever.

In 1955 she married equestrian Olympian Norman Brinker, moved to Dallas, Texas and became a tennis correspondent for various newspapers, and a consultant, and found the Maureen Connolly Brinker Foundation which has worked with junior tennis prospects, including a young Andy Roddick. Connolly wrote book for her daughter, Cindy, Little Mo's Legacy, inspiring mother-daughter lessons. That same daughter, Cindy Brinker Simmons, became president of the foundation. In 1957 Connolly wrote her autobiography, Forehand Drive.

Maureen Connolly Brinker died of ovarian cancer in Dallas Texas on June 21, 1969, at only thirty-four years of age. She has been inducted into the International Tennis Hall of Fame, the International Women's Sports Hall of Fame and the San Diego Hall of Champions. Now there is a Maureen Connolly Brinker Players Cup for junior girls from the United States and Great Britain. Glynnis O'Connor portrayed Connolly in the 1978 television movie, Little Mo.

#34- *Gerty Cori (1896-1957)*
The Cori Cycle

Gerty Theresa Radnitz, one of the greatest woman scientists of the twentieth century, was born on August 15, 1896 in Prague, Bohemia, then part of the then Austro-Hungarian Empire, now part of the Czech Republic. She was the daughter of Martha and Otto, who was a sugar chemist. She wanted to go into medicine, but did not have the basic requirements. In one year she mastered eight years of Latin and five years of science and mathematics, and was accepted in 1914 to Karl-Ferdinands University, graduating in 1920.

While there she met Carl Cori, and soon after their graduation she converted from Judaism to Catholicism, and were married in a Catholic ceremony. They moved to Vienna, but soon left for America and to Buffalo, New York in 1928, where they became American citizens. They worked together there, at the Roswell Park Cancer Institute. Carl Cori was warned that it was not proper for a man to work with his wife, and was told his job could be on the line. But they still continued to work together, writing over fifty papers, eleven by Gerty Cori alone, creating what came to be known as the Cori Cycle.

This was the discovery of the conversion of glucose to muscle glycogen, a pathway in the human body by which glycogen, carbohydrates that are changed into a type of sugar called glucose, which is the chief source of fuel for living cells, is broken down and stored as a source of energy in the muscles and liver as lactic acid, and returns to the muscles, and is metabolized, or chemically changed, back to lactate. It was important in the prevention of lactic acidosis, an increase bringing on excessive quantities of acid, leading to academia, excess acid in the blood.

Eventually they moved to Washington University in St. Louis, Missouri, and although they did the same work, she was ranked lower and paid far less. It took at least thirteen years for her to reach equity and named professor of biology, chemistry and pharmacology. Together they published their research.

In 1947 Gerty Cori, along with her husband and another chemist, won the Nobel Prize in Science, again due to their studies on glycogen. She was the first American woman biochemist win the prize in physiology or medicine.

The couple won many awards and recognition together, including being honored in 2004 when the American Chemical Society deemed the Cori laboratory at Washington University to be National Historic Landmark, as well as both honored with a 1946 award from the American Chemical Society (Midwest) and in 1947 the Squibb Award in Endocrinology. But Gerty Cori received much on her own. In 1948 she was awarded the Garvin-Olin Medal for distinguished work by a woman in chemistry, and later the Sugar Research Prize and the Borden Award. She was given honorary doctorates from Boston University, Yale University, Columbia University, Smith College and the University of Rochester, and was elected a fellow of the American Academy of Arts and Sciences. President Harry Truman named her to the board of directors of the National Science Foundation. The consensus is that although they sometimes worked as a team, Gerty Cori was more the genius and more the productive one.

In 1947, at around the same time she was receiving the Nobel Prize, Gerty Cori was diagnosed with myelosclerosis, a disease of the bone marrow, enduring it until her death in Missouri on October 26, 1957. She probably contracted it while studying the effects of x-rays. She has been inducted into the National Women's Hall of Fame, and a postage stamp was issued in her honor in 2008. Her biography is Glories of the Human Mind.

#35- *Susan Ahn Cuddy* (1915-2015)

Iconic Gunny

Dosan Ahn Chang Ho and Helen Lee Ahn were the first married Koreans to emigrate to the United States in 1902. They were activists in the independence of Korea from the conquering Japanese and their daughter, Susan Ahn (later Curry), who was born in Los Angeles, California on January 16, 1915, aided them in their activism while still a youngster. She grew up in a home that was open to Korean immigrants and exiles. They even founded the Young Korean Academy. Susan went on to Los Angeles City College and then San Diego State University. She had become an exceptional softball and baseball player, even becoming the first Asian American to run a college sports program.

With her intense hatred of Japan, it should be no surprise that after Japan's attack on Pearl Harbor in Hawaii that Susan Ahn joined the United States Navy in 1942, the first-ever Asian American to do so, eventually rising to the rank of lieutenant. All this was done in a time not only of anti-Asian sentiment, but still a lingering shadow of sexism. She was enrolled in the United States Reserve Midshipmen's School at Smith College in Massachusetts.

Susan Ahn became the first female gunnery officer ("gunny") in the navy, and becoming a naval instructor, teaching aviators aircraft control in a cockpit simulator. There were those that objected to an Asian female telling them what to do, but she always straightened them out. After this she became the first Korean American that went to work for US Naval Intelligence After the war, and during the "cold war" Susan Ahn Cuddy worked for the National Security Agency in Washington, D.C. as a code-breaker. She was in charge of three hundred think-tank linguists in the Russian section. The agency then awarded her a fellowship to study at the University of Southern California (USC), later working on top secret projects for the Department of Defense on a number of top secret projects.

She retired in 1959, but back in 1947 Susan Ahn "committed" another first. In defiance of miscegination (marriage between races) laws that were still on the books, she married navy chief petty officer Frances X. Cuddy, of Irish descent, at a naval chapel in Washington D.C. Her brother Philip Ahn was a film actor and restauranteur of note.

Trailblazing Susan Ahn Cuddy's military and governmental service, perserverence, dedication and fundraising efforts have been recognized many times. She has received the Southern California Edison Heritage Month Calendar Leadership Award, the United States Seabee Museum Recognition of Service, the United States Navy Fleet Readiness Center Recognition Award, the United States Navy Assault Craft Commendation of Service, the March First Women's Association Appreciation Award, the National College Leadership Conference Appreciation Award, and the American Courage Award from the Asian American Justice Center. In addition she was a California State Assembly Woman of the Year, and received awards from the Los Angeles City Council, the Los Angeles County Board of Supervisors ("Susan Ahn Cuddy Day"), the American Cancer Society, and even the Los Angeles Dodgers. Susan Ahn Cuddy passed away on June 24, 2015, at one hundred years of age, at her home in California, and buried next to her husband who died in 1994.. Her legacy is captured in the biography, which is entitled Willow Tree Shade. There was also a play, Born to Lead: The Susan Ahn Cuddy Story.

In 2016 artist Jacqueline Barrera won the North Carolina Veterans of Foreign Wars patriotic art contest with a beautiful portrait of Susan Ahn Cuddy in uniform, surrounded by an American flag and American eagle.

Group Four

Bette Davis - Katherine Graham

#36- Bette Davis (1908-1989)

"Bette Davis Eyes"

Ruth Elizabeth Davis, always known to her family as "Betty." was one of the greatest and most authentic actresses ever. She was born on April 5, 1908 in Lowell, Massachusetts. Her parents, Harlow and Ruth, divorced when she was young. She moved with her mother to New York City in 1921, where Betty enrolled in John Murray Anderson's Dramatic School. She changed the spelling of her name to Bette, liking the Balzac charater La Cousine Bette. In 1923 she made her stage debut in an off-Broadway stock company. In 1929 she was on Broadway in Broken Dishes.

She arrived in Hollywood in the early 1930s, signed with Universal Studios briefly, and then on to Warner Brothers. In 1931 she was in Way Back Home. In 1932 she appeared in The Man Who Played God, and credited George Arliss with giving her what she felt was her big break and a five year contract. In another one of her early roles in Of Human Bondage, LIFE magazine cited it as "probably the best performance recorded on the screen by an actress." She went on to win the Venice Film Festival Volpi Cup for Marked Woman in 1937.

She tried a prolonged battle unsuccessfully to pull out of her contract, but went on to be nominated for best actress five years in a row, from 1938 to 1942, and nominated ten times in all, winning twice. Bette Davis was the first person to be nominated ten times. She was probably the most celebrated actress during this period. She won for Dangerous and Jezebel. She was nominated for Dark Victory, The Letter, The Little Foxes, Now, Voyager, Mr. Skeffington, All About Eve (in which she uttered the lines, "Fasten your seatbelts, it's going to be a bumpy night"), and The Star. Some of Bette Davis' other well-known films are Hush Hush Sweet Charlotte, A Pocketful of Miracles, The Private Lives of Elizabeth and Essex, The Virgin Queen, All This and Heaven, Too, Hollywood Canteen, Watch on the Rhine, The Corn is Green, A Stolen Life, The Man Who Came to Dinner, The Petrified Forest and possibly her worst film, Beyond the Forest (in which she said the well-known line, "What a dump"). She had wanted the role of Scarlet O'Hara in Gone With the Wind, but did not get it. She was also nominated for another of her more well-known films, What Ever Happened to Baby Jane? In a 2017 well-received television mini-series entitled Feud: Bette and Joan with actress Susan Sarandon in the role of Bette Davis, chronicled the rivalry, bitterness and tempestuous relationship between Davis and Joan Crawford, during and after the making of the movie.

In 1941 she was briefly the president of the Academy of Motion Picture Arts and Sciences, and during World War ll, in addition to selling war bonds, she co-founded the Hollywood Canteen which supplied top tier entertainment to the troops. In 1980 she would be given the

Distinguished Civilian Service Medal for her Canteen work. By the later 1940s some of the films she was in were not the same quality as before, and she was not in as much demand. In the 1960s she did quite a bit of television appearances. In the early 1970s Bette Davis toured Australia and the United Kingdom with "Bette Davis in Person and on Film." A bit later she had some stage, film and television flops, but in 1977 the American Film Institute granted her a Lifetime Achievement Award. And she was in demand again. She made a television mini-series, The Dark Secret of Harvest Home, and a television movie, Death on the Nile, receiving a 1979 "Emmy" for Strangers: The Story of a Mother and Daughter. In 1980 and 1982 she was again nominated for an Emmy for television roles, and even went on and made some Disney movies. She continued acting until the late 1980s. She was made a Fellow of the British Film Institute. In 1983 she was given the Women in Film Crystal Award, and in 1987 she was chosen as one of the Kennedy Center honorees.

Not long before her death in 1989 LIFE magazine did a retrospective of the many great films of 1939, and Davis was singled out as "the most significant actress of her era," especially her performance in Dark Victory. The American Film Institute again recognized her achievements in 1999 with their American Film Institute....100 Years...100 Stars, listing her as the number two actress. France awarded her the Legion of Honor and Italy the Campione d'Italia. In 2006 Premiere magazine listed Bette Davis portrayal of Margo Channing in All About Eve as the fifth best performance of all time. Although Davis did not get an Oscar for that film, she did win at the Cannes Film Festival, and received both the New York Film Critics Award and the San Francisco Critics Circle Award. That is when she got her handprints in front of Hollywood's Grauman's Chinese Theatre. Empire magazine listed her as number fifteen of the top movie stars of all time. In 2008 a postage stamp was issued in her honor.

Throughout all the time, she had a difficult personal life. Davis married Harmon Nelson in 1932 and went through an ugly divorce in 1938. She married Arthur Farnsworth in 1940, and he died in 1943. She married William Grant Sherry in 1945 and divorced in 1950, and finally married fellow actor Gary Merrill in 1950, and that lasted only until 1960. Her daughter, known as BD, who she was supporting, wrote a nasty tell-all book about their mother-daughter relationship. All who knew them both felt there was little substance in the accusations. Bette Davis responded with her 1987 memoir, This 'N That, contradicting her daughter. In 1962 she had written a prior memoir, Bette Davis, The Lonely Life. Throughout her career, her mannerisms, such the way she held a cigarette, and her speech pattern, gave much fodder to imitators. In 1931 Bette Davis was about to be fired from the set of Bad Sister, when a cinematographer commented about her lovely eyes, and her job was saved. In 1940 there were a number of "eye" close-ups in All This and Heaven, Too. And that was why the eyes were sung about in the very popular song, "Bette Davis Eyes" by Kim Carnes in 1981.

She portrayed unsympathetic, intense, shrewish and forceful women and said of herself, "I have been uncompromising, peppery, monomaniacal, tactless, volatile, and off times disagreeable." And it was true that she did not along very well with many of her co-stars.

In addition to her other memoirs she also wrote one memoir entitled, Mother Goddam. In 1983 she was diagnosed with breast cancer and had a mastectomy. This was followed by four strokes, leaving her partially paralyzed. She died in France, too weak to travel home, from the effects of breast cancer, on October 6, 1989. Boston University has an extensive archive of Bette Davis material, while the executors of her estate formed the Bette Davis Foundation which awards scholarships to aspiring actors and actresses.

#37- *Dorothy Day (1897-1980)*

Original Hippie/Servant of God

The very complex and controversial journalist/activist Dorothy Day was born in Brooklyn, New York on November 8, 1897 to John and Grace Day. Due to her father's accepting a job as a sports writer in San Francisco, California, the family moved to nearby Oakland. When the earthquake of 1906 hit, among other things, John Day lost his job. The family then moved to Chicago, Illinois. Her parents had her baptized into the Episcopal Church at age ten and she began reading both her catechism and the Bible. Dorothy began attending the University of Illinois-Urbana-Champagne on a scholarship.

She only stayed there two years, and left, heading to New York City, working for the socialist magazine, The Liberator, and entered into a now rather wild, uninhibited lifestyle. Her reading turned to the Russian writers and works of social conscience. Dorothy Day was becoming a political radical. She was arrested as part of Alice Paul's "Silent Sentinels" pushing for women's suffrage. She lived in the bohemian Greenwich Village, began many a romantic liaison, even had an abortion, and was an admirer of the Russian revolution.

She married Berkeley Tobey, separated from him, became involved with Forster Battterham, with whom she had a daughter Tamara. But about this time, she began an inner change, and became interested in Catholicism and converted in 1927, and ended her relationship with Batterham because he would not marry her in a religious Catholic ceremony.

Day moved briefly to Los Angeles, California to work for the motion pictures, but was soon back in New York. She had purchased a cottage there on Staten Island, and began working for the Staten Island Advance with gardening pieces. But she also began writing book reviews for the Catholic periodical, Commonweal. She had become somewhat of a radical convert.

1932 was another turning point. After supporting protesters in Washington, D.C. she realized there was no support or leadership in any way from the Catholic Church. She had met one

Peter Maurin and together they founded the rather socialist Catholic Worker. They stated that "our manifest is the Sermon on the Mount, which means that we will try to be peacemakers.... We love our country, we love our president. We have been the only country in the world where men of all nations have taken refuge from oppression." It made sure there was coverage on striking workers, and on working conditions, particularly for women and African Americans.

This was part of her Catholic Workers Movement, which espoused pacifism, aiding the Great Depression poor and homeless, and nonviolent-driven action. Folks were urged to support union workers. But Dorothy Day's philosophy was that of "distribution," a middling ground between socialism and capitalism. The movement gained momentum and by 1941 there were more than thirty workers communities. In 1949, in one of her most defiant gestures, she feuded with New York's Francis Cardinal Spellman over the fate of cemetery workers, indicating that the rich church should take care of the poor working men.

This pacifism was deeply imbedded in her beliefs, and during the 1930s Spanish Civil War she would not agree to the Catholic Church's support of the Francisco Franco rebels, especially because they promoted atheism. This caused her a large loss of support, especially for the Catholic Worker.

She had become a postulant (someone aspiring to join) with the Fraternity of Jesus Caritas, who lived their lives based on Christ's life, but without work: only prayer, reading and retreats. Her sojourn was not long. But in the 1940s Dorothy Day became affiliated with the Benectine order and became an oblate (a person living in society, but adhering to the rules of the order) of St. Procopius Abbey in Chicago. She stayed with this the rest of her life. She also continued her total pacifism during World War II.

In the 1960s she took heart in the Second Vatican Council putting forth a message of non-violence and anti-war. At the same time, she disliked the current popular "hippie" culture because she felt they had no principles and promiscuity was rampant, and they seemed to be atheists, sometimes violent, and promoted a class hatred. She was, however, somewhat pleased when radical hippie leader Abbie Hoffman called her the "Original Hippie," probably because of her frequent defiant and radical stands, and the fact that she had been sent to jail on numerous occasions for her civil disobedience. She was even arrested in her seventies when she joined Cesar Chavez' protest for the farm laborers of California.

In 1971 Day traveled throughout the world as a peace activist, including Poland, the Soviet Union, Hungary, Romania, and India, where she met with Mother Teresa.

Over the years she had expressed either admiration or empathy with certain controversial world leaders. She felt Ho Chi Minh of communist Vietnam was a patriotic man of vision protecting his country from foreign invaders. She even admired the aspirations and promises of Cuban leader Fidel Castro in his early days in power, but not later.

There seemed to be a strain among certain elements about her being a radical and at the same time a devout Catholic convert. She once wrote a response: "How can you believe in the Immaculate Conception, in the Virgin Mary, in the Resurrection? I could only say that I believe in the Roman Catholic Church and all she teaches. I have accepted her authority with my whole heart... We are taught that faith is a gift, and that sometimes I wonder why some have it and some do not. I feel my own unworthiness and can never be grateful enough to God for this gift of faith."

Among her writings were: The Eleventh Virgin, From Union Square to Rome, The Long Loneliness, Loaves and Fishes: The Inspiring Story of the Catholic Worker Movement, all somewhat autobiographical. She also wrote Therese: A Life of Therese of Liseux. There are numerous biographies written on Day.

Dorothy Day has been honored on numerous occasions, with many college facilities and other types of housing named in her honor. In 1972 the Jesuit magazine, America, used an entire issue to profile Dorothy Day on her seventy-fifth birthday. She has received the Pacem in Terris Peace and Freedom Award and The Gandhi Award. The Isaac Hecker Award from the Paulist Center Community in Boston was given to her for her "selfless commitment to people who are homeless, jobless and powerless." The University of Notre Dame awarded her the Laetare Medal because she was "universally acknowledged as the matriarch of American Catholic radicalism." She has also been inducted into the National Women's Hall of Fame.

Dorothy Day died of a myocardial infarction (heart attack) in New York City on November 29, 1980. Terence Cardinal Cooke presided over a memorial mass in her honor at St. Patrick's Cathedral. In 1996 actress Moira Kelly portrayed Day in the film, Entertaining Angels: The Dorothy Day Story. The Tribeca Film Festival presented the documentary, Dorothy Day: Don't Call Me A Saint in 2006. The source of her stating, "Don 't call me a saint. I won't be dismissed so easily," is lost, but by many it is only her humility being expressed, and the fear that a saint would not be taken seriously. However, in 1983 the Claretian Missionaries proposed her for sainthood. This missionary society is known for its dedication to outreach and solidarity with immigrants and refugees, with evangelization and with interreligious dialogue. Pope John Paul II opened the case, leading to possible canonization (sainthood) allowing her to be called "Servant of God." In 2012 the proposal was turned over to the United States Conference of Catholic Bishops. Pope Francis spoke highly of her as one of the four great examples of praiseworthy Americans when he spoke before the United States Congress.

#38- *Julia de Burgos (1914-1953)*

Rebellious Poet

Poet and activist Julia Connstancia de Burgos Garcia was born to poor farmer Francisco and his wife Paula on February 17, 1914 in Carolina, Puerto Rico. When she was in her teens the family moved to Rio Piedras. In 1931 she began attending the University of Puerto Rico, graduating with a teaching degree at nineteen years of age.

Julia got a teaching position in Naranjito, but also became a writer for children's radio, and in 1934 married Ruben Rodriguez Beauchamp (getting divorced in 1937), and in 1936 became the Secretary General of the Daughters of Freedom, the women's branch of the Puerto Rican Nationalist Party, which sought independence for Puerto Rico. She privately published Poemas exactos a mi Misma, which included the poem,"A Julia de Burgos," and Cancion de la verdad sencilla (Song of the Simple Truth), receiving a prize from the Institute of Puerto Rican Literature for the latter. In 1946 she received another prize from them for "Ser o no ser la divisa" (To Be or Not to Be is My Motto).

By this time Julia de Burgos had also had some poetry published in periodicals, poems that were lyrical, poems that were intimate, and yet poems that told of the struggle of Puerto Rico. Her first full published work was Rio Grande de Loiza: "Great river. Great flood of tears... save those greater that come from the eyes of my soul for my enslaved people." She became romantically involved with Dr. Juan Isidro Grullon, and they traveled to Cuba. However, when things began to go sour, she left and came to New York City. There she became a journalist for the progressive Pueblos Hispanos. However, she returned briefly to Cuba, hoping for reconciliation, but returned to New York City.

When she returned she was gratefully assisted by the Circle of Iberio-American Writers and Poets, and in 1943 she married musician and poet Armando Marin and they moved to Washington, D.C. for a while. In 1946 Julia de Burgos was diagnosed with cirrhosos of the liver, and in 1952 had a papilloma (growth) removed from her throat.

Since the 1920s there had been a resistance to the United States, being considered a colonial power by some nationalistic Puerto Ricans. In the 1930s the Nationalist Party was involved in a revolt that came to be known as the Ponce Massacre, with nineteen people being killed, and the leaders sent to prison. In 1948 a law was passed to suppress governmental opposition, but was immediately assailed as a violation of the first amendment, the freedom of speech. The nationalists planned a number of revolts in late 1949, but the plans were discovered. They took over the town of Jayuga, capturing the police station, burning the post office, cutting the telephone lines, and raising their own Nationalist Party flag. It is known as the

Jayuga Uprising. They were, however, brutally crushed, but the participants have come to be considered heroes. In Mayaguez plaques have been placed honoring them. One of the plaques lists the women participants, and Julia de Burgos' name is there.

On June 28, 1953, Julia de Burgos, possibly Puerto Rico's greatest twentieth century poet, left the home of a friend in New York with whom she had been staying, after recently being again released from the hospital, and she disappeared. No one knew what happened to her. But it was later discovered that on July 6, over a week later, she passed out on a street in Spanish Harlem, and died of pneumonia in a hospital there, only thirty-nine years of age. She had no identification papers on her, and no one claimed the body, and so she was buried in a potter's field, which is a place of burial for unknown persons, on Hart Island, off the eastern part of the Bronx, in Long Island Sound.

Eventually the whole situation was uncovered and her body was sent to Puerto Rico, with the help of that same Circle of Iberio-American Writers and Poets, and given a hero's burial in Carolina, with a monument erected later. Posthumously she was awarded a doctorate from the University of Puerto Rico. There are schools named in her honor in Puerto Rico, New York City and Philadelphia, and parks in Puerto Rico, Chicago and Connecticut. Yale University's Latin Cultural Center is named in her honor. Soon after her death the Journal Artes y Letras put out a special issue, "Homenaje (Homage) a Julia de Burgos."

She had also written "Poema para Mi Muerte" (My Death Poem), and in early 1953, during her last hospitalization, possibly in anticipation of her own death, she wrote "Farewell from Welfare Island." Welfare Island is now renamed Roosevelt Island (located in the East River off Manhattan) since 1971. Prior to that Welfare Island was principally an island of hospitals, one of which had Julia de Burgos as a patient.

"The past is only a shadow emerging from nowhere. Life was somewhere forgotten and sought refuge in depths of tears and sorrows....my cry into the world. My cry that is no more mine, but hers and his forever, the comrades of my silence, the phantoms of my grave...forgotten but unshaken...deep into Welfare Island my farewell to the world."

Other works by Julia de Burgos are: Yo Misma Fui Mi Ruta (I Was My Own Path), Alba de Mi Silencio (Dawn of my Silence), and Alta Mar y Gaviota (High Sea and Gulls). In 1978 a "biopic" was produced, Vida y poesia de Julia de Burgos (Life and Poetry), and in 2002 there was a documentary, Julia, Todo en mi (Julia, All in Me). Composer Leonard Bernstein's Songfest: A Cycle of American Poems for Six Singers and Orchestra has part of it de Burgos' poem, "A Julia de Burgos." A United States postage stamp has been issued in her honor, and she has been inducted into the New York Writers Hall of Fame. Her writing was the expression of a woman who refused to be contained by what males felt should be her standards of behavior.

#39- Ruby Dee (1922-2014)

Legend

Actress, writer and activist Ruby Ann Wallace was born in Cleveland, Ohio on October 27, 1922 to cook Edward and Gladys Wallace, although her mother left the family while Ruby was young. She was raised in Harlem, New York, graduated from Hunter College, and became an apprentice at the American Negro Theater. In 1941 she married blues singer Frankie Dee Brown, and Ruby began using his middle name as her last name. They divorced in 1945, but she kept that name.

Ruby Dee's first Broadway play was as a native girl in South Pacific. Her first film was That Man of Mine in 1946. In that same year she appeared in Broadway play, Jeb, and it was there that she met her future husband and also future legend, Ossie Davis. They married in 1948.

Her theater accomplishments, as well as those on the television screen are worth noting. As well as in the film, she was first in the stage version of A Raisin in the Sun, and was the first African American woman to take the lead role at the American Shakespeare Festival in both Taming of the Shrew as Kate (an Obie award) and in King Lear as Cordelia. On television she was part of the cultish Peyton Place series and Roots: The Next Generations (an Emmy nomination), as well as the soap opera, Guiding Light, and television films, Decoration Day (an Emmy Award), To Be Young Gifted and Black, Their Eyes Were Watching God, Feast of All Saints, Long Days Journey Into Night, and America (nominated for an Emmy). She also appeared as a guest star in many well-known television series, such as The Golden Girls, CSI, Touched By an Angel, China Beach, Evening Shade, The Fugitive, Police Woman, The Defenders and narrated a number of documentaries, including Betty and Coretta and for the American Masters series "The Underground Railroad" and "Edgar Allan Poe."

Over the years Ruby Dee appeared in a great many notable films: The Jackie Robinson Story (which first brought her some fame), A Raisin in the Sun, Do the Right Thing, Jungle Fever, St. Louis Blues, Buck and the Preacher, 1982, and American Gangster (an Oscar nomination and Screen Actors Guild Award). Over the years of fine acting Ruby Dee has been that recipient of the Emmy Award (television), and in addition to Taming, she won the Obie Award (Off-Broadway) for Anna Lacosta, The Glass Menagerie and Checkmates, the Grammy Award (Recording) with Ossie Davis, "In This Life Together," and the Drama Desk Award for The Wedding Band and Boesman and Lena, and nominated for that Academy Award (Film). She has been the recipient of the Kennedy Center Honors, a Screen Actors Guild Lifetime Achievement, a Women in Film Crystal Award, a Women of Vision Award, been given the Springarn Medal, and the Eleanor Roosevelt Val-Kill Award, and is in the American Theater Hall of Fame, and with Davis, received the National Medal of Arts.

But she was so much more than an actress. She wrote poetry, Glowchild, and wrote a play, Ten Ways to Count to Ten.

As civil rights activist, she had been a part of many protest marches, was a member of CORE (Congress of Racial Equality), NAACP (National Association for the Advancement of Colored People) and the Southern Christian Leadership Conference, and becoming friends with both Martin Luther King and Malcolm X. In 1963 she was the Mistress of Ceremonies for the March on Washington for Jobs and Freedom, and a recipient of the Lifetime Achievement Award from the National Civil Rights Museum and the Urban League's Frederick Douglass Award, and with Davis is in the NAACP Hall of Fame. Ruby Dee suffered from breast cancer, and passed away at her home in New Rochelle, New York on June 11, 2014.

#40- Emily Dickinson (1830-1886)

The Belle of Amherst

Pale, auburned-hair Emily Elizabeth Dickinson began her seemingly uneventful life on December 10, 1830 in Amherst, Massachusetts to Edward and Emily Dickinson. She left there on only a few occasions in her life, and died there of Bright's disease (now known as acute nephritis, a kidney disease) on May 15, 1886. She was of a prominent family. Her paternal grandfather was one of the key founders of Amherst College. At sixteen she briefly attended Mary Lyons' Mount Holyoke Seminary, one of the first times leaving home. It has never been clear as to why she left.

Despite this life of hers, she is considered among America's greatest poets, of either gender, and of any time period. Benjamin F. Newton, one of her father's law students, aroused her poetic instincts. He brought her books of William Wordsworth and Ralph Waldo Emerson. She cared deeply for him, and was quite upset when he married, and then died prematurely. In 1854 she met Reverend Charles Wadsworth in Philadelphia, on her way home from Washington, D. C., where her father was serving in Congress. This was also one of those few times away from Amherst. Emily Dickinson fell in love with Wadsworth, and although they had met a few times, it seems he was unaware of her feelings. When he left to go to San Francisco, she was devastated. She never left Amherst again. It seems he did visit her much later in life, and when he died in 1882, she had somewhat of a breakdown.

After that initial loss of Wadsworth, all of her energy went into her poetry. They were mostly written on brown bags, on scraps of paper, and on envelopes. These poems are the essence of New England, with traditionally controlled emotion, but with the aim of a loosening of the old ways, on nature, on need, on life, on death, on God, on love, and on time and eternity. She composed approximately eighteen hundred poems, with only a few published in her lifetime. Although the early 1860s were her most creative, Thomas Wentworth Higginson gave her much advice, but never followed through to help the poems get published.

Her early poems were rather sentimental, but In the 1860's things changed and she became more creative. Now, mysteriously, she almost always dressed in white, and had to spend much time as a housekeeper and caregiver for her ailing mother. Her later life may also have brought her some romance with the widower judge Otis Phillips Lord.

The popularity of this girl/woman has only grown over the generations. Her mysticism makes for grand poetry, the mind and spirit being a person's "undiscovered continent." The ordinary is no longer ordinary.

"A word is dead When it is said, Some say. I say it just begins to live That day." "I Died For Beauty, "A Narrow Fellow In The Grass," "I Never Saw A Moor," "I Never Lost But Twice," "I Heard A Fly Buzz" and "If You Were Coming In The Fall" are among the "Nun of Amherst's" more popular poems.

Her half-rhymes and slant rhymes, her imagery and compression and her delicacy of presentation displayed her immeasurable talent. "Because I could not stop for Death- He kindly stopped for me." She is so provocative and yet so gentle. A few years after her death her sister Lavinia published one hundred fifteen of Emily Dickinson's poems. Some of her poems were published by friends in 1890, including Higginson. In 1914, The Single Hound brought fame to her name, but it was not until 1955 that the first complete collection of her poems was published. Up to that time every editor tried to re-write her poems to fit the current trend. Thomas H. Johnson's The Poems of Emily Dickinson finally changed that. In 1981 The Manuscript Books of Emily Dickinson was the first time her poems were put in chronological order. In 1994 critic Harold Bloom declared her to be among the top twenty-six central writers of western civilization.

The Jones Library in Amherst has a special collection of seven thousand pieces of Emily Dickinson material. And Amherst College has manuscripts and letters. Evergreens, the home of brother Austin Dickinson, is now the Emily Dickinson Museum. There also exists an Emily Dickinson International Society. In 1971 an eight cent commemorative stamp was issued, and she has been inducted into the National Women's Hall of Fame. Alfred Hobeggar wrote My Wars Are Laid Away in Books: The Life of Emily Dickinson in 2001. The 1975 Broadway play, The Belle of Amherst, about Dickinson, won awards and was adapted to television, as well. In 2016 actress Cynthia Nixon portrayed Dickinson in a biographical A Quiet Passion.

#41- *Dorothea Dix (1802-1887)*

Dragon and Advocate

Dorothea Lynde Dix, the first American woman to fight for humane treatment for the mentally ill, was born on April 4, 1802 in Hampton, Maine to her parents, preacher Joseph and his wife Mary. They moved to Worcester, Massachusetts, but at twelve years of age she went to live with her well-to-do grandmother in Boston, fleeing from an impoverished home life. Although she was quite ill on many occasions, she still was able to open and run a school for young ladies from 1821 until 1835 in her grandmother's home. While teaching, she also managed to write a textbook, Conversations on Common Things, and also wrote a dictionary of flowers, The Garland of Flora.

She did some traveling with friends in Europe for health reasons, but while there met with a number of reformers and activists working for the cause of the mentally ill. And when she returned to Massachusetts in 1841, she accepted a position teaching Sunday school at the East Cambridge House of Corrections. This was the start of her second career. She found the place disgusting and unsanitary. It was not heated, smelled awful, with mentally ill persons locked up with the common criminal populace. Some prisoners were kept in outhouses, others in chains, sexually abused and even sold. Her efforts for reform were assisted by Dr. Samuel Gridley Howe, Horace Mann and Senator Charles Sumner, but still the path to improvement was not easy. Newspapers called her a meddler, a busybody, and even a slanderer, but she did succeed because of her single-mindedness and her zeal.

She began to be curious about a good many institutions, such as other prisons, insane asylums and almshouses, and started donating much of her time to these people who were under-cared for and suffering. In 1843 Dix presented her "Memorial to the Legislature of Massachusetts." Her words, in which she wanted to "call your attention to the present state of Insane Persons, confined within this Commonwealth, in cages, stalls, pens! Chained naked, broken with rods, and lashed into obedience." This helped get an expansion of the Worcester insane asylum.

But Massachusetts was just the start. On she went to New Hampshire, Rhode Island, New Jersey, New York, Maryland, North Carolina, Tennessee, Pennsylvania, Illinois, Indiana, Missouri, Mississippi, Louisiana and other states, as well as to Canada and Europe. Dorothea Dix is credited for obtaining funding for over two dozen asylums for the mentally ill, and more than a dozen schools, and the needed improvement of many others. Dix wished to set up an Army nursing corps at the onset of the Civil War, and got her wish, and became the Superintendent of Women Nurses. It was not only herself, but Clara Barton, eventual founder of the American Red Cross, earning her reputation as "The Angel of the Battlefield," who helped. She was called "Dragon" Dix because she doggedly fought with everyone to get the job done, including the military officers when they refused her demands for the treatment of her nurses. As much as she was an advocate for her nurses, she was disliked by them also, and by the doctors who did not like her giving orders. Despite her good work, the "dragon" was dismissed, but not before she was awarded two national flags for the "Care, Succor and Relief of the Sick and wounded Soldiers of the United States during the recent war," and was also made "President for Life" of the Army Nurses Association.

Much due to her efforts, in 1854 a bill was passed in the Congress of the United States to set aside a large tract of federal land to be used for the care of the insane, and also for others with various handicaps. She changed the attitude toward the mentally ill, but President Franklin Pierce felt the responsibility for these people rested with the individual states, and so he vetoed the bill. Dix was so upset with this action she left for Europe and worked there. Upon returning to the United States she continued to work this cause of reform in a field that was finally getting some due recognition, writing and offering guidance, until so ill, she placed herself in a New Jersey hospital, and then worked from there. Dorothea Dix died on July 17, 1887 at the New Jersey State Hospital in Trenton, where she had spent the last six years of her life, one of the hospitals she was responsible for founding. It had been her headquarters during her final years, where she kept up a correspondence, still advocating for the mentally ill, although incapacitated. She is buried in Cambridge, Massachusetts.

The Bangor, Maine Mental Health Institute has been renamed the Dorothea Dix Psychiatric Center. There is a Dorothea Dix Museum on the grounds of the Harrisburg State Hospital in Pennsylvania. She has been honored with an 1983 postage stamp, and is remembered on the Boston Women's Heritage Trail, as well as there being a transport ship, the USS Dorothea L. Dix. She is, of course, a member of the National Women's Hall of Fame.

#42- Amelia Earhart (1897-1937)

Queen of the Air

Adventurous tomboy Amelia Mary Earhart, the daughter of Samuel and Amelia, was born in Atchison, Kansas on July 24, 1897, and became the most celebrated female aviator in history. The family moved to Iowa, where Amelia saw her first airplane at a state fair. They went on to move to Minnesota and Chicago in 1915. A few years later she drove up to Toronto, Canada, where her sister was living. There she did volunteer work at a military hospital caring for the World War l veterans returning home. When the Spanish flu epedemic broke out she stayed to help. At this time she developed an eye infection that would plague her for the rest of her life, including three sinus operations. She briefly worked as a social worker and teacher in

Massachusetts. In 1919 she began attending Columbia University, but dropped out to be with her parents who had moved to California.

In Long Beach, California, in 1920, she and her father went on a ten-minute airplane ride. That was all it took. Earhart decided she wanted to fly and worked as a truck driver, photographer and stenographer to earn the money needed for flying lessons. She took her first lesson in 1921, and soon bought a second-hand bi-plane. On October 22, 1922, she reached an altitude of 14,000 feet, a record for female pilots. On June 17, 1928 she became the first woman to fly across the Atlantic Ocean, albeit as a passenger. They flew from Newfoundland to Wales. In England she bought another plane and had it shipped back to America. When the crew returned home they had a tickertape parade and a White House meeting with President Calvin Coolidge. They began calling her the "Queen of the Air" and "Lady Lindy" (referencing Charles Lindbergh). But it must be noted that as accomplished as Earhart turned out to be, she was quite accident prone, wrecking a number of planes.

Later that year she flew solo across the United States and back. In 1929 George P. Putnam who coordinated the flight, urged the shy, but charismatic Amelia to go on a lecture tour, which made her a celebrity. Earhart became an associate editor at Cosmopolitan magazine, campaigning for greater acceptance of aviation. She also began making product endorsements, which gave her money to continue flying, and worked with many fledgling aviation clubs. From 1930 to 1935 she set seven aviation records, and became an official of the National Aeronautical Association, and founded and was first president of "The Ninety-Niners," a female pilot organization. In 1931 she again set the women's altitude record at 18, 415 feet. In May, 1932 she flew from Newfoundland to Northern Ireland making an Atlantic solo, only the second person to do this. In January, 1935, she flew solo from California to Hawaii. At this time she also became a visiting professor, counselor and consultant at Purdue University.

In 1931, after many refusals she had finally agreed to marry Putnam. A few years later their home in Rye, New York burned down and they decided to move to California. Here she eventually opened the Earhart-Mantz Flying School. This is when she decided to begin planning for a circumnavigational flight, in a Lockheed Electra 10E. Purdue established the Amelia Earhart Fund for Aeronautical Research, and helped sponsor her around-the-world trek, as an encouragement for air travel. The first attempt would be westward, but after flying from California to Hawaii they had problems, and the flight was cancelled.

The second flight, on June 29, 1937, went eastward from California, to Florida, to Puerto Rico, to South America, to Africa, including Egypt, to India, to Lae, New Guinea. They left there and Amelia Earhart and her navigator Fred Noonan disappeared somewhere in the vicinity of Howland Island in the Pacific Ocean. There could have been any number of problems and there are many theories. Her last message received was, "Circling...cannot see island...gas is running low." The official search for them lasted until July 19, and then George Putnam set up the greatest rescue search in history of aviation up to that time, but no trace was found. Over the years some Oriental islands have claimed to have found her body, or to have made her acquaintance, but nothing was substantiated. She was officially declared dead in 1939.

There are schools, air fields, roads and scholarships named in her honor, as well as a postage stamp issued with her likeness in 1963. She was awarded honorary degrees from Ogelthorpe University and Thiel College, was made an honorary major in the United States Army Reserve and there is a USNS Amelia Earhart since 2007. She had been given the Distinguished Flying Cross, plus awards from Great Britain, Mexico, Belgium, Romania and France's Legion of Honor, as well as a gold medal from the National Geographic Society. She had been given keys to the cities of Buffalo, Pittsburgh and Atlantic City, and medals from New York City, Chicago, Philadelphia, Boston, and the Commonwealth of Massachusetts. In her hometown in Kansas there is the Amelia Earhart Birthplace Museum. And on Howland Island there is an Earhart Light.

There was a fictionalized film version of her life in 1943, Flight For Freedom. Actress Susan Clark portrayed her in 1976's television movie, Amelia Earhart, and Hilary Swank did the same in the 2009 film, Amelia. She was also portrayed by Amy Adams in the comedy film, Night at the Museum 2. In 1993 there was a documentary as part of the American Experience: "Amelia Earhart: The Price of Courage." She has been inducted into the National Women's Hall of Fame, the Aviation Hall of Fame, the Colorado Hall of Fame, and even the Motorsports Hall of Fame.

Amelia Earhart will always be a symbol of calmness under pressure, courage, persistence, independence.

#43- *Gertrude Ederle (1905-2003)*

Queen of the Waves

Gertrude Caroline Ederle was born on October 23, 1905 in New York City to German immigrants, butcher Henry and Anna. As a young girl she learned to swim at New Jersey beaches, near where her family had a summer place. She joined the Women's Swimming Association, and very soon, while still quite young, set the record for the 880-meter free-style, the youngest ever to set a world record. From the age of sixteen to twenty, she went on to set eight world records. Eventually she would set twenty-nine national and world swimming records. In 1922, in one day at Brighton Beach, Brooklyn, New York, she broke seven records.

In the 1924 Olympics in Paris, she had become the heavy favorite to win gold medals. She did in the 4x100 meter relay, but only managed third place and bronze medals in the 100-meter free-style and the 400-meter free-style. She was very disappointed in herself.

She decided to turn professional, and in 1925 swam the twenty-two mile stretch from Battery Park in New York City to Sandy Hook, New Jersey, setting a record of seven hours, eleven minutes. That record stood for eighty-one years. Presently there is an annual event there called the "Ederle Swim."

In that same year, on August 18, she made her first attempt to be the first female to swim the English Channel. However, when one of her crew jumped into the water to assist her, and she did not need the assistance, she was disqualified. The next year on August 6, 1926, her body coated with oil and lanolin (a protective waterproof lubricant) to protect her from both the cold water and jelly fish, Gertrude Ederle, accompanied by two tug boats, stepped into the water at Cape Gris-Nez, France and swam the English Channel to Kingsdown, Kent, England in fourteen hours, thirty-four minutes, a record (for both male and female swimmers) that stood for twenty-four years. She had told her handlers this time that under no circumstances were they to jump in to help her, unless she specially asked. It was her defining moment. She returned home to a ticker-tape parade of over two million people. President Calvin Coolidge called her "America's Best Girl"

She went on to many speaking engagements and took part in vaudeville (a type of entertainment that presented a whole variety of acts), giving swimming demonstrations, and even made a film, Swim Girl, Swim. As a result of measles when Ederle was young she had become partially deaf, and took upon herself to teach deaf children to swim at the Lexington School for the Deaf.

In 1933, while still a young woman, Ederle fell down the steps in her apartment and twisted her spine. The consequence left her bedridden for years. In 1939, however, she did appear in showman Billy Rose's Aquacade at the New York World's Fair There were other performers, but she was the star.

For a while she lived in Queens, New York, but the last years were in Wycoff, New Jersey, where Gertrude Ederle passed away on November 30, 2003, and is buried in Woodlawn Cemetery in the Bronx, New York. She has been inducted into the National Women's Hall of Fame, the International Swimming Hall of Fame and the Women's Sports Hall of Fame. Her biography is American Girl.

#44- *Gertrude Belle Elion (1918-1999)*

Drug Pioneer

Gertrude Belle Elion was born January 23, 1918 in New York City to a father, Robert, who was a Lithuanian immigrant dentist, and her mother, Bertha, a Polish immigrant. Her grandfather died of cancer when she was young, and it had a great impact on her. She wanted to find cures.

At nineteen years of age, in 1937, she graduated summa cum laude from Hunter College with a degree in chemistry, and with a master's degree from New York University in 1941 in medical science. She worked for a while as a substitute high school teacher, since she had been turned down for fifteen fellowships, due to a still remaining gender (anti-female) bias. She wound up as a food quality supervisor at a supermarket chain, checking on things such as pickles and egg yolks.

But then in 1944 she got a job with a pharmaceutical firm, Burroughs-Wellcome (now GlaxoSmithKline) in Tuckahoe, New York, and began working with George H. Hitchings. She began attending Brooklyn Polytechnic Institute (now the NYU Tandon School of Engineering) in search of a doctoral degree. However, the commute was too much, and she had to drop out. She never did get that doctorate. But later in life not only was she awarded honorary doctorates from Harvard University and Polytechnic University, but also more than twenty other honorary degrees.

But she did continue to work with Hitchings on drugs, such as tioguanine and 6-MP (also known as mercaptopurine) which dealt with leukemia, cancer and auto-immune diseases. From 1967 to 1983 she was the Head of the Department of Experimental Therapy at Burroughs-Wellcome, and from 1971 to 1983 was an adjunct professor of pharmacology and experimental medicine at Duke University. During her career she was also a member of the National Cancer Institute, the American Association for Cancer Research and the World Health Organization. Elion and Hitchings compared normal cells with pathogens, disease-causing agents. They designed drugs that would block viral infections and kill pathogens, but not harm the normal cells. This led to more help with leukemia, kidney transplant reception, malaria, meningitis, septicemia, herpes gout, and cancer. She oversaw the adaptation of azidothymidine (AZT) as the first drug to fight Aids. In 1988 she and Hitchings and one other were awarded the Nobel Prize in Physiology or Medicine for the development of multiple drugs for Aids, especially AZT, and the first immunosuppressive drug used for organ transplants.

From 1983 until her death in 1999, Elion was a research professor at Duke, but remained just about full-time in the laboratory overseeing the seeking of a cure for AIDS.

In addition to the Nobel Prize, Gertrude Elion was elected to the National Academy of Sciences and the Institute of Medicine, made a fellow of the American Academy of Arts and Sciences, honored with the National Medal of Science, the Garvin-Olin Medal, the Lemelson-MIT Lifetime Achievement Award, and even membership as a Foreign Member of the Royal Society, the oldest and probably the most eminent science academy. She is in the Engineering and Science Hall of Fame and the first woman elected to the Inventors Hall of Fame. She is also in the National Women's Hall pof Fame.

When Burroughs-Wellcome moved to the famed Research Triangle of North Carolina, she moved to nearby Chapel Hill. Biochemist and pharmacologist extraordinaire Gertrude Belle Elion died there on February 21, 1999.

45. Mitsuye Endo and Tsuyako Kitashima

In February 1942, shortly after the devastating bombing of Pearl Harbor in Hawaii by Japan on December 7, 1941, President Franklin D. Roosevelt issued Executive Order 9066, authorizing the forced removal of people of Japanese ancestry along the Pacific coast, forcing them into detention "camps" on the interior of our nation. The two outstanding women here fought against this order, one during the "removal" and the other afterward.

As a point of knowledge: "issei" are Japanese immigrants; "nisei" are the children of the immigrants; and "sansei" are the grandchildren.

45A- Mitsuye Endo (1920-2006)

Quiet Civil Rights Hero

Mitsuye Endo was born in Sacramento, California on May 20, 1920 to parents who were Japanese immigrants. It was difficult for Japanese Americans to get jobs unless they worked for Japanese-owned businesses or for the government. Endo got a job with the State of California Department of Motor Vehicles as a typist.

However, soon after Executive Order 9066, she, and over one hundred thousand other Japanese Americans, were forced from their homes and lost their jobs.

First she and her family were sent to Walarga, near Sacramento, and then to the Tule Lake Relocation Center, and finally to the Topaz War Relocation Center in central Utah. Many legal challenges were filed against the government, but all failed or were only partially successful.

Lawyer James Purcell, working on behalf of the Japanese American Citizens League, took on the challenge. He interviewed hundreds of these detainees, hoping to find one to use as a test case against the United States government. He finally settled on Mitsuye Endo because she had a brother who was serving in the army, she had never been to Japan, and she was a Methodist, as opposed to an Oriental religion.

They challenged the constitutionality of the forced removal because Endo represented a loyal American, and the denial of allowing her to report to work as a state employee, and attempted to force the government to admit to anti-democratic tendencies. They initially granted her release, but only if she would go to the eastern part of the United States. Others did this. She refused, feeling she should be allowed to go anywhere she wanted. This kept her court case alive, not allowing the government to get off the hook. She defied and challenged them and remained at the camp, as a great sacrifice to herself. She was an ordinary woman who made an extraordinary choice.

The ACLU (American Civil Liberties Union) of northern California came to her aid in 1944, filing a legal brief of "Amicus Curiae" (Friend of the Court), sent to the United States Supreme Court. In December 1944 the court ruled in her favor, with Associate Justice Frank Murphy stating, "detention in Relocation Centers of persons of Japanese ancestry regardless of loyalty is not only unauthorized by Congress or the Executive, but is another example of the unconstitutional resort to racism in the entire evacuation program." It was passed 9-0. She and any others were to be released in January 1945. The government pulled their own manuever to avoid negative appearances and released them ahead of time in late 1944, but Mitsuye Endo had forced their hand.

Following the relocation, Mitsuye Endo moved to Chicago and became a secretary on the mayor's Committee on Race Relations. In 1947 she married Kenneth Tsutsumi, whom she met in the Utah camp. She went on to live a quiet life, having three children, and never talking about her wartime triumph. She avoided the publicity and usually avoided interviews, except for a short oral presentation, And Justice For All, in 1984.

Mitsuye Endo died on April 14, 2006 in Chicago from cancer. There has been a push to award Endo the Presidential Medal of Freedom posthumously.

45B- Tsuyako Kitashima (1918-2006)

Sox

Tsuyako Kitashima, nickenamed "Sox" because her friends could not pronounce her name, was born to Japanese immigrants and owners of a strawberry farm in Hayward, California on January 1, 1918. She became an ardent activist in seeking reparations for the relocation of Japanese Americans.

When the relocation order came in 1942 her family was moved to the Tanforan race track in San Bruno, California, where they slept in horse-smelling stalls. Then a more permanent move was to the Topaz War Relocation Center in central Utah. "Sox" Kitashima endured the relocation during World War II, but when it was over she began her full effort for recompense and reparations. She married Tom Kitashima and spent thirty years in administration at the San Francisco Medical Center.

She spent a great deal of time speaking to students about the relocation. In the 1980s Tsuyako Kitashima became a spokeswoman for the National Coalition for Redress and Reposition. In 1981 she lobbied and addressed the Landmark Commission of Wartime Relocation and Internment of Civilians. It was through her efforts that the Civil Liberties Act of 1988 had the United States government offer an apology and compensatory payments to those Japanese Americans who had been detained during World War II.

In 1998 she was honored with the Free Spirit Award from the Freedom Forum, which came with $10,000. She became the "Grandmother of Japantown" and was a member of the advisory council of the San Francisco Commission on Aging, and volunteered with Kimochi in Japantown, a non-profit organization to help seniors. Tsuyako "Sox" Kitashima died of a heart attack in San Francisco on December 29, 2006.

#46- Edna Ferber (1887-1968)

America

Edna Ferber, who has probably had the most larger-than-life stories of the American scene made into motion pictures, was born on August 15, 1887 in Kalamazoo, Michigan, but after moving with her Jewish parents, storekeeper Jacob and Julia, to Illinois and Iowa, grew up in Appleton, Wisconsin. She was deeply hurt by the amount of anti-Semitism she and her family had to endure, particularly in Iowa. She had wanted to be an actress, but to help support her blinded father she began working on Appleton's Daily Crescent at seventeen. This was followed by employment with Milwaukee's Journal and the Chicago Tribune. She worked so hard that she was exhausted, and forced herself to take a break. During this leave, she tried her hand at writing. She wrote "The Homely Heroine" which was published in Everybody's Magazine. That was the start.

She then turned to writing stories, with the first about a writer/newspaper woman in Milwaukee, Dawn O'Hara, in 1911, which was part of her portraying strong female characters. It was a huge success and the following year came Buttered Side Down, short stories about Appleton, and in 1913 Emma McChesney, a traveling saleswoman, was created in Roast Beef, Medium. Emma appeared in an additional thirty stories, including Personality Plus and Emma McChesney and Co., prompting Ferber to devote full time to writing.

So Big was set in Illinois and Edna Ferber's works each began having a different American setting. Not only was it awarded the Pulitzer Prize, but films of it were made in 1925, 1932 and 1953. In 1926, Show Boat, later both a stage musical and a motion picture, told of the life of an actress on a Mississippi riverboat. Cimarron, in 1929, told of the Oklahoma land rush. It, too, became a film (which was awarded the Best Picture Oscar), and a remake in 1960, and a television series. In 1935, Come and Get It was set again in Wisconsin. In 1941 New Orleans and upstate New York were the settings for Saratoga Trunk, also made into a musical. In 1945 it was The Great Son in Seattle, in 1948 it was Ice Palace in Alaska, also made into a film, and in 1952 it was Giant in Texas, which was also made into a film and a musical. It seemed all of America was her literary canvas.

She eventually settled in New York City, becoming a member of the famous Algonquin Hotel "Round Table" along with Dorothy Parker and others. She wrote a number of plays, such as Dinner at Eight, Stage Door, and The Royal Family, with George S. Kaufman. Also with Kaufman she wrote Minick and The Land Is Bright. Other works by Ferber are American Beauty, Gigolo, The Girls, and Mother Knows Best.

She also wrote two autobiographies, A Peculiar Treasure in 1939, and A Kind of Magic in 1963. Edna Ferber died of stomach cancer in New York City on April 16, 1968. In the 1994 film, Mrs. Parker and the Vicious Circle, one of the characters is Edna Ferber, and in the 2013 film, The Son, there is a fictionalized version of her. In 2002 an Edna Ferber 83-cent stamp was issued, and a school in Appleton is named for her, and she has been inducted into the Michigan Hall of Fame. All in all, Edna Ferber wrote twelve novels, twelve short story collections, nine plays (most of them co-written) and two autobiographies.

#47- *Geraldine Ferraro (1935-2011)*

New York Icon

Geraldine Anne Ferraro was born in Newburgh, New York on August 26, 1935, to Italian immigrant restauranteur Dominick, and his wife seamstress Antonetta Ferraro. Her father died when she was only eight years old and her mother, investing poorly, lost quite a bit. As a result, losing much, they had to move to the South Bronx, where she grew up. Geraldine graduated from Marymount Academy in Tarrytown at sixteen years of age, as the person "most likely to succeed" and earned a scholarship to Marymount Manhattan College, graduating with a degree in English in 1956. For five years she taught in the Astoria neighborhood of Queens, New York. In 1960 she began attending Fordham University law school, and married real estate businessman John Zaccaro. They moved to the Forest Hills neighborhood in Queens, and Ferraro worked on legal matters for the real estate firm for over thirteen years.

She became president of the Queens County Women's Bar Association (an association of lawyers), and in 1974 became an assistant district attorney, creating and working primarily in the special victims bureau. Four years later, after becoming familiar with local Democratic Party workings, she submitted her name as a candidate for the United States House of Representatives. There was a three-way primary which she won, and then went on to win the election. Once in Congress she gained respect and became a force with which to be reckoned. She was on the House Budget Committee, the House Select Committee on Aging, the Steering and Policy Committee (the committee which determines what will or will not be brought up to the entire House), the Post Office and Civil Service Committee, and the Public Works and Transportation Committee, bringing about stricter regulations for transporting hazardous waste material. Ferraro also became secretary of the House Democratic Caucus (only Democratic officials included). She also became a strong advocate for equity in women's wages and pensions and retirement, fighting vigorously against Ronald Reagan's economic policies. She was on the rise! In 1980 Ferraro co-founded the National Organization of Italian American Women, whose goals were not only educational and professional, but also to fight ethnic stereotyping.

In the presidential election of 1984 the Republican Party ran Ronald Reagan. The Democratic Party nominee was Walter Mondale. He and the party felt it was time for a female candidate for vice president, and it came down to two, with the feisty and spirited Geraldine Ferraro coming out as the candidate, the first woman and the first Italian American candidate for vice president on a major party line. The speech she made, which brought tears to the eyes of many at the convention, has been rated number fifty-six in the Top 100 Speeches of the Twentieth Century. "The daughter of an Italian immigrant from Italy has been chosen to run for vice president in the land her father came to love."

Although the Mondale-Ferraro team got a good bump up in the polls after the convention, the immense charisma and popularity of Ronald Reagan was too much. And there still existed a good deal of gender bias. Too often it was said or inferred, "Are you tough enough?" It also came out in October in the New York Post that Ferraro's late father had been arrested just before he died for being involved in the "numbers" game, an illegal lottery. This happened when Ferraro was young, and she knew nothing about it. To make matters worse, when her husband belatedly released his tax returns, it showed that the family was worth over four million dollars, and it showed some questionable matters. This rather destroyed the Ferraro image of the little girl who was so poor.

After the election Geraldine Ferraro finished her term as in congress, and what followed was a life of ups and downs. She was much in demand for speaking engagements and wrote an autobiography, Ferraro: My Story. Also, all charges were dropped on John Zaccarro's tax situation. However, her son was arrested on drug charges and sent briefly to prison.

She got herself involved in many worthwhile efforts, becoming a board member of the National Democratic Institute for International Affairs and the Council on Foreign Affairs. She became president of the International Institute for Women's Political Leadership, and was part of the Pension Rights Center, and wrote, Changing History: Women, Power and Politics. Geraldine Ferraro was on the board of the National Breast Cancer Fund and the New York Easter Seal Society, which is a non-profit charitable association to aid people with disabilities or special needs. In 1998 she wrote a second autobiography, Framing A Life: A Family Memoir. That same year she was diagnosed with blood cancer, but did not disclose this until 2001. She did go to Washington, D. C. to promote cancer research. In 2002 she moved to Manhattan.

She and former Republican congresswoman Lynn Martin teamed up and formed G & L Strategies, advising corporate entities how to create more women in leadership positions, and making the workplace a better place for female employees. In 1992 and in 1998 she sought the Democratic nomination for the United States Senate from New York. In the first primary she lost to Robert Abrams who went on to lose the election. In 1998 she lost the primary to Chuck Schumer who did go on to win. With that loss, Ferraro retired from politics, although she worked for Hillary Clinton in the 2008 primaries.

For a few years she was a political commentator for Fox News and on CNN's Crossfire political talk show. In 1993, President Clinton named her to the United Nations Commission on Human Rights, with her eventually becoming ambassador, until 1996. In 2011 Geraldine Ferraro went to the Cancer Institute in Boston, but was transferred to Massachusetts General Hospital where she died of multiple myeloma (cancer) on March 26, 2011. At the time of her death, Hillary and Bill Clinton stated that "she was a one of a kind- tough, brilliant and never afraid to speak her mind...a New York icon." She has been inducted into the National Women's Hall of Fame, received the Lifetime Achievement Award of the Sons of Italy, the Edith I.

Everything

Spivak Award from the New York County Lawyers Association, and has received honorary degrees from Hunter College, Case Western Reserve University, Marymount Manhattan College, Muhlenberg College, and others, including New York University Law School.

#48- Ella Fitzgerald (1917-1996)

Scat

Ella Jane Fitzgerald, Lady Ella, was born on April 25, 1917 in Newport News, Virginia to William and Temperance. She moved with her mother to Yonkers, New York in the early 1920s with her first observation of formal music at the Bethany African Methodist Church there. Her mother died in 1932 in a car accident, and Ella moved in with an aunt. She went on to become one of the greatest jazz, blues, and swing singers. Her upbringing was hard, and for a while she even worked as a teenager as a "lookout" in a bordello, and as a "numbers" runner, an illegal lottery. She was caught and sent to the Colored Orphan Asylum in the Bronx, New York and then on to the reform school, New York Training School for Girls in Hudson, New York. Eventually, she escaped and became homeless.

In November of 1934, bedraggled and unkempt, she went on in "Amateur Night" at Harlem's Apollo Theater, singing "Judy" and "The Object of My Affection" and won the first prize of twenty-five dollars. Soon after in January, 1935 she worked with Tiny Bradshaw at the Harlem Opera House. She auditioned for the Chick Webb Orchestra at a Yale University dance and was a success. Ella was then asked to join, and began appearing at the Savoy Ballroom, and traveling throughout the United States. This was the real beginning of her fame. With Chick Webb she recorded "Love and Kisses," "If You Can't Sing It, You Have to Swing It" and, possibly her best-known song, "A Tisket a Tasket."

When Webb died in 1939, she took over the orchestra, calling it Ella and Her Famous Orchestra. In the time she spent with these two orchestras, she recorded one hundred and fifty songs. In 1942, Ella Fitzgerald went solo, signing with Decca Records. She also began her long and successful association with jazz impresario and promoter Norman Granz. She worked for a while with Dizzy Gillespie, where she began her famous "scat" singing, possibly the best known was "Flying Home," a classic in jazz vocals. Ella Fitzgerald's scat was a very pleasing, melodic jazz singing of nonsense sounds. Ella Fitzgerald brought scat to a truly art form. "Oh Lady Be Good" was also extremely popular. Under Granz' promoting she began the series "Jazz at the Philharmonic". In 1941 she married drug dealer Benjamin Kornegay, a man unworthy of her, but it was annulled a few years later. From 1947 to 1952 she was married to bassist Ray Brown.

She moved to Verve Records, founded by Granz, in mid-1950s. Out of this came the Great American Songbook.

There was a Cole Porter songbook, and one for Duke Ellington, and one for Gershwin, and others, eight in all. And then later there were the very successful "live" albums: Ella in Berlin, Ella in Rome, Ella in London. In the early 1960s she bought a home in Denmark and lived there briefly.

Along the way Ella got into the movies, as well: Pete Kelly's Blues, St. Louis Blues, Let No Man Write My Epitaph, and even an Abbot and Costello film, Ride 'Em Cowboy. She also appeared in a great many television variety shows, and even a few dramas. And she made numerous television commercial advertisements, the most memorable for Memorex, a tape recording device. She recorded over two hundred albums, and was voted best female vocalist three years in a row, in addition to being named #13 on VH1's list of Greatest Women of Rock and Roll. In 1958 she became the first African American woman to win a Grammy award.

And this Queen of Jazz was a great collaborator, teaming up with such all-time greats as the Ink Spots, Louis Armstrong, Count Basie and Duke Ellington ("Dream a Little Dream of Me," "Cheek to Cheek," "It Don't Mean a Thing if it Ain't Got That Swing," "Into Each Life Some Rain Must Fall.").

Over her long and illustrious career she received so many honors: Presidential Medal of Freedom, Kennedy Center for the Performing Arts Honor, National Endowment of the Arts Medal of Art, Grammy Lifetime Achievement Award (to go along with her fourteen Grammys), Society of Singers Lifetime Achievement Award (afterwards called the "Ella"), George and Ira Gershwin Lifetime Achievement, and the USC Magnum Opus Award. And she is in the National Women's Hall of Fame, as well as the Big Band and Jazz Hall of Fame. There are bronze sculptures of Ella Fitzgerald in her one-time hometown of Yonkers, New York, and one in California's Chapman University. There is even a 2007 postage stamp issued in her likeness. In "another" hometown, in 2008 Newport News, Virginia opened its Ella Fitzgerald Theater, and she has her "Star" on the Hollywood Walk of Fame. In 2016 the Apollo Theater held a centennial celebration (a bit early) of Ella Fitzgerald.

In the late 1980s she began to suffer a number of health problems. There were respiratory problems, exhaustion, heart failure. She had a five-way bypass operation in 1986,and both legs amputated due to diabetes in 1993. Ella Fitzgerald's last recording was in 1991 and last performance was in 1993, and she went blind. About this time she set up the Ella Fitzgerald Charitable Foundation. The First Lady of Song died on June 15, 1996 in her home in Beverly Hills, California of diabetes melitus.

"The only thing I like better than singing is more singing."

#49- Betty Friedan (1921-2006)

The Feminine Mystique

The bad-tempered, flamboyant, abrasive Betty Naomi Goldstein Friedan, who influenced a whole generation of writers, journalists, educators, union organizers, anthropologists, and, especially feminists and women's rights activists, was born in Peoria, Illinois on February 4, 1921 to parents jeweler Harry and poet Miriam.

She graduated summa cum laude, with a degree in psychology from Smith College in 1938, where she showed a distinct flair for poetry, but went on, but only briefly, to do graduate work at the University of California at Berleley. She moved to New York, becoming politically involved, working as a somewhat left-wing journalist for the Federated Press and the United Electrical Workers UE News from 1943 until 1952. After that she did freelance work for Cosmopolitan magazine.

Her 1963 best-seller blockbuster work, The Feminine Mystique, the cornerstone work that brought about what has been labeled the "second wave of feminism." Simply put, it dealt with what Friedan called "the problem with no name." The problem, it seemed, was that in modern society women's priorities were set at being the traditional housewife and mother, and deferring to the husband's career, neglecting what might have been any other fulfillment she may have wanted, leading to a restrictive dissatisfaction. That book, and her 1966 co-founding of NOW (National Organization for Women), galvanized a resentment that was simmering inside many women. She was its first president until 1970. The purpose was to bring women up to equality with men in the workplace, including pay differential, and with the equal rights amendment, discrimination, and opportunities.

She married thatrical producer Carl Friedan in 1947. They divorced in 1969, and he died in 2005.

In 1969 she founded the National Association for the Repeal of Abortion Laws, and the next year organized and led the Women's Strike For Equality, marching with at least twenty thousand people in New York City on the fiftieth anniversary of the passage of the nineteenth amendment, giving women the right to vote. Although Betty Friedan and Gloria Stienem were rivals in the feminist movement, in 1971 they teamed up with Bella Abzug and founded the National Women's Political Caucus. Later in her career she wrote The Second Stage, which was somewhat of a follow up to The Feminine Mystique, in that she now attacked those who would go to extremes in the movement, and defended those women who did choose to be homemakers. Betty Friedan was given the Eleanor Roosevelt Award in 1989, the Humanist of the Year Award from the American Humanist Society, the Mort Weisinger

Award from the American Society of Journalists and Authors, and was featured in the 2013 documentary, Makers: Women Who Make America. Other books by Fridan were: The Fountain of Age, Beyond Gender, It Changed My Life: Writings on the Women's Movement, and her autobiography, Life So Far.

Pugnacious Betty Friedan died in Washington, D. C. of congestive heart failure on her birthday, February 4, 2006. Betty Friedan is in the National Women's Hall of Fame. Glamour magazine named her one of the "75 Most Important Women of the Past 75 Years." She received honorary doctorates from Columbia University, Smith College, Bradley University and State University of New York at Stony Brook.

#50- Margaret Fuller (1810-1850)

Brilliant

Bad tempered, overly confident, but absolutely brilliant, Sarah Margaret Fuller, daughter of lawyer Timothy and Margaret Fuller, was born in Cambridge port, Massachusetts on May 23, 1810, and went on to demonstrate and prove she had one of the keenest minds, male or female, that America had ever produced. She dropped the "Sarah" from her name at age nine. And while her father served as a congressman, she lived off and on in Washington, D.C. When her father died she had to fend for herself and began teaching back home in New England. For a bit of time she taught in Bronson Alcott's Temple School, but she was forced to leave when he could not pay her salary, even though she supplemented her salary with translation work.

From 1840 to 1844 she conducted her series of "Conversations," which was a successful group for women to gather. Her comprehensive, intensity and quick wit made her an overwhelming success. She knew what she wanted to say and had the knack of knowing when to say it. She spoke of history, literature, fine arts, nature, and mythology. Her audiences were awed by this amazing woman. By this time she was considered to be the best-read person in all of New England. And it led the way for other female speakers to follow.

She had also become an editor of the transcendentalist The Dial, becoming one of the most influential members of that movement, and making friends with the likes of Ralph Waldo Emerson, Nathaniel Hawthorne, and Henry David Thoreau, and herself becoming a member of the Transcendentalists. A transcendentalist philosophy is one in which the nature of a human is good, but can be corrupted by culture or society. Her Woman of the Nineteenth Century, published by The Dial, was the first major feminist work in America, and was a call for the fulfillment and development of women as individuals, spiritually, politically and emotionally. She was, indeed, ahead of her time and an early advocate of the emancipation of slaves, suffrage, employment and prison reform. She traveled, particularly in the northern areas of the United States, leading to her 1844 Summer on the Lakes, which detailed her experiences with the Chippewa and Ottawa Native American tribes. Horace Greeley admired it and invited Margaret Fuller to go to New York and become a literary critic for the Herald Tribune. Within two years she became regarded as the most able of critics. But in 1846 she went to Europe as the first-ever woman foreign correspondent.

While in Italy she aligned herself with Giuseppe Mazzini's revolutionaries, and even married one of his close allies, disinherited nobleman Giovanni Angelo Ossoli, living in Florence and Rome, and giving birth to a son, Angelino. She also did volunteer work in hospitals, but with Mazzini defeated, she decided to come home.

On July 19, 1850, the ship, "Elizabeth," with Margaret Fuller and her family on board, sank off Fire Island, New York. She was only forty years old. During her life and afterwards, as well, she had many notable admirers, besides the ones already mentioned, such as Walt Whitman, Edgar Allan Poe, Elizabeth Barrett Browning, Elizabeth Cady Stanton, and Susan B. Anthony, who especially considered Fuller to be an inspiration. It is assumed that Hawthorne's Hester Prynne's radical stand in The Scarlet Letter is based on Margaret Fuller's personality. At Home and Abroad and Memoirs of Margaret Fuller Ossoli were published posthumously, but her history of Rome, which included that recent revolution, was lost. She had also written Life Without and Life Within.

She has been inducted into the National Women's Hall of Fame, and through the efforts of Julia Ward Howe in 1901, there is a memorial to her on Fire Island. Her answer to THE question: "If you ask me what office women should fill, I reply...any."

#51-Althea Gibson (1927-2003)

She led the way

Althea Gibson, daughter of sharecroppers Daniel and Annie Gibson, was born in Silver, South Carolina on August 25, 1927. Due the hardship of the Great Depression, they moved up to Harlem, New York in 1930. Althea became quite proficient in paddle tennis, winning the New York City championship at age twelve.

In 1940 some neighbors collected funds to have her admitted to the Cosmopolitan Tennis Club in Harlem and in the next year she entered their tournament and won. She went on to win the American Tennis Association New York State championship. In 1944 and 1945 she won the National Championships, made it to the finals in 1946, and won it every year from 1947 to 1955, ten years in a row. In 1946 she moved to North Carolina to attend and graduate high school and in 1949 she attended Florida A & M University on a scholarship, graduating in 1953. But the 1950s would be the decade of Althea Gibson, with her grace and power she dominated. In 1950 she made it to the second round at the US Championships (now called the US Open), erasing tennis' color line. The next year she made it to the third round there, and the same at Wimbledon, as well as winning the Caribbean Championship. In 1952 she again made it to the third round of the US Championships. Her five-foot eleven-inch frame was beginning to show that she would go on to become one of the greatest women players of all time.

In 1953 she reached the quarterfinals of the US Championships and became ranked #7 in the world, and made it to the first round and third round in the next two years. Althea Gibson took time off to teach at Lincoln University in Missouri. In 1955 the State Department asked her to go on a goodwill tour with exhibition matches. She traveled through Mexico, India, Pakistan, Thailand and what was then Burma and Ceylon. She remained in Asia and Europe for a while, winning sixteen out of eighteen matches.

In 1956 not only did she win the French Open, becoming the first Black to win it, and followed this with a victory in the doubles. She also made it to the finals in the Australian and US Championships, and also won doubles at Wimbledon and at the French and made it to the mixed doubles finals at Wimbledon: also the Italian championships and the Asian championships.

She went on to be part of the Wightman Cup team that defeated Great Britain in 1957 and won in Wimbledon in 1957 and 1958, and the US Championships in those same years. At the 1957 Wimbledon, Queen Elizabeth made her first appearance at this tournament, and personally presented Althea Gibson with the award. In 1957, besides winning Wimbledon, she made it to the Australian finals, and made it to the Wimbledon mixed doubles finals. In 1958 she made it to the finals at Wimbledon.

In both 1957 and 1958 she was ranked #1, and named Associated Press' "Female Athlete of the Year." Gibson once said, "In sports you simply aren't considered a real champion until you have defended your title successfully. Winning it once can be a fluke; winning it twice proves you are the best." In New York City they gave her a ticker-tape parade and a bronze medallion. In 1958, after winning fifty-six international and national titles, she retired at age thirty because there was very little money in amateur tennis. She played professionally by putting on demonstrations and match games, but competitive professional women's tennis was a long way off. She did not see herself as a civil rights leader, but only wanted to play tennis and win.

Althea Gibson then went into the entertainment business, releasing an album, Althea Gibson Sings, appeared in a movie, went on television, did some sports commentary, and did commercials. In 1960 her memoir, I Always Wanted To Be Somebody, was published. In 1964 she joined the Ladies Professional Golf Association (LPGA), the first African American to do so, but the best she ever did was to finish twenty-seventh in 1966, and retired from golf in 1978. She had also married William Darben in 1965, but it only lasted until 1976. In the 1970s she became director of Women's Sports and Recreation for Essex County, New Jersey, and in 1976 New Jersey Athletic Commissioner, the first African American woman to hold such a position. That same year Gibson competed and did very well on television's Superstars, a decathlon-type competition that pitted athletes of different sports against each other. In 1977 she unsuccessfully tried for the New Jersety state senate, but did become supervisor of the Governor's Council on Physical Fitness and Sports. Throughout the 1970s and 1980s she began running tennis clinics in many major cities and worked tirelessly as a coach and mentor. Later in life Althea Gibson made a tennis comeback that was unsuccessful.

For a short while in the 1980s she was married to coach Sydney Llewellyn, but in the late 1980s she had two cerebral hemorrhages, and in 1992, a stroke. She was financially devastated, and only through the help of donations was one million dollars raised. After this she became somewhat of a recluse, not wanting anyone seeing her in such poor condition. In 2003 she suffered a heart attack, and she died on September 28, 2003 of respiratory and bladder infections, and is buried in East Orange, New Jersey. She was a competitor in both tennis and golf. She was the first African American woman placed on the cover of both Sports Illustrated and Time, was part of the first group inducted into the International Women's Sports Hall of Fame in 1980. There is now a Althea Gibson Cup for seniors. She also wrote a second memoir, So Much To Live For. Gibson led the way for players like Arthur Ashe and Zina Garrison and so many more.

Althea Gibson is also inducted into the International Tennis Hall of Fame, the Florida Sports Hall of Fame, the Sports Hall of Fame of New Jersey, the New Jersey Hall of Fame, the International and the National Women's Hall of Fame, the Black Athletes Hall of Fame and the National Lawn Tennis Hall of Fame. Her Wimbledon trophies are in the Smithsonian Institution in Washington. She was presented the Candace Award in 1988 from the National Coalition of 100 Black Women, and in 1991 the Theodore Roosevelt Award from the NCAA. In 2007, on the fiftieth anniversary of her Wimbledon victory, she was inducted into the US Open Court of Champions. There is a statue of her in Newark, New Jersey.

#52- *Lillian M. Gilbreth (1878-1972)*

Genius in the Art of Living

Pioneer industrial and organizational psychologist, Lillian Evelyn Moller, was born on May 24, 1878 in Oakland, California to building supply merchant William Moller and his wife Annie. She earned a degree in English literature from the University of California/Berkeley in 1900, and a master's degree in 1902. Over her lifetime she would be regarded as an expert in psychology, engineering and homemaking. Her biggest achievements were in organization and innovation, and efficiency both in the workplace and in the home.

After obtaining her degree she took a vacation, and, in Boston, met Frank Gilbreth. In 1904 she married him, and the two of them would be forever remembered in two books, Cheaper By the Dozen and Belles on their Toes, written by two of their twelve children, Ernestine and Frank, Jr., about the life of living in the home of efficiency experts. They did, actually, have thirteen children. One of her children, number nine, Frederick, lived until 2015.

In 1910 they moved to Rhode Island where Lillian M. Gilbreth got a doctorate in psychology in 1915 from Brown University. Frank Gilbreth was extremely interested in the concept of efficiency in the workplace. Together they began studying the principles of scientific management. Together they wrote a number of books on the subject, but even though Lillian Gilbreth had the doctorate and did most of the research, and Frank had no college at all, publishers insisted that Frank's name be listed first because he was a man.

They founded Gilbreth, Inc. for the purpose of studying time efficiency. It was a unique first effort to bring psychology to an organization, to make industry compatible to both employer and employee. What they did was advance industry and workplace effectiveness which was beneficial to both. They examined what would make the workplace psychologically more manageable and effective in all ways. They suggested such concepts as better lighting, motivation, standardization and simplification of job duties, regular break time, incentive salary plans, suggestion boxes, and even free books. They also studied the effects of stress and fatigue on time management.

Frank Gilbreth died in 1924, and Lillian now turned her attention to those same principles, but now in the home, to domestic management and home economics. She wanted the homemaker to have simpler and easier ways of getting housework done, so that if she wished, she would have time for outside employment. This was important for women during the Great Depression. Such simple but profound innovations came from the mind of this mother of the modern home: shelves on refrigerator doors, on-the-wall light switches, the foot-pedal trash pail, and the standard and appropriate height of kitchen appliances, such as stoves and sinks.

In addition, in 1926 she became a lecturer at Purdue University, and in 1935 became Purdue's first female engineering professor, and full professor in 1940. She retired in 1948. She became friends with Herbert Hoover and his wife, and was named president of the Emergency Commission for Employment. During World War II her expertise was sought and used by the United States Navy, the Office of War Information and the War Manpower Commission. After World War II she was employed by the Chemical Warfare Board, on President Harry Truman's Civil Defense Board, and the Defense Advisory Committee on Women in the Services.

In 1944 California Monthly declared Gilbreth "a genius in the art of living," and in the same year the American Management Association awarded her the Henry Laurence Gantt Medal. In 1965 the National Academy of Engineers awarded her the Hoover Medal. She became a member of the American Society of Mechanical Engineers and was the first honorary member of the Society of Women Engineers. Lillian M. Gilbreth received over twenty honorary degrees, most notably from Princeton University, Brown University, Bryn Mawr College, Rutgers University and the University of Michigan. In 1964, at age eighty-six she was teaching at Massachusetts Institute of Technology. In 1984 she became the first female psychologist honored with a postage stamp. Lillian M. Gilbreth died on January 2, 1972, at the age of ninety-three. This woman who perfectly combined career and family has her portrait hanging in the National Portrait Gallery, and she has been inducted into the National Women's Hall of Fame. Her autobiography is As I Remember It.

#53- *Katherine Graham (1917-2001)*

Katherine the Great

Renowned publisher Katherine Meyer Graham was born in New York City on June 16, 1917 to banker and financier Eugene Meyer and his wife Agnes, an art lover and political activist. Katherine spent most of her youth in what was referred to as "the castle" in Mount Kisco, New York and in another home in Washington, D. C. Most of her upbringing was done by nannies, governesses and tutors. She started higher education at Vassar College, but switched to the University of Chicago, graduating in 1938.

In 1933, her retired father bought the Washington Post newspaper. When Katherine graduated college she went to work for a short while with the San Francisco News, but soon went to work for her father in Washington.

In 1940 she married Philip Graham, a Harvard Law School graduate and law clerk for Associate Justice of the Supreme Court Felix Frankfurter. In 1946 Eugene Meyer turned the Washington Post over to Philip Graham. Under his leadership the paper did prosper, even acquiring Newsweek magazine and some television and radio stations. Eventually they would have a daughter and three sons. Katherine Graham was in the heart of Washington's fabulous social world. Over the years she would count the Kennedys, the Johnsons, the Reagans, Warren Buffet, and Henry Kissinger as friends. After a series of traumatic events due to mental illness, alcoholism and infidelity, Philip Graham had a nervous breakdown, and on August 3, 1963 committed suicide. Katherine Graham took over the helm of the Washington Post upon her husband's death, first in an "acting" capacity, but then as the publisher, a real working publisher, from 1963 until 1979, and was chairman of the board of directors from 1973 to 1991. At first, as a woman, she was not taken seriously, but soon showed why Deborah Davis' biography was entitled Katherine the Great. She would go on to become one of the most courageous, and the most powerful woman in publishing and The Washington Post one of the two greatest newspapers in America. In 1972 she became the first woman to be a CEO of a Fortune 500 company. The Fortune 500 is a list of the 500 companies that represent a large majority of the finances in America, according to income and other financial guideposts.

Those early 1970s were Katherine Graham's entry into national prominence. She hired Benjamin Bradlee as editor, and in 1971, when Daniel Ellsberg, who had been part of the creating the "United States-Vietnam Relations, 1945-1967: A Study Prepared by the Department of Defense" released part of it first to the New York Times and then to the Washington Post, the Post was given a court order not publish. The "Pentagon Papers" as they came to be called revealed that President Lyndon Johnson had lied to the public and to Congress about bombing in countries that bordered Vietnam. She fought back and it went all the way to the Supreme Court, with Graham receiving the favorable ruling, and a big gain for freedom of the press. Justice Black commented that "only a free and unrestrained press can effectively expose deception in government." The 2017 film, The Post, deals with this incident, with Meryl Streep portraying Katherine Graham.

In 1972 there was a break-in at the Democratic Party National Headquarters at the Watergate office complex in Washington, D. C. Early on most publications rather downplayed it, but Graham and Bradlee gave reporters Bob Woodward and Carl Bernstein room to investigate, and they exposed a great deal of cover-up and illegal acts. In the end the most time in prison for the five burglars was eighteen months, and for those other twelve connected with the Committee for the Re-Election of the President, no one served more than four years in prison, but the disgrace and deception was huge, and it lead to the eventual resignation of Richard Nixon as president of the United States. Woodward and Bernstein wrote a blockbuster book in 1974, All the President's Men, detailing all the events in what was to be called the "Watergate scandal." A film of the same name was released in 1976, with Robert Redford portraying Woodward and Dustin Hoffman portraying Bernstein. Over the years Katherine Graham was honored often. She was the recipient of the David Rockefeller Award, the Elijah Parish

Lovejoy Award, the S. Roger Horchaw Award for the Greatest Public Service by a Private Citizen, and the Walter Cronkite Award for Excellence in Journalism. She became a fellow of the American Academy of Arts and Sciences, and was listed as one of the International Press Institute's 50 World Press Freedom Heroes of the past 50 years.

In 1997 she was awarded the Freedom Medal, and posthumously, in 2002, given the Presidential Medal of Freedom, and has been inducted into the National Women's Hall of Fame. While in Sun Valley, Idaho in 2001, Katherine Graham fell. She was taken to a hospital in Boise where she died three days later of complications from the head injury on July 17. She was eulogized by, among others, Henry Kissinger, Nancy Reagan and Queen Noor Al Hussein of Jordan in Washington's National Cathedral. She is buried in Georgetown, Washington, D. C. Her memoir, Personal History, won the Pulitzer Prize for biography.

Group Five

Alice Hamilton –
Florence Griffith Joyner

#54- Alice Hamilton (1869-1970)

OSHA

Alice Hamilton was born in New York City on February 27, 1869 to merchant Montgomery and Gertrude Hamilton. While she was still young the family moved to Fort Wayne, Indiana. She always wanted to be a medical missionary, traveling all about the world healing people. After a good deal of training and preparation, including the Fort Wayne College of Medicine, she was accepted into the University of Michigan Medical School, getting her degree in 1893. From there she did internships in Minneapolis and Boston. Then it was off to Europe to study further on bacteriology and pathology (the study of diseases), but some of the European schools were not quite accepting of women. Alice came home and did some post-graduate work at Johns Hopkins University in Baltimore, and then in 1897 she became a professor of pathology at the Woman's Medical School of Northwestern University in Chicago. This privileged woman actually also took up residence in Jane Addams Hull House in order to better observe and study why typhoid and tuberculosis was so rampant in that poor area. These ailments resulted in fever, pain, rashes and lung disease. Her investigation led to the discovery of improper sewage disposal, and led to the replacement of the chief sanitary inspector of Chicago. In addition, Alice Hamilton found that the study of industrial health problems was practically non-existent in the United States.

She began to realize that workplace poisons, particularly lead, were affecting the people. This is when she began her warfare against industrialized toxins. In 1902 she became involved with the Memorial Institute for Infectious Diseases in Chicago, and in 1908 she managed to receive an appointment to the Illinois Commission on Occupational Diseases. This commission urged the passage of laws in Illinois and other states, making sure that businesses took whatever safety measures were needed. Over the next ten years they discovered how many harmful things existed: carbon monoxide, mercury, radium, hydrogen sulfide, tetraethyl lead, benzene and carbon disulfide to name a few. These combined caused cancer, lowered intelligence, muscle weakness, harm to the nervous system and bone marrow, and pain.

In 1911 she received a special invitation to join the Bureau of Labor Statistics of the United States Department of Labor, and her pioneering work brought about widespread health reforms. Her study on the effects on the human body led to findings of occupational illnesses, especially due to industrial metals and chemicals. In 1919 she became an assistant professor (the first woman) at Harvard University's Department of Industrial Medicine. From 1924 until 1930 she was on the League of Nations (the organization before the United Nations) Health Committee (the only woman). She retired in 1935, but became a medical consultant to the United States Division of Labor Standards. Over the years she wrote Industrial Poisons in the United States and Industrial Toxology.

And while living at Hull House and in the company of Jane Addams, she began getting active in the advocacy of women's rights and involved in the peace movement. Hamilton even traveled with Addams and others to the 1915 International Congress of Women in The Hague, Netherlands.

From 1944 to 1949 Hamilton was president of the National Consumers League. Eleanor Roosevelt presented her with the Chi Omega sorority National Achievement Award, and in 1947 she was honored with the Lasker Award from the United States Public Health Service for "public service."

In 1995 a postage stamp was issued in her honor, and in 1956 she was Time magazine's Woman of the Year. She is not only in the National Women's Hall of Fame, but also in the Connecticut Women's Hall of Fame and the Michigan Women's Hall of Fame. Alice Hamilton died at the age of 101 at her home in Hadlyme, Connecticut on September 22, 1970. What Alice Hamilton had done was to make sure that workers were entitled to a safe workplace environment. Practically no one else had put that concept forward.

Three months after her death the government finally passed the Occupational Safety and Health Act (OSHA). In 1987 the National Institute for Occupational Safety and Health named their research facility the Alice Hamilton Laboratory for Occupational Safety and Health. Since 2002 there is an Alice Hamilton Award from them for published scientific research in the field of occupational health. It is through the tireless quest of this woman that the workplaces factories and mines of the United States are less dangerous. Her autobiography is Exploring the Dangerous Trades.

#55- Lorraine Hansberry (1930-1965)

"...an inspiration of generations yet unborn."

Lorraine Hansberry was born on May 19, 1930 in the Southside of Chicago. She was a member of Carl and Nannie's no-nonsense family, with a father, who was a real estate broker and N. A. A. C. P. activist, who had even run for congress, and teacher mother. He fought against housing restrictive practices, taking it up to the United States Supreme Court. They won, and the family moved into an all-white community, where Lorraine learned about racial taunting. She wanted to be an artist, and to further that goal she spent time in Guadalajara, Mexico and the University of Wisconsin only to find out that art was not her forte'. In 1950 she came to New York City, settled in Harlem, worked for the Pan-African newspaper, Freedom, as a "jill-of-all-trades", and attended the New School for Social Research. She also worked for civil rights and women's rights, as well as against colonialism and imperialism, which were the evils of controlling one country by another by various means. And in 1953 married music publisher Robert Nemiroff and moved to Greenwich Village. They later divorced in the 1960s, but remained friends.

1959 saw Loraine Hansberry's A Raisin In The Sun arrive at Broadway's Ethel Barrymore Theatre, recalling her own family's housing problems, it exploded into legend. The title was taken from lines in a Langston Hughes poem: "What happens to a dream deferred? Does it dry up like a raisin in the sun?" It was the first play written by an African American woman to be produced on Broadway, and not only won the Drama Circle Award (the youngest person ever), but Variety selected Hansberry as the most promising playwright of the season. The world now knew she was a major playwright. It was translated into thirty-five languages. Sidnet Poitier appeared in it both on Broadway, and in the film version. Her The Sign in Sidney Brustein's Window in 1965 also opened on Broadway. It was the tale of a Jewish man's work with liberal causes contributing erosion in his marriage. She also wrote The Drinking Gourd, a play on slavery and What Use Are Flowers, which were never produced. Les Blancs was her last Broadway play. She was working on a novel, In Defense of Life and doing the text of The Movement: Documentary of a Struggle for Equality, a photographic presentation.

In 1967 a seven and one-half hour radio broadcast was done of her works. As a speaker at a conference to young people she once said: "though it be thrilling to be merely young and gifted in such times, it is doubly dynamic --to young, gifted and black." In 1969 the autobiographical To Be Young, Gifted and Black was made into a long-running off-Broadway play. Her friend Nina Simone took those words and helped create a song and performed it with the same title, and it was a hit. In 1973 Raisin was a musical and won a Tony Award. A 2004 revival of Raisin in the Sun was nominated for a Tony award. In 2008 a television production of Raisin in the Sun garnered two N. A. A. C. P. Image awards. Hansberry has been inducted into the National Women's Hall of Fame and in 2002 she was named one of the "100 Greatest African Americans," and in 2013 inducted into the American Theatre Hall of Fame. A number of schools in New York City and New Orleans are named for her, as is San Francisco's Lorraine Hansberry Theatre.

In 1963 Lorraine Hanberry had two operations for pancreatic cancer. Both were unsuccessful, with her dying on January 12, 1965 in New York City. She is buried in Croton-on Hudson, New York. She was only thirty-four years old. The great singer/actor/activist Paul Robeson gave one of the eulogies. James Baldwin stated of her: "Her creative ability and her grasp of the deep social issues confronting the world today will remain an inspiration of generations yet unborn." Everything in Hansberry's writing points to African Americans as normal and complex human beings, possessing dignity, and like all humans, having both failings and successes.

#56- *Helen Hayes* (1900-1993)

First Lady of the American Theatre

Helen Hayes, born Helen Hayes Brown, arrived in this world on October 10, 1900 in Washington, D.C. to jack-of-all-trades Francis Brown and his wife, actress Catherine. At five years of age she made her first professional appearance with the Columbia Players in Washington. From 1908 to 1912 she toured with Lew Fields and John Drew, Jr., and appeared in, among other plays, The Prince Chap, Old Dutch, and Little Lord Fauntleroy. She even appeared in a film Jean and the Calico Doll, and as teenager she acted in The Prodigal Husband, Pollyanna, She Stoops to Conquer, Penrod, Dear Brutus, Clarence, and Babs.

These plays kept her working, but it was not until 1925 that she got noticed. Quarantine and Caesar and Cleopatra, first, and then What Every Woman Knows. She was seen as too pretty for the Cleopatra role, but the latter play turned out to be the beginning of her acceptance as an mature performer. From 1926 to 1928 she was married to John Swanson, but in 1928 she married playwright Charles MacArthur, and their marriage lasted until his death in 1956. In 1931 they moved to southern California.

Her very first film role was in The Sin of Madelon Claudet and for that she received her first "Oscar" at the Academy Awards. The 1930s saw her in such well-known films as Arrowsmith, The White Sister, Vanessa: Her Love Story, a film version of What Every Woman Knows and A Farewell To Arms, but she also returned to the stage triumphantly in Mary of Scotland, and a four-year run, in possibly her greatest success, as Victoria Regina. The 1940s was a continuance of success as in Twelfth Night, as Harriet Beecher Stowe in Harriet, Happy Birthday (a Tony award) and as the mother in The Glass Menagerie.

The 1950s was when she excelled in both film and on stage. Anastasia (nominated for a Golden Globe award), The Wisteria Trees and My Son John were on film, while she appeared on stage in Time Remembered (a Tony award), a revival of The Skin of Our Teeth, Mary Rose, and A Touch of the Poet, for which she also received the Tony award, and The Cherry Orchard, The Chalk Garden, and Good Morning Miss Dove. In 1955 the first of two different Helen Hayes Theatres in the Broadway district opened.

Helen Hayes also excelled in television productions. She was nominated for an Emmy Award for Miss Gilling and the Skyscraper, Victoria Regina, and The Snoop Sisters. And she did win an Emmy for 1958's One Red Rose for Christmas, 1971's Do Not Fold, Spindle or Mutilate, and in 1975 in appearance on the television program, Hawaii 5-O, and for 1978's A Family Upside Down. She also got to portray Agatha Christie's Miss Marple in two television productions, A Caribbean Mystery and Murder With Mirrors.

She became the first to do the "triple play" winning an Oscar, an Emmy and a Tony. She also went on to win a Grammy award for a "Spoken Word" album in 1977. She was also nominated twice for Golden Globe awards, and nine times for Emmy awards. She was also the recipient of the Straw Hat Achievement Award from the Council of Stock Theaters and a member of the American Theatre Hall of Fame. All these point to her being considered the "First Lady of the American Theatre." She was presented with the Presidential Medal of Freedom in 1986 and the National Medal of Arts in 1988, and since 1984 there have been the Helen Hayes Awards for theatrical excellence in the Washington, D.C. area. In 2011 her likeness was portrayed on an American postage stamp, and she is in the National Women's Hall of Fame.

In the 1960s Helen Hayes went on an thorough tour of South America and Europe with the American Reparatory Company, and then stayed with Phoenix Reparatory Company which produced School for Scandal in New York. Both her memoirs, The Gift of Joy, and her autobiography, On Reflection, also appeared in this decade. Later My Life in Three Acts came later. She also began teaching speech at the University of Illinois, but continued acting, as in the film, Airport, for which she received another Oscar. Helen Hayes also made a number of Disney films. Her last play was in 1970 with James Stewart in Harvey.

One of her proudest achievements was the Helen Hayes Hospital for people with physical disabilities, in West Haverstraw, New York which she supported for many years. It is now the New York State Rehabilitation Hospital.

James MacArthur of the original "Danno" of Hawaii 5-O television series, in which she made that appearance, and the film, Swiss Family Robinson, was her adopted son. Helen Hayes died of congestive heart failure in Nyack, New York on March 17, 1993.

#57- *Lillian Hellman* (1905-1984)

Lilly

Playwright and screenwriter Lillian Florence Hellman was born on June 20, 1905 to Max and Julia in New Orleans. Her formative years were spent there and in New York City. She briefly attended both New York University and Columbia University.

In 1934 while working as a book reviewer, play reader and press agent, she wrote her first play, The Children's Hour, the tale of a child's accusatory lie about a homosexual relationship between two teachers. The play was a huge success. As great as it was, her next endeavor,

The Little Foxes in 1939, was undoubtedly her best work, about the Hubbard clan, and the overbearing desire for power and wealth through any means. Both of these plays were made into successful films with Bette Davis nominated for an Oscar for The Little Foxes. Another success had been In Days To Come.

Also in the 1930s Hellman spent time in Spain giving support to the anti-Franco forces. This period of time was the subject of much controversy later in life, with Hellman and others disagreeing on what exactly happened there. It also had some bearing when the Joseph McCarthy Un-American hearings came about in the 1950s.

The 1940s saw her write Watch on the Rhine, The Searching Wind and Another Part of the Forest, which was a further tale of the Hubbards. These, too, were made into films. In 1951 came a story of middle age, The Autumn Garden. In 1942 she was nominated for an Academy Award for the screenplay of The Little Foxes, and again 1944 for The North Star. The era of Senator Joseph McCarthy and his House on Un-American Activities Committee arrived, and with it a summons for Lillian Hellman and her friend, writer Dorothy Parker, both suspected of being communists. Hellman stood firm and courageous and would not reveal the information McCarthy wanted. She was blacklisted, which meant that because she disagreed with the powerful McCarthy, she was discriminated against and even refused employment.

In 1955 she edited the letters of one of her heroes, Anton Chekhov, and adapted Jean Anouihl's play, L'Aloutte, titling it The Lark for Broadway. It was the trial of Joan of Arc. And continuing her very varied literary career, she wrote a text, also called a libretto, for Candide in 1956. In 1960 the Tony nominated Toys in the Attic dealt with family relationships, and was, also, made into a film.

Although she had married and divorced playwright Arthur Kober when she was young, and lived the turbulent life, they moved to Hollywood, where she would meet and have a more mature relationship was with writer Dashiell Hammett, who died in 1961. In 1966 she had some of his short novels and stories published postumously, titled The Big Knockover. In 1969 her memoir, An Unfinished Woman, was published. It included some memories of her friend Dorothy Parker, who had recently passed. It was given the National Book Award. This was followed by Pentimento, and the 1977 Oscar-nominated film, Julia, based on one story from Pentimento. Maybe: A Story was a fictionalized memoir and Scoundrel Time was an actual memoir. She also taught at a number of universities, including Harvard and Yale, in the 1970s.

Lillian Hellman was one of the most brilliant twentieth century playwrights in America, living in an exciting literary time. She was an artist who chastised America for not going after tyrants such as Hitler and Mussolini when they were young. Irresponsibility, injustice, selfishness, exploitation and other issues were dealt with artistically, yet with power. Over her career she was awarded the prestigious Edward MacDowell Medal, the Brandeis University Creative Arts Medal, the Albert Einstein College of Medicine Achievement Award, was made a fellow of the American Academy of Arts and Sciences, and a member of the American Academy of Arts and Letters and honorary degrees from Yale, Columbia, Smith College, Mt. Holyoke College, Brandeis, and Wheaton College. Lillian Hellman died of a heart attack on Martha's Vnneyard on June 30, 1984. In 1993 Peter Feibleman's Cakewalk had Hellman as a central figure, and in 1999, Kathy Bates played her in the television movie, Dash and Lilly.

#58- Katherine Hepburn (1907-2003)

The Great Kate

Dr. Thomas and suffragist Katherine Hepburn's daughter, Katherine Houghton Hepburn, winner of four best actress Oscars, the most ever, was born in Hartford, Connecticut on May 12, 1907. She attended Bryn Mawr College where she really first took up acting, and was a success in The Woman In the Moon. She married Ludlow Smith in 1928, and for the next four years did acting with a stock company. Although she and "Luddy" always remained friends, they did divorce in 1934. She got decent reviews in small roles in The Czarina and Printed Word.

In 1932 came her big break. She appeared on stage in The Warrior's Husband, which led to her first film, A Bill of Divorcement. She received high praise, and then more praise as she portrayed Jo in a film version of Louisa May Alcott's Little Women, winning the best actress award at the Venice Film Festival. In that same year appeared in Morning Glory, for which she received her first Academy Award nomination and Oscar in 1934.

As quickly as success came, it left. She appeared on Broadway in The Lake, and critic Dorothy Parker said Hepburn's emotional display as an actress, "ran the gamut from A to B." It was a flop. She did bounce back with her second Oscar nomination for Alice Adams. But for a while it looked like she had reached her peak and was fading. She appeared in Mary of Scotland, Quality Street, Bringing Up Baby, Holiday, and Edna Ferber's Stage Door, but none of these films did all that well. The big powers of Hollywood began to be upset with Hepburn because she had decided not to accept roles she did not like, and became listed as "box office poison." Annoyed with the system, she bought out her contract and left Hollywood.

She had gotten into a relationship with the wealthy Howard Hughes, and with his assistance, Hepburn bought an interest in the play The Philadelphia Story. She thought she was perfect for the role of Tracy Lord, and she was correct. The play opened in 1939 and ran for a year, and given the New York Critics Award. Then on to Hollywood with The Philadelphia Story, receiving another, and her third, actress nomination, and a New York Film Critics Award, seemingly back on the road to success. Soon after this she made her first film with her long-time partner, Spancer Tracy in Woman of the Year, and with that her fourth Oscar nomination. In 1953 she was nominated for a Golden Globe for Pat and Mike, also with Tracy. In her career she would be nominated for eight Golden Globe nominations, but would win none.

She was again nominated for the fifth time for her role in The African Queen, and in 1955 went on tour with the Old Vic Company. Summertime brought her a sixth nomination, as did The Rainmaker the very next year, a seventh. And soon came Suddenly Last Summer, with her eighth nomination, The Desk Set and her portrayal of Mary Tyrone in Long Day's Journey Into Night, for which she received the Cannes Film Festival best actress award and her ninth Oscar nomination.

From 1953 to 1963 Katherine Hepburn had been nominated as best actress five times. She had also appeared in the Stratford Shakespeare Festival in Stratford, Connecticut. The 1940s saw her in Adam's Rib, State of the Union, Without Love, and a film version of Pearl Buck's The Dragon Seed. Guess Who's Coming To Dinner reunited her on film with Spencer Tracy. They were both nominated for Oscars, this being her tenth. At this time it tied her for most nominations with Bette Davis, and when she won the Oscar, it tied her for the most wins, two. Although it was a huge success, Spencer Tracy died soon after its wrap.

But soon after came The Lion in Winter, which was not only a huge success, but gave her a record-breaking (at the time) eleventh Oscar nomination, and when she won, she was the first to win three. Her portrayal of the aging, witty, biting Eleanor of Aquitaine was glorious, and possibly the best performance of her legendary career. To enhance that career even more, she returned to Broadway, wonderfully portraying Chanel in Coco, and getting nominated for a Tony award, and in 1981 also for West Side Waltz. She was voted "Woman of the Year" by McCall's magazine in 1970, well into her sixties, and in both 1976 and 1983 People's Choice Award's Favorite Motion Picture Actress. Now it was time for television. There was an Emmy-nominated performance in The Glass Menagerie, and a follow-up triumph in Love Among the Ruins, winning herself the Emmy. In 1979 she again acted on television and was Emmy nominated for The Corn Is Green, and was nominated for an Emmy for Mrs. Delafield Wants to Marry in 1986, and for a Golden Globe for The Man Upstairs in 1993.

Katherine Hepburn had not always been popular or successful, but she had always been great. Of course there was On Golden Pond, for which she, as Ethel Thayer, was nominated for the twelfth time, and winning the Oscar for the fourth time, and was nominated for a Golden Globe. Some later films were The Madwoman of Chaillot, Rooster Cogburn, and Olly Olly Oxen Free. In 1994 she appeared in her last film, in a small but pivotal role, in Love Affair, starring Annette Bening. In that same year she did appear in the television film, One Christmas, for which got a Screen Actors Guild nomination. During her career she acted with the greatest of male co-stars, such as Cary Grant, Jimmy Stewart, Humphrey Bogart, Charlton Heston, Warren Beatty, John Barrymore, Sidney Poitier, Peter O'Toole, Laurence Olivier, Henry Fonda, John Wayne, Anthony Hopkins, and, of course, Spencer Tracy, and was always equal to the task.

She passed away on June 29, 2003 at her home, Fenwick, in Connecticut. In 1991 her autobiography, The Stories of My Life, had been published. Katherine Hepburn was given a Lifetime Achievement Award from the Screen Actors Guild in 1980,and one also in 1989 from the American Comedy Awards. In 1999 the American Film Institute named her the "greatest female star of the classic Hollywood era." She has, of course, her spot on the Hollywood Walk of Fame since 1960. In Connecticut there is the Katherine Hepburn Cultural Arts Center, which, among other things, bestows the "Spirit of Katherine Hepburn Award. She was in her life, and in many of her award-winning roles, a spirited, outspoken, eccentric, unconventional and fiercely independent woman.

#59- *Billie Holiday (1915- 1959)*

Lady Day

Sadie Fagan gave birth to a daughter, Eleanor, who later became known as the legendary and great jazz, swing, r&b (rhythm & blues), blues and torch singer and songwriter Billie Holiday, in Philadelphia on April 7, 1915, and she grew up in Baltimore. For a while Sadie was married to a Philip Gough, and Eleanor used his surname at times. At an early age little Eleanor was placed in The House of the Good Shepherd, a Catholic home for girls. However, at thirteen she rejoined her mother in Harlem in New York City, and started working in a house of prostitution, at first just doing errands, but was eventually arrested for prostitution.

Still in her teens, she began singing, inspired by the recordings of the great Bessie Smith. And she, too, became very popular, and even made records, initially with the Brunswick label. Later she would also record with Columbia and Decca. She changed her professional name to "Billie Holiday" because she greatly admired singer Billie Dove, and it seems possible that she felt musician Clarence Holiday was her father. She performed with some of the great bands of the time, such as Count Basie, Benny Goodman, Teddy Wilson and Artie Shaw, and picked up the title "Lady Day," from her friend, saxaphonist Lester Young. She was also the lady with the gardenia in her hair.

By 1940 she was on top, having even made a film, "New Orleans." When she made "What a Little Moonlight Will Do" she really reached the pinnacle. The very controversial "Strange Fruit" and her "God Bless the Child" sung in her own distinct bittersweet vocal style were among her best songs, also. She was inspired by the jazz musicians with whom she performed, and she "improvised" her voice to match them. But "What Is This Thing Called Love" in 1947 was probably her biggest hit, and she sold out concert venues. Four straight years in the 1940s she was given Esquire magazine's Best Jazz Female Vocalist award.

And then it went downhill, after achieving so much fame and praise. She even was sent to prison in West Virginia for a while for drug offenses.

In 1949 she again was brought up on drug charges, but managed to get acquitted. The 1950s found her making successful tours of Europe, appearances on television and at Carnegie Hall, but her addiction came to be too much. She was again arrested for drugs in New York City, but she was in the hospital where she died of cirrhosis of the liver on June 17, 1959. She had just made her last appearance in New York City, and she was broke. She was buried in St. Raymond's Cemetery in the Bronx, New York. Although Billie Holiday had many relationships, she had been married twice, to Jimmy Monroe and Louis McKay, but had no children.

Her 1956 autobiography, Lady Sings the Blues, was published, and a film by the same name was made in 1972, with Diana Ross in the "Oscar" nominated title role. Audra McDonald portrayed Billie Holiday in Lady Day At Emerson's Bar and Grill, and was awarded a Broadway Tony award for her effort.

Billie Holiday was a phenomenal singer who could not beat the odds, but nevertheless was a legend, and has had the greatest of influences on many later singers. She has been inducted into two different jazz halls of fame, and the Rock and Roll Hall of Fame, the National Women's Hall of Fame, and the Maryland Women's Hall of Fame. In 1999, television station VH1, slected her as #6 of the 100 greatest rock and roll performers.

In 1987 she was posthumously given a Grammy "Lifetime Achievement Award." Six of her songs are also in the hall of fame: "I'll Be Seeing You," God Bless The Child," "Embraceable You," "Strange Fruit," "Crazy He Calls Me," and "What Is This Thing Called Love." Her likeness was place on a 1994 postage stamp. She has been portrayed in the movie Malcolm X and in the "God Bless the Child" episode of television's Touched By An Angel. Among the tributes to Billie Holiday were Langston Hughes' poem, "Song for Billie Holiday." singing group U2's "Angel of Harlem," and Frank Sinatra's "Lady Day."

#60- Jeanne M. Holm (1921-2010)

The General

Jeanne Marjorie Holm was born in Portland, Oregon on June 23, 1921. Her father died when she was quite young, and she was raised by a single mother until she was fifteen, when her mother remarried. For a while she worked as a silversmith and for an ambulance corps.

In 1942 Holm enlisted in the Women's Army Auxiliary Corps, and was sent to Officer Candidate School at Fort Des Moines, Iowa. In January, 1943 she became the equivalent of a second lieutenant. During World War II she was assigned to Fort Ogelthorpe in Georgia, where she became a commander of basic training, and later commander of a hospital company in West Virginia.

She left the military in 1946 to attend Lerwis and Clark College, but two years later was recalled to duty. She would eventually earn her degree in 1956. Her first duty was in Berlin, Germany dealing with the blockade, set up by the East German communists. Then it was back to the United States and Camp Lee in Virginia where she worked at the Women's Army Corps Training Center. In 1949 she transferred to the United States Air Force. Holm was then sent to Erding Air Depot in Germany as an assistant director for plans and operations. She became War Plans Officer during the Berlin airlift (to overcome the "wall"), and during the Korean War.

Following this she was the first woman accepted to the Air Command Staff College at Maxwell Air Force Base in Alabama, and then was assigned to the United States Air Force Headquarters in Washington, D. C. as deputy in charge of Staffing and Personnel. Her advancement continued as Chief of Manpower as part of Allied Air Force in Southern Europe, stationed in Naples, Italy for four years, as part of NATO (North Atlantic Treaty Organization). In 1961 she was a congressional staff officer with the Manpower organization. For her efforts, Jeanne M. Holm was awarded the Legion of Merit.

Four years later she became Director of Women in the Air Force, and under her guidance the enlistment doubled, and the jobs and assignments expanded, not only in numbers, but also in importance. She had become a driving force for changing roles for women in the air force, and the military, in general. She was awarded the Air Force Distinguished Service Medal.

After feeling rather frustrated, and somewhat alone, in still trying to open doors for women in the military and some of her other attempts to improve and expand their lot in an atmosphere of male dominance and rigidity, she was ready to retire in 1970. She led the fight to have women accepted in the service academies, to be included in college R.O.T.C. (Reserve Officer Training Corps) programs and to see women as pilots. However, the next year she was promoted to brigadier general, the first woman in the Air Force to reach such a rank. And two years later was promoted to major general, the first woman in any branch of the armed services to reach such a rank, becoming director of the Secretary of the Navy Personnel Council. She did retire in 1975. After retirement she became a special assistant to President Gerald Ford in the Office of Women's Programs. She held similar positions in the Carter and Reagan administrations. Holm also was on the Board of Trustees of the Air Force Historical Association, and was on the Board of Directors of the Camp Fire Girls.

Over the years she received the Distinguished Alumni Award from Lewis and Clark College, and the Eugene Zuckert Leadership Award from the Arnold Air Society, and a Citation of Honor, and later the Lifetime Achievement Award, from the Air Force Association. In addition to all of these accolades Jeanne M. Holm received the following: Women's Air Corps Service Medal, World War II Victory Medal, American Campaign Medal, Army of Occupation Medal, Small Arms Expert Ribbon, and the Medal for Human Action. She also received the National Defense Service Medal with a bronze service star, Air Force Longevity Service Award with silver and bronze oak leaf clusters. There is a Jeanne M. Holm Center for Officer and Citizen Development at the Air University at Maxwell Air Force Base.

Jeanne M. Holm died in Maryland on February 15, 2010 from cardiovascular disease, complicated by pneumonia, and is buried at Arlington National Cemetery. She had written two books: Women in the Military: An Unfinished Revolution and In Defense of a Nation. She has been inducted into the International Women in Aviation Hall of Fame and the National Women's Hall of Fame.

#61- *Grace Murray Hopper* (1906-1992)

Amazing Grace

Walter and Mary Murray's daughter, Grace Brewster Murray, was born on December 9, 1906 in New York City. She would go on to become not only a rear admiral in the United States Navy, but also one of the pioneers of twentieth century computer science. It was said of her when she received the Society of Women Engineers Achievement Award that it was in "... recognition of her significant contributions to the burgeoning computer industry as an engineering manager and originator of automatic programming systems."

Grace graduated from Vassar College with a bachelor's degree in mathematics and physics, and then got her master's degree from Yale University in 1930 and a doctorate from there in mathematics in 1934. She had begun teaching mathematics at Vassar, becoming an associate professor in 1941. In the meantime she married New York University professor Vincent Foster Hopper in 1930. The marriage only lasted until 1945, but she kept the married name of Hopper.

In 1943 Grace Murray Hopper took a leave of absence from Vassar and joined the United States Navy Reserve, and trained at the Naval Reserve Midshipmen's School at Smith College in Massachusetts, graduating first in her class, first becoming an ensign, and soon after a lieutenant, assigned to the Bureau of Ships Computation Project at Harvard University.

In 1944 she was one of the first computer programmers of the Mark I computer. Hopper wrote three papers on the Mark I, which was also known as an Automatic Sequence Controlled Computer. She invented the first compiler for a computer programming language, and in doing so, popularized a machine-independent programming language, which led to COBOL (COmmon Business-Oriented Language). In her words, she "translated mathematic notation into machine code...so I decided data processors ought to be able to write their programs in English, and the computers would translate them into a machine code. That was the beginning of COBOL, a computer language for data processors." To this day it is still important and needed. A compiler is a program converting instructions into a machine-code form so that it can be read by the computer.

Hopper had requested a transfer to the regular navy, as opposed to the reserves, but was turned down due to her age, thirty-eight. She, instead became a research fellow at Harvard University.

Five years later she went to work for the Eckert-Mauchly Corporation (which later was acquired by the Remington Rand Corporation) as a senior mathematician, joining the team that developed UNIVAC (UNIVersalAutomaticComputer), the first commercial computer in the United States. Hopper also led the way to realize computers could do more than just mathematics. Hopper was named director of automatic programming, and her department created some of the first compiler-based programming languages: MATH-MATIC and FLOW-MATIC. The navy promoted her to lieutenant commander and then commander.

In 1966 she retired from the navy, but the next year was recalled, becoming Director of the Navy Program Language Group, as part of the Office of Information Systems Planning, and promoted again, to captain. In the 1970s Grace Murray Hopper became an advocate for replacing large centralized computer systems with networks, and developed the standards for testing computers. In the 1980s this job was taken over by the National Institute of Standards and Technology (NIST). She was given the Meritorious Service Medal and promoted to commodore, and in 1985 became rear admiral. It was probably about this time, due to her high rank and considerable accomplishments, that she acquired the nickname, "Amazing Grace."

After retirement she lectured on early computers, and worked as a senior consultant with Digital Equipment Corporation until her death on January 1, 1992 in Arlington, Virginia. She is buried at Arlington National Cemetery. Hopper was recognized for her accomplishments with the Naval Campaign Medal, World War II Victory Medal, National Defense Service Medal (twice), Armed Forces Reserve Medal (three times), the Legion of Merit, National Medal of Technology, and The Distinguished Service Medal. The Government Technology Leadership Awards have now become known as the "Gracies." The Office of Naval Intelligence now has a Grace Hopper Informational Services Center. The guided-missile equipped destroyer USS Hopper is named for her.

And in the world of computer technology she was honored, as well, with the Data Processing Management Association Man of the Year Award, the American Association of Women Achievement Award, the first recipient to be a Fellow of the Computer History Museum, the Toastmasters International Golden Gavel Award, and was elected a Fellow of the American Academy of Arts and Sciences, and the first woman named Distinguished Fellow of the British Computer Society. Hopper has received honorary doctorates from Marquette University and Western New England College.

In 1971 the Association for Computer Machinery created the "Grace Murray Hopper Award" for outstanding young computer professionals. Grace Murray Hopper was awarded the Presidential Medal of Freedom, posthumously, in 2016.

#62- *Lena Horne* (1917-2010)

Stormy Weather

Lena Mary Calhoun Horne, a descendent of pre-Civil War southern senator John C. Calhoun, was born on June 30, 1917 in Brooklyn, New York to gambler Edwin (Teddy) and actress Edna Horne. Her ethnicity was quite a mix of African, European and Native American. Her father was gone by the time she was three years old, and by five she was sent to Georgia to live with relatives, including uncle Frank S. Horne, who later became an advisor to President Franklin D. Roosevelt. At twelve years of age, she was back in New York. This also did not last long. At sixteen she dropped out of school and went to live with her father in Pittsburgh, Pennsylvania. She was again back in New York when she got a job in the chorus of Harlem's famous and legendary Cotton Club.

She stayed with the Cotton Club, becoming its female vocalist with its orchestra, and even made recordings with them for Decca records, leading to a regular spot on a radio program. Lena Horne made her film debut in Dance With Your Gods in 1934 and appeared in Lew Leslie's Blackbirds of 1939, and around this time she married Louis Jordan Jones, but it only lasted until 1944. She was now in Hollywood as a featured singer at a new Little Troc nightclub on the famous Sunset Strip. Lena also made the film Panama Hattie at this time.

Back in New York she was a hit at Cafe Society, and in 1943 began a long, career-making stand at the Savoy Plaza. She was featured in LIFE magazine. It led to an unheard of movie contract (partially negotiated by the NAACP), with the provision that she would not do typical African American domestic-type roles. Many of the films, however, like Swing Cheer and Broadway Rhythm were only singing parts.

At this time Lena Horne first gave the world her take on equality. She volunteered to perform for the USO (United Service Organizations, formed to provide entertainment to United States armed forces), but was scheduled to perform for segregated military personnel. She refused and instead performed for a group that included white German prisoners seated in front of African American soldiers. She left the stage and proceeded to stay by the first row of African Americans, with her back to the Germans.

In 1943, in her silky voice, she sang the title song for the film Stormy Weather, and this became her signature song throughout her career, and is even the title of a biography on her written in 2009. Horne also appeared in Cabin in the Sky, and later Ziegfeld Follies. Her roles in films were few because the studios felt all her scenes would have to be re-done with white actresses for southern audiences, and that would every expensive. Horne wanted the key role in Show Boat, but the studio felt an interracial relationship would not be very popular. She went back to her singing career and was with the Billy Eckstine Orchestra, and in 1947 married Lennie Hayton.

As part of her civil rights involvement in the late 1940s she joined the Progressive Citizens of America. As a result, Senator Joseph McCarthy's Committee on UnAmerican Activities blacklisted her, attempting to prevent her being hired, and although it did hurt her career for a short time, she was able to continue her successful career. She appeared successfully on Broadway in the late 1950s in Jamaica with Harry Belafonte.

She became a prominent nightclub performer in Europe, Canada, and Las Vegas, New York and Los Angeles, and other American cities, and did make a few films in the 1950s, Meet Me in Las Vegas and Duchess of Idaho. That was about it in films until 1969 in Death of a Gunfighter. But it had left time to continue her civil rights activism and Horne took part in the magnificent March on Washington in 1963. Except for her iconic role of Glinda in The Wiz in 1978, this was a rather quiet decade for her.

By this time Lena Horne had become a sultry icon of jazz and pop music, but had decided to retire. But yet, in 1981 she appeared on Broadway in Lena Horne: The Lady and her Music. It was sold out for over three hundred performances, and then toured the United States and Europe.

Throughout her career Lena Horne received many honors. She received an honorary degree from Howard University, was awarded a Critics Circle Award, the Pied Piper Award from ASCAP (American Society 0f Composers, Artists and Publishers), the Sammy Cahn Lifetime Achievement Award, A Lifetime Achievement Award from the Society of Singers, a Drama Desk Award for Outstanding Performance in a Musical, received two different Hollywood Walk of Fame spots, one for recording and one for film, hosted Broadway's Tony Awards, and received the Springarn Medal from the NAACP (National Association for the Advancement of Colored People), as well as their Image Award. There was a planned biography tribute with singer Janet Jackson to portray Horne. However when the infamous and controversial "wardrobe malfunction" happened in front of millions of viewers with Jackson at the half-time Super Bowl show, Horne and her people decided to cancel the production, not wanting Jackson in the part.

Lena Horne's acclaim was such that she also received television's Emmy award, Broadway's Tony award, received four Grammy awards, including one for Lifetime Achievement, was inducted into the International Civil Rights Walk of Fame at the Martin Luther King, Jr. Historic Site, and was a Kennedy Center Honoree.

Lena Horne died of congestive heart failure in New York City on May 9, 2010. She co-wrote her autobiography, Lena, in 1965.

#63- Whitney Houston (1963-2012)

The Voice

Whitney Elizabeth Houston, the daughter of entertainment executive John Russell Houston, Jr. and gospel singer Emily (Cissy) Houston, was born in Newark, New Jersey on August 9, 1963. Her family was entertainment royalty, having Dionne Warwick and Leontyne Price as cousins and Darlene Love as a godmother. She sang in her church choir, becoming an angelic soloist at age eleven. She sometimes also accompanied her mother when she sang in nightclubs, and even was a back-up singer.

However in the 1980s she became a fashion model, appearing in Seventeen, Cosmopolitan, Glamour and Young Miss, and did commercials for all sorts of different products, especially soft drinks.

In 1983 she signed a contract with Arista Records, and her debut album, selling twenty-five million copies, Whitney Houston, reached the number one spot on the music charts, as did the singles "How Will I Know" and "Saving All My Love For You". The biggest hit of all, though, was "Greatest Love of All." She began making videos for MTV and her popularity increased immensely. It was the bestselling album of 1986. Two years later her Whitney album appeared, also debuting and rocketing to the top of the charts, an unheard of four singles from this album also making it to the top: "I Wanna Dance With Somebody," "So Emotional," "Didn't We Almost Have It All" and "Where Do Broken Hearts Go." With singles released from these first two albums she had a record seven consecutive number one hits.

In 1989 she founded the non-profit Whitney Houston Foundation for Children which concentrated on homelessness, children's diseases and empowerment. Her third album, I'm Your Baby Tonight, with both that title song and "All the Man That I Need" also making it to the top. By this time she was already being referred to as "The Voice," due to a combination of purity, power, talent and fluidity. In 1991 at Super Bowl XXV in Tampa, Florida, Whitney Houston sang what has come to be considered one of the greatest renditions of "The Star Spangled Banner." Simply put, it was unforgettable. In that same year she put on the "Welcome Home Heroes" concert at the Norfolk (Virginia) Naval Station, which was the highest ratings ever on television cable station HBO. In 1992 she married "bad boy" rapper Bobby Brown, and that lasted until 2007.

And now she began her film carteer. In 1994 she appeared with Kevin Costner in The Bodyguard. The soundtrack from the film won Album of the Year, and the theme song, her iconic "I Will Always Love You" became Record of the Year. Both were the bestselling of all time by a woman. In that same year Houston was a guest at the White House dinner honoring South Africa's Nelson Mandela. She next acted in Waiting To Exhale (her "Shoop Shoop" song from here went on to the top) and then The Preacher's Wife with Denzel Washington. This latest became the bestselling gospel soundtrack in history, and in addition, Whitney Houston was honored with the NAACP's Image Award for achievement by an actress in a motion picture. She would go on to win a total of nineteen Image awards over her career. In 1998 she was nominated for a television Emmy award for her portrayal of the Fairy Godmother in Cinderella.

The RIAA (Recording Industry Association of America) declared her to be the top selling rhythm and blues singer of the twentieth century, and Artist of the Decade in 1999. In 2009 the Guinness World Records organization acknowledged Whitney Houston as the most awarded female act of all time, having sold almost two hundred million records and receiving awards, not only from music and film organizations, but also from international, charitable and educational associations. She even was once voted "America's Greatest Smile" by the American Dental Hygienists' Association. Her seven studio albums and two soundtrack albums have proven to be very influential. Her popularity was widespread, every "type" loved her singing.

There are so very many conflicting reasons why this great artist rose to such great heights and then fell too hard to the depths. By the beginning of the twenty-first century she had become all-too-well acquainted with cocaine and other drugs. She spent time in rehabilitation in 2004, 2005 and 2011.

Whitney Houston died on February 11, 2012 of accidental drowning in her hotel bathtub in Beverly Hills, California due to a drug overdose. At her funeral both Stevie Wonder and Alicia Keys performed, and Dionne Warwick, Kevin Costner and record executive Clive Davis, who had nurtured her career, spoke. She was buried in Westfield, New Jersey. In 2017 the

Tribeca Film Festival made a tribute to Clive Davis, and during the show, Jennifer Hudson sang a medley of Whitney Houston songs, and went into the audience to dance with Davis to "I Wanna Dance With Somebody." The crowd went wild.

In 2010, VH1 declared Whitney Houston one of the 100 Greatest Acts of All Time. She has a place on both the Harlem and New Jersey Walks of Fame, received the BET Lifetime Achievement Award, the Quincy Jones Award, a Soul Train Music Award, an honorary doctorate from Grambling State University, has been inducted into the New Jersey, Georgia and Rhythm and Blues Halls of Fame. In 2017 an unauthorized documentary, Whitney: Can I Be Me, was released. She had accumulated thirty Billboard Music awards, twenty-two American Music awards, six People's Choice awards, six Grammys, and two Emmys, and so many more. Not bad for a relatively short career. At the 2017 American Music Awards singer Christine Aguilera paid tribute to Whitney Houston, singing a medley of her songs from The Bodyguard.

Her elementary school has been renamed the Whitney E. Houston Academy of Creative and Performing Arts.

#64- Julia Ward Howe (1819-1910)

"Battle Hymn of the Republic"

Writer, abolitionist and humanitarian Julia Ward Howe was born on May 27, 1819 in New York City, the daughter of Samuel Ward III, a wealthy banker and descendent of Rhode Island founder, Roger Williams. Her mother, Julia, a poet and descendent of Revolutionary War hero, Francis Marion, known as the "Swamp Fox," died when Julia was only five years old, and so her father had her tutored privately until the age of sixteen. Her father died in 1839 and she went to live with her brother Sam, who had married Emily Astor, of the famous Astor family. There she was introduced to New York City society.

In 1843 she married reformer Dr. Samuel Gridley Howe, eighteen years her senior, the founder of the Perkins School for the Blind, noted for later teaching Anne Sullivan and Helen Keller. The relationship seems always to be a strained one. Although liberal in many areas, Dr. Howe was stubborn as to the role of women. For a while they lived at Perkins, but from 1845 to 1863 they moved to Green Peace, their home in Boston, which became a center of Boston's intellectual life. Besides having six children, editing her husband's work, Julia Ward Howe wrote Words for the Hour and Passion Flowers, and a play, The World's Own, which opened in New York. In 1852 they separated, with Julia living in Rome, but they reconciled their rocky marriage.

While her husband was working with the United States Sanitary Commission during the Civil War in Washington, D.C. in 1861, she became visibly upset at the sight of injured and sick soldiers, and was inspired to write the famous "Battle Hymn of the Republic." There are five stanzas. Included here is just the first one, and the chorus.

"Mine eyes have seen the glory of the coming of the Lord;
He is trampling out the vintage where the grapes of wrath are stored;
He hath loosed the fateful lightning of His terrible swift sword;
His truth is marching on.

(Chorus)

Glory, glory Hallelujah!
Glory, glory Hallelujah!
Glory, glory Hallelujah!
His truth is marching on."

It was published in The Atlantic Monthly in 1862, and sung to the tune of "John Brown's Body." It became very popular, and at times used to keep spirits up. This made her one of the most famous women in nineteenth century America.

But these ravages of war were not Julia Ward Howe's only concern. In 1870 she became co-editor of The Woman's Journal, and wrote the "Appeal to Womanhood throughout the World," which led to the founding in 1871 of the Women's International Peace Association in America, with her as president. She also helped found the Woman's Suffrage Association, and was its president for a number of years. In addition, she started the New England Women's Club in 1871.

But much of Julia Ward's life did not come to fruition until, in 1876, her husband passed away, and Julia Ward Howe became a new woman, and started a new life! Not only did she write the Memoir of Dr. Samuel Gridley Howe. She also wrote The Life of Margaret Fuller, From the Oak to the Olive, Northern Lights, From Sunset Ridge: Poems Old and New, Reminiscences and At Sunset. Julia Ward Howe had not been particularly happy in her marriage, and much of her literature shows this. Howe also wrote the plays Hippolytus and Leonora. Julia also traveled out west on a lecture tour. She was given an honorary degree from Smith College, and over the years she had become friends with a number of notable writers of the time, especially Henry Wadfsworth Longfellow and Ralph Waldo Emerson.

Also her activity in the area of abolition and women's rights and prison reform and education now grew. She served as president of the American Woman Suffrage Association on two separate occasions. She also wrote travel books, having traveled to Cuba, the Dominican Republic and Europe, and children's literature, and even a mysterious unpublished novel referred to as "the Laurence manuscript," but later called The Hermaphrodite, a person who is double-sexed.

In 1908 she was the first woman elected to the American Academy of Arts and Letters. She also campaigned for Mother's Day.

In 1917 two of her daughters received the Pulitzer Prize for their biography, Julia Ward Howe.

She died on October 17, 1910 of pneumonia in Portsmouth, Rhode Island. She has been inducted into the Songwriters Hall of Fame, the Rhode Island Hall of Fame and the National Women's Hall of Fame. In 1987 there was a postage stamp issued in her honor. There are any number of schools named for her, as well. Her Rhode Island home, Oak Glen, is on the national Register of Historic Places.

#65- Mahalia Jackson (1911-1972)

Queen of Gospel

Mahalia Jackson (born Mahala), nicknamed "Halie," the great contralto gospel singer, one of the greatest musical figures in American history, and civil rights activist, was born on October 26, 1911 in New Orleans, Louisiana. She was raised in a three-room home, housing thirteen people. Her father was Johnny Jackson and her mother, Charity Clark, died when she was very young, and Halie was raised by her hard-driving Aunt Duke, and she had many chores and tasks, and beatings, as well. And there was little time for schooling.

Although she loved the singing of Bessie Smith, she was most at home on Wednesdays, Fridays and Sundays with the Mount Moriah Baptist Church Choir. At sixteen, however, she left New Orleans with her Aunt Hannah and they took a train to Chicago. At first the only work she could find was as a domestic, and singing at funerals. She began singing with the Greater Salem Baptist Church Choir and the Johnson Gospel Singers, and they were good enough to begin touring.

In 1929 she met composer Thomas A. Dorsey, who became known as the "Father of Gospel Music," and they began a long collaberation, including "Take My Hand, Precious Lord," which became her signature song. In the early 1930s Jackson made some recordings for the Decca label, but they were not successful, and around this time she added that "i" to her name. In 1936 Jackson married Isaac (Ike) Hockenhull, but they were divorced by 1941, due to his gambling and to his unsuccessful insistance that she turn from gospel singing to secular singing. She had said "I sing God's music because it makes me feel free."

She signed with Apollo Records in the later 1940s, and recorded "Move On Up a Little Higher" in 1948. White disc jockey Studs Terkel played on his radio show, mixed in with rhythm and blues recordings, and thereby popularized it. Mahalia Jackson became a star. It was sold out in most stores and sold over eight million copies. In 1998 that song itself was inducted into the Grammy Hall of Fame.

Mahalia Jackson now performed in concert halls, including New York City's famed Carnegie Hall, and she followed up with such gospel classics as "Let the Power of the Holy Ghost Fall on Me," "Silent Night," "I Can Put My Trust in Jesus," "Go Tell It On the Mountain," "The Lord's Prayer," How I Got Over," "His Eye Is On the Sparrow," "I Believe," "Didn't It Rain," and "Nobody Knows."

As successful as Jackson was, however, she still felt the pang of prejudice. When she bought her home in Chicago she saw a great deal of resistance, but she stayed there. With the 1950s she became much more involved with the civil rights movement and with Dr. Martin Luther King, Jr. She was with him at the Montgomery, Alabama bus boycott concert, singing, "I've Heard of a City Called Heaven," "Move On Up a Little Higher," and "Silent Night." At the monumental March on Washington she was there and sang, "How I Got Over" and "I Been 'Buked and I Been Scorned." At King's funeral she sang "Take My Hand, Precious Lord." She also sang at President John F. Kennedy's Inaugural Ball in 1961.

Her rights involvement, however, did not interfere with her career. She toured Europe and was proclaimed the "World's Greatest Gospel Singer." and the "Angel of Peace." The Mahalia Jackson Show had a short radio life in 1954, and in 1956 appeared on the famous television program The Ed Sullivan Show and also appeared as the main attraction at the Newport Jazz Festival. From 1961 to 1969 she was constantly touring Africa, Europe, Japan, India and the Caribbean. She even sang before Liberian president William Tubman in 1970. In the film St. Louis Blues she played the part of Bessie May and sang a number of songs, and in The Best Man she appeared as herself. In the 1958 film Imitation of Life she sang "Trouble of the World" and 1970 she was on Sesame Street and singing "He's Got the Whole Word In His Hands." She had a short-lived marriage to Sigmund Galloway from 1964 t0 1967.

In her career Mahalia Jackson made thirty albums and over forty-five singles. What the World Needs Now in 1969 was her last album, and her last concert was in Munich, Germany in 1970. One of her more notable albums was a joint venture with Duke Ellington, Black, Brown and Beige. She received four Grammy awards, including a Lifetime Achievement Award, and has been inducted into the Grammy Hall of Fame. She has also been inducted into the Rock and Roll Hall of Fame, Gospel Music Hall of Fame, Louisiana Music Hall of Fame, and on the Hollywood Walk of Fame, and was awarded the Order of Lincoln, Illinois' highest honor. This revered woman was included as a character in the 2014 film Selma.

Mahalia Jackson died on January 27, 1972 in Evergreen Park, Chicago, Illinois, at the Little Company of Mary Hospital. The mayor of Chicago, Richard Daley, and Coretta Scott King gave eulogies. Aretha Franklin, whom Jackson had mentored, sang, "Precious Lord, Take My Hand." In her birthplace of New Orleans, she was eulogized by public officials and comedian/civil rights activist Dick Gregory. Lou Rawls sang "Just a Closer Walk With Thee." She was laid to rest in Providence Memorial Park in Metarie, Louisiana. She had founded the Mahalia Jackson Scholarship Foundation and built the Mahalia Jackson Theatre.

#66- Mother Jones (1830s-1930)

The Most Dangerous Woman in America

The fearless Mary Harris Jones, later referred to as "Mother Jones," was born in Cork, Ireland, sometime in the 1830s. With her parents, Richard and Ellen Harris, she emigrated to Canada to escape Ireland's Great Potato Famine, and then on to Maine as a tutor and then to Monroe, Michigan as a convent teacher. A move to Chicago came next with Mary as a dressmaker. Mary claimed she switched from teaching to dressmaking because she preferred sewing to "bossing little kids." She then went to Memphis, Tennessee and opened a dress shop. In 1861 she married George E. Jones, a member and organizer of the National Union of Iron Mongers.

In 1867 a yellow fever epidemic swept through Memphis, taking with it Mary's husband and all four of her children. Trying to rebuild her life, Mary Harris Jones moved back to Chicago and opened another dress shop. As if fate was after her, the great Chicago fire of 1871 destroyed her shop and her home.

She joined the many others helping to rebuild Chicago, and joined the Knights of Labor. By this time, Jones had seen enough to realize that there was an enormous disparity between workers and their bosses, and felt something had to be done. The rest of her life became dedicated to the rights of those workers, becoming a community organizer and representative of organized labor. In Mary Harris Jones, the spirit of civil disobedience in the fight for those rights, became paramount. She traveled to Kansas City, to Birmingham, Alabama, to Pennsylvania, to West Virginia, to Colorado and everywhere she felt workers were being abused, particularly in the mines and railroads. "Working men deserve a wage that would allow women to stay home and care for their kids." Jones did not necessarily agree with the women's rights groups of the time since she felt childhood neglect and delinquency were partially due to women not at home caring for their children. However, she vigorously encouraged wives and daughters to get out and support the strikers.

In 1873 she was there for the Pennsylvania coal miners and in 1877 with the railroad workers. But, her involvement and initiating strikes, however, sometimes led to violence. In 1886 the Haymarket Riot led to the fall of the Knights of Labor. But she continued on working tirelessly for the United Mine Workers and the American Railway Union. Though she is less known today than she should be, Jones was an effective, passionate, charismatic, and even sometimes purposeful humorous speaker, and had already become known as "Mother Jones," seen very demurely dressed in black with a white lace collar. She once said, "Pray for the dead and fight like hell for the living." In 1902 a Virginia district attorney declared, "She is the most dangerous woman in America. She comes into a state where people and prosperity reign,... crooks her little finger and twenty thousand content men lay down their tools and walk out."

Child labor abuses were also on her agenda. In 1903 she organized the "Children's Crusade" and marched with about one hundred mine-worker children from Philadelphia to the Oyster Bay, New York summer home of President Theodore Roosevelt. They carried signs: "We want to go to school and not the mines." They never got to see the president, but the march did bring the child labor situation more into the public consciousness.

A 2003 book, Kids on Strike! told this story. Due to her involvement in the 1912 West Virginia miners' strike, she was brought to trial in a military court, and sentenced to twenty years in prison. While she was under house arrest she came down with pneumonia, and after a few months was pardoned. This period of Jones' life is depicted in the 1978 novel, The Scapegoat. Her efforts there got the United States Senate to investigate the plight of the miners. She went to the same situation in Colorado mines, and was again imprisoned. This time, mine owner, John D. Rockefeller, Jr., met with her and instigated reforms.

She just never seemed to stop. In 1898 she had helped found the progressive Social Democratic Party and in 1905 the Industrial Workers of the World. Jones continued her union organizing into the 1920s and wrote the Autobiography of Mother Jones in 1925. Mary "Mother" Jones passed away on November 30, 1930 in Adelphi, Maryland, a suburb of Silver Springs, and is buried in the Union Mines Cemetery in Mount Olive, Illinois. The United Mine Workers erected a granite monument, and on October 11, 1936, fifty thousand people came to her grave to see the monument. October 11 is now "Mother Jones Day."

In the 1970s a radical magazine decided to call itself Mother Jones. In the coal miners' strike of 1989-1990 in Virginia, women came in support, addressing themselves as "Daughters of Mother Jones." There is a school in Adelphi, Maryland named in her honor, and in 2012 a plaque was created in her honor in her birthplace in Cork, Ireland, and they celebrate a Mother Jones Festival. Besides being honored with an induction into the National Women's

Hall of Fame, she is remembered and mentioned in numerous songs, poems and plays. She has also been referred to as "The Miner's Angel" and "the grandmother of all agitators."

#67- Florence Griffith Joyner (1959-1998)

Flo-Jo

Florence Delorez Griffith Joyner, who would become known to the world as "Flo-Jo," was born on December 21, 1959 in Los Angeles, California to Robert and Florence. In the family, though, she was called Dee Dee. She would go on to be known as fastest woman of all time. Some people use their entire lifetime to show their greatness and some do it in a moment. Flo-Jo did it in moments.

Her father moved to the Mojave Desert, and would dare his daughter to catch the jackrabbits in the area, and she became fast enough to do it. In elementary school she joined the Sugar Ray Robinson Organization to run in track meets. By the time she graduated Jordan High School she had set the records in long jump and in sprints. She qualified for the 1980 Olympics, but the United States decided to boycott the games.

She attended California State University at Northridge where she was on teams that won national championships in two years, but had to drop out due to financial problems, and worked as a bank teller and hair stylist. But she then, with aid, attended UCLA (University of California, Los Angeles), and in 1983 got her degree in psychology.

In the 1984 Olympics in Los Angeles she not only achieved her first Olympic medal, a silver in the 200 meter race, but she also married triple jump champion Al Joyner. In the 1987 World Championship she garnered another second place in the 200 meters and first with the 4 x 100 meter relay team. By this time she already started showing her own distinctive and flashy style, with long, long, exotically polished fingernails, and unique fashion running outfits in bold colors and designs, jewelry, and uncommonly long (for a track runner) hair. Flo-Jo became beloved by the world, unabashedly capturing their attention.

The 1988 Olympics in South Korea were Flo-Jo's moment. In the quarterfinals she ran a 10.49-second 100 meters, breaking the world record. She also ran a 21.77-second 200 meters, also a world record in the preliminary rounds, breaking her own record in the semi-finals with a 21.56, and again breaking the record in the finals with a 21.34. Until this day, these records still stand. In addition she went on to win gold in the 4 x 100 meter relay, and a silver medal in the 4 x 400 relay.

These achievements had her named Amateur Athlete of the Year and the recipient of the James E. Sullivan Award, the UPI Athlete of the Year, and Track & Field Woman Athlete of the Year, a similar award from IAFF, and named the L'Equipe Champion of Champions. Following the Olympics were accusations that she had made use of performance enhancing drugs. However, she had passed all drug tests, and Prince Alexandre de Merode, chairman of the International Olympic Committee medical committee stated, "We performed all possible and imaginable analyses on her. We never found anything. There should not be the slightest suspicion." In 1988 she had been subjected to eleven separate drug tests.

Flo-Jo retired from track after 1988 and devoted herself to business opportunities, and did very well in toys and clothing design, including professional basketball team uniforms. She was appointed co-chair of the President's Council on Physical Fitness in 1993.

In 1995 she was inducted into the USA Track & Field Hall of Fame. In 1996 she announced she was "unretiring" and intended to run the 400 meters because she did not have the record for that distance. Unfortunately she developed tendonitis in her right leg, and had to give it up. For a while she dabbled in acting, sports casting, lecturing, writing and painting, and her latter work was displayed as part of the Art of the Olympics.

On September 21, 1998, Flo-Jo died in her sleep of an epileptic seizure at her home in Mission Viejo, California. In 2000, the elementary school she attended was renamed in her honor.

Group Six

Helen Keller- Mary Lyon

68. *Helen Keller and Anne Sullivan*

68 A- *Helen Keller (1880-1968)*

A Remarkable Life

Helen Adams Keller was born normal in every way to Arthur and Kate on June 27, 1880 in Tuscumbia, Alabama, and, though far removed, was related to the Massachusetts Adamses and the Virginia Lees. At about one and a half years of age she came down with either meningitis or scarlet fever, or what was commonly called then as "brain fever." It left her without sight or hearing. After a number of years, having had no success in helping her, her parents with the help of Alexander Graham Bell, who, in addition to being an inventor, was also an educator, put them in touch with the Perkins Institute For the Blind in South Boston. On March 3, 1887, Perkins Institute sent Miss Anne Sullivan to Tuscumbia to teach young Helen. This relationship would last almost fifty years, and was the true beginning of Helen Keller's remarkable life.

She learned the deaf and dumb language by touch and the Braille system, and eventually, to type. The first word was "doll," but it was not until the word "water" was discovered that it all started to come together. The story of this early learning experience has been shown in the William Gibson's television production, play and film, The Miracle Worker. Her later life was made into a television movie, The Miracle Continues in 1984. Her advancement was amazing and she was brought to Perkins Institute.

Helen Keller took speaking lessons at the Horace Mann School for the Deaf in Boston, and later went to the Wright-Humason School for the Deaf in New York City. She wanted more than just these types of schools. She wanted to go to Radcliffe College, and in preparation attended the Cambridge School for Young Ladies. Anne Sullivan was always with her, repeating the lessons by touch. She was accepted to Radcliffe in 1900. Author Mark Twain became an admirer, and introduced Keller to oil tycoon Henry Huttleston Rogers, who, in turn, financed her education.

Again she was accompanied by Sullivan, used Braille, and took examinations on a special typewriter. Helen Keller graduated Radcliffe College "cum laude" in 1904. In addition, she managed to write her autobiography, The Story of My Life, first released in the magazine Ladies' Home Journal, and then in 1902 in book form. For a while she lived with Anne Sullivan, but in 1914, Keller hired a secretary, Polly Thomson, to relieve Sullivan's load. Sullivan died in 1936. Thomson herself died in 1960 and Winifred Corbally became the companion.

In 1932 she was granted five thousand dollars as the year's greatest achiever by Pictorial Review, and soon after elected to the National Institute of Arts and Letters. President Franklin D. Roosevelt awarded her the Distinguished Service Medal for her leadership of youth and development of American character. Radcliffe presented Keller with the Alumnae Achievement Award in 1954, and her home in Tuscumbia, "Ivy Green," was declared a national museum the same year. Ten years later she received the Presidential Medal of Freedom, and soon afterward elected to the National Women's Hall of Fame, the Alabama Women's Hall of Fame, the Alabama Writers Hall of Fame, and the Connecticut Women's Hall of Fame. In 2009 a bronze statue of her was added to the National Statuary Hall Collection for the state of Alabama. Even beyond these awards, she received praise and recognition from many other countries she visited, over forty, including the Philippines, Japan, Lebanon, Brazil and Scotland. France awarded her the Legion of Honor. As if this was not enough praise, she met every president of the United States from Grover Cleveland to Lyndon B. Johnson. Tewksbury, Massachusetts erected a Anne Sullivan-Helen Keller sculpture. She has also been honored with a postage stamp in her likeness in 1980, and in 2003 on the Alabama state quarter.

Even though she had already written an autobiography, she went on to write Out of the Dark, The World I Live In, Midstream- My Later Life, My Religion, Peace at Eventide, Teacher, Helen Keller's Journal, and Helen Keller in Scotland. In addition there have been so many documentaries on her life.

Following World War ll she had visited the wounded and handicapped trying to buck up their courage and bring them hope. Throughout her life she lectured on the problems of the physically handicapped, and helped found the National Committee for the Prevention of Blindness and the American Foundation for the Blind. The foundation's archival material on Keller was lost on 9/11/2001 when the World Trade Center towers were destroyed. She was also very politically active, joining both the Socialist Party and the Industrial Workers of the World, and helping to found the American Civil Liberties Union (ACLU) in 1920.

Helen Keller had a series of strokes in the early 1960s, and died on June 1, 1968 in Connecticut and was buried near Anne Sullivan and Polly Thomson at the National Cathedral in Washington, D.C.

The 1999 Gallup Poll included her as one of the "Most Widely Admired People of the 20th Century." There are schools and hospitals and thoroughfares named after her throughout the world. June 27 has been declared "Helen Keller Day" in the United States. Helen Keller's journey through life does serve as the most excellent example of what any individual can achieve.

68B-Anne Sullivan (1866-1936)

The Miracle Worker

Joanna Mansfield Sullivan, always called Anne or Annie, was the daughter of Thomas and Alice Sullivan. She was born on April 14, 1866 in Feeding Hills, Massachusetts. Although she became the miracle working teacher and companion of Helen Keller, she had a horrible childhood. Some of her siblings were in good health, but some were not. Her mother died when Anne was young, and her father abandoned the sickly children and left with the healthy ones. Anne had seriously poor eyesight caused by trachoma at age five, and her younger brother was also sickly. They had no relations, and were placed in the Tewksbury Almshouse, where her brother died shortly thereafter. Anne survived, but spent the next four years in degrading squalor amongst drunks and addicts.

In 1880 she was placed in the Perkins Institute For the Blind where she learned an manual alphabet. After two operations, her eyesight improved quite a bit, and she graduated in 1886 as valedictorian. That same year she was informed that the Keller family in Alabama needed a teacher for their blind and deaf daughter, Helen. Sullivan spent months preparing, arriving at the Keller home in the spring of 1887. It was the beginning of great change for both Anne and Helen Keller.

She tried teaching Helen the manual alphabet with the word "doll" and a doll. Helen proved to be reluctant and stubborn, and even destructive, even causing Anne Sullivan harm. She determined that to end this failing, and to begin real progress Helen had to be removed from her spoiling and catering parents. They were moved into a separate home away from the main house. They did make progress, but a "water" incident some time later was the moment of no return. When Helen felt the water, and had the word spelled to her, the concept that all items have names became clear. In 1888 they both went up to the Perkins Institute to continue their progress. The institute presented a report that made Anne Sullivan and Helen Keller famous, and created the idea and atmosphere that Perkins was a top school. In 1891 Anne wound up having a strained relationship with Perkins, but they made up, but the rift never completely healed.

During this period of time, Anne's vision suffered, and she had to leave Keller for a while for treatments. When she returned, the Keller's could no longer afford to pay her, but Anne stayed on, anyway. Helen Keller now wanted a first class education, and appealed to Radcliffe College. Anne Sullivan was accused of overworking Keller in her preparation, and efforts were made to separate them. Sullivan stood fast, stayed with Keller, and Helen graduated Radcliffe. Sullivan had done all the translating of Helen's work.

After the graduation, Sullivan needed an operation on one of her feet and complications from her rough upbringing. She had also met Harvard professor and literary critic, John Macy. They married and lived with Helen Keller, but it was too stressful for Macy, and he left. In that same year, 1912, Anne Sullivan had a exhaustion breakdown. Keller hired one Polly Thomson as secretary to relieve some of Anne's workload. In 1916 she spent time in Puerto Rico and Lake Placid, New York to recuperate.

Sullivan returned to help and accompany Keller on her travels for lectures and tours. She had freed Helen from her quiet and darkness in the past, and although Anne Sullivan's methods were outside of the mainstream, they became a blueprint for others to follow. Helen Keller, of course, was the star, the attraction, and Sullivan got very little attention or credit for most of her life, even went blind toward the end of her life.

However, in 1936, when Anne Sullivan was seventy years old, she and Keller were awarded the Roosevelt Memorial Association medal. Both were also awarded honorary degrees from Temple University, with fellowships from the Educational Institute of Scotland, and recipients of the order of St. Sava from the Serbian Orthodox Church. Additionally, Anne was given an honorary degree from Harvard University.

Later in 1936, on October 20, Anne Sullivan died in her home in Forest Hills in Queens, New York City after having suffered a coronary thrombosis and going into a coma. Her ashes were placed in the National Cathedral in Washington, D. C. She is the first woman so honored based on her own achievements.

Helen Keller summed up her feelings about Anne Sullivan: "All the best of me belongs to her; there is not a talent, or an inspiration or joy in me that has not been awakened by her loving touch." Keller's book, Teacher, is about Sullivan. But she really was much more than her teacher.

In 1959 William Gibson's The Miracle Worker opened on Broadway, with Anne Bancroft portraying Sullivan and Patty Duke as Keller. It depicts Anne Sullivan's struggles and successes with young Helen. It later became a successful film, for which Bancroft received an Academy Award, as did Duke. There was a television remake in 1979 with Patty Duke then portraying Sullivan. It was done again in 2000, and a Broadway revival came about in 2010. Anne Sullivan has been inducted into the National Women's Hall of Fame.

#69- *Stephanie Kwolek (1923-2014)*

Kevlar

Pioneering chemist Stephanie Louise Kwolek was born on July 31, 1923 in New Kensington, a suburb of Pittsburgh, Pennsylvania to Polish immigrants John and Nellie Kwolek. Her foundry worker father died when she was ten years old, but her mother was determined to see her children educated. Stephanie, desiring to be a doctor, graduated from Carnegie Mellon University with a degree in chemistry in 1946. She took a "temporary" job with DuPont's textile fiber laboratory in Buffalo, New York, hoping to make enough money to get through medical school. The temporary job lasted forty years. As it turned out she found she loved the work at DuPont, finding it so interesting that she gave up any desire to become a doctor, rather becoming one of the first women research chemists, and an award-winning one at that.

In 1950 Kwolek moved to Dupont's newly-opened Pioneering Research Laboratory in Wilmington, Delaware. She researched and created a way to get lightweight, yet strong fibers to be used in tires. This work led to work with polymers, which are various chemical compounds made of smaller identical molecules linked together, such as in nylon, which had been discovered in 1939. She lowered the temperature with a liquid crystalline solution, and in the mid-1960s she unexpectantly developed it into poly-para-phenylene terephthalamide, whose trade name is kevlar, first marketed in 1971.

Kevlar is a synthetic material, like nylon, but which is five times as stong as steel. It has been found to have many valuable uses, such as in spacecraft shells, armored limosines, yacht sails, canoes, radial tires, brake pads, frying pans, safety helmets, gloves, bridge cables, ropes, skis, tennis racket strings, parachutes, but most importantly, bullet-proof vests worn by law enforcement and military personnel, beginning in 1975. Thousands of lives have been saved because of kevlar. Its commercial uses have generated billions of dollars in sales. Stephanie Kwolek, herself, made little direct money from this invention, turning the rights over to Dupont, but she did hold the patent for at least another seventeen inventions. Over the years she has received the Chemical Pioneer Award, the Kilby Award, the Award for Creative Invention, the Lemelson-MIT Lifetime Achievement Prize, the National Medal of Technology, the IRI Achievement Award, the Perkins Medal, the Lavoisier Medal, the Potts Medal, has received numerous honorary degrees, and been inducted into both the National Inventors Hall of Fame, the Plastics Hall of Fame, the Delaware Womens Hall of Fame, and the National Womens Hall of Fame.

There is a children's book, "The Woman Who Invented the Thread That Stops Bullets: The Genius of Stehanie Kwolek." She also devised the "nylon rope trick" which is used in many classrooms.

She retired in 1986, but stayed on as a consultant, serving on the National Research Council and the National Academy of Sciences. Stephanie Kwolek died at ninety years of age on June 18, 2014 in Wilmington, Delaware.

#70- *Hedy Lamarr* (1914-2000)

The Most Beautiful Woman in Film... and Most Interesting and Intelligent

The beautiful Hedwig Eva Maria Kiesler was born in Vienna, Austria, to bank director Emil Kiesler and his wife Gertrud, on November 9, 1914. She had a short, but controversial film career in Germany and Czehoslovakia, beginning in her teens. The first was Geld auf der Strase (Money on the Street) in 1930. The controversy arose mainy from the 1933 film, Exstase (Ecstacy), in which she appears as a young, but neglected wife who is seen in the nude running and swimming. At this same period of time she married arms dealer Fritz Mandl. While married to Mandl she got see first-hand his dealings with both Nazis and Fascists, and learned something about the military. Mandl also proved to be a very controlling and demanding husband, and she ran away, escaping him. She met American movie mogul Louis B. Mayer who offered her a contract, less notoriety, urged her to change her name, and promoted her as the "world's most beautiful woman." She became Hedy Lamarr, one of the most well-known, popular and finest actresses from the 1930s to the 1950s. She portrayed two of the most seductive women in film history, the amoral, seductive Tondelayo, and the Biblical traitor Delilah.

As a very in-demand actress, she got to act with the greatest leading men of the era: Clark Gable, Spencer Tracy, Bob Hope, Ronald Colman, James Stewart, Robert Taylor, William Powell, Ray Milland, Robert Cummings, George Sanders, and Robert Young. Her first American film in 1938 was Algiers with Charles Boyer, and her most well-known was Samson and Delilah with Victor Mature in 1949, the highest grossing film of the year. Other more notable films were Tortilla Flat, The Female Animal (her last film, in 1958), Comrade X, and White Cargo, in which she played Tondelayo. Unfortunately, her personal life was not as successful. She divorced Mandl in 1937, but then went on to more marriages, among them: Gene Markey, actor John Loder, Teddy Stauffer, W. Howard Lee, and Lewis J. Boies, all ending badly. She did have three children.

Making use of what she had learned from observing Mandl's dealings, along with composer George Anthuil, she devised a radio guidance system method called frequency-hopping which manipulated and continually changed the radio signals given off by torpedoes, and, therefore preventing the threat of jamming. She patented it as "Secret Communications System." She offerered this to the United States Navy, but they preferred she concentrate on selling war bonds during World War ll. However, by the 1960s, during the Cuban missile crisis, an updated version was put into use. The principle she developed, called spread spectrum technology, is now what is used in GPS, WI-FI, cellular phone and Bluetooth technologies. It is, indeed, a basic part of secure military operations and mobile telephone technology. She never profited from her phenomenal invention.

In 1997 the visionary Hedy Lamarr was given the Electronic Frontier Foundation Pioneer Award and the Bulbie Gnass Spirit of Achievement Bronze Award (considered the "Oscar" of science achievement). In 2014 Hedy Lamarr was inducted posthumously into the National Inventors Hall of Fame. She has been featured on both the Science and Discovery channels. She had also invented an improved traffic light, and a tablet that dissolved in water to make a carbonated drink. She was also honored on the Hollywood Walk of Fame. Actress and inventor: Hedy Lamarr was a very intelligent and interesting woman. The set in 1965's The Sound of Music, was set in Lamarr's mansion (at the time). In the 2012 film, The Dark Knight Rises, Hedy Lamarr's persona was the inspiration of the character Catwoman.

Hedy Lamarr became an American citizen in 1953. In 1966, Andy Warhol made a film, Hedy. Later in her life impoverished Hedy Lamarr was arrested twice for shop-lifting, but charges were dropped. She moved to Florida, and became a recluse, seeing very few people, but being on the telehone hours at a time. In 2004 there was a documentary Calling Hedy Lamarr. She died, in obscurity, of heart failure, in Casselberry, Florida, near Orlando, on January 19, 2000. There have been two off-Broadway plays about her: Frequency Hopping and Hedy! The Life and Times of Hedy Lamarr.

#71- Dorothea Lange (1895-1965)

Documentary Photographer

Born Dorothea Margaretta Nutzhorn in Hoboken, New Jersey on May 26, 1895 to parents Heinrich Nutzhorn and Johanna Lange, she dropped the name of her abandoned father, and took her mother's maiden name, becoming Dorothea Lange. By the time she had to adjust to a gone father, she had already had to deal with contracting polio at age seven, leaving her with a lifelong limp.

Lange attended Columbia University, and apprenticed herself to several different photographic studios. But in 1918 she decided to travel the world, but got only as far as San Francisco when unforeseen circumstances found her with little funds. She settled down in San Francisco and nearby Berekeley, which would be considered her home for the rest of her life. She soon opened her own portrait studio, and married painter Maynard Dixon.

With the onset of the Great Depression, Lange discovered her calling and soon was on her way to becoming a renowned documentary journalist. The impoverished people of the streets were her first subjects. "White Angel Breadline" led to a job with the Resettlement Administration, later renamed the Farm Security Administration. Her work for the FSA gave humanity to those suffering from the Depression. She opened her first exhibit in 1934: she had come to the forefront of documentary and journalistic photography.

In 1935 she divorced Dixon and married economist Paul Schuster Taylor. They traveled together, her photographing the sharecroppers and migrant workers suffering in rural poverty, and Taylor documenting it. They would distribute the photos free to the newspapers, bringing public attention to the situation.

Possibly her most famous and iconic photograph is "Migrant Mother" of Florence Owens Thompson in Nijomo, California. It is a stark shot of the mother with her children clinging to her. It now hangs in the Library of Congress. Lange once said, "I saw and approached the hungry and desperate mother, as if drawn by a magnet...There she sat in that lean-to tent with her children huddled around her, and seemed to know that my pictures might help her, and so she helped me." A school named for Lange sits on that site.

In 1936 many of the photos were included in John Steinbeck's The Harvest Gypsies. In 1939 came "An American Exodus; A Record of Human Erosion." In 1941 she was awarded a Guggenheim Fellowship, but chose to photographically record the internment and incarceration of Japanese-Americans from the west coast. She showed the first permanent camp at Manzanar. Some of her images were heart-breaking, such as the Japanese-American children saluting the American flag and the grandfather with his granddaughter. The United States Army did not want these shown, and confiscated most of them. However, in 2006 Impounded: Dorothea Lange and the Censored Images of Japanese American Internment was released.

After World War II famed photographer Ansel Adams invited Dorothea Lange to be part of the founding faculty of the California School of Fine Arts. She also took on a series of assignments for LIFE magazine, particularly "Mormon Villages" and "Irish Countryman" and traveled the globe from Asia to the Middle East to South America.

In 1965 she worked on a retrospective of her work for New York City's Museum of Modern Art, but passed away before it opened in 1966. She had suffered from post-polio syndrome, and Dorothea Lange, who demonstrated the potential of photography, died from esophageal cancer in San Francisco on October 11, 1965. She has been inducted inti the California Hall of Fame and the National Women's Hall of Fame.

#72- Estee Lauder (1908-2004)

The Sweet Smell of Success

Passionate Josephine Esther Mentzer supposedly was was born on July 1, 1908 in Corona, a neighborhood in the borough of Queens, in New York City. Her parents were immigrants, her father Max a Czech hardware store shopkeeper, and her Hungarian mother was Rose Schotz. Growing up she was nicknamed Estee, and she wanted to be an actress (and she actually did a little before her children were born). She helped her father at the store, but as she got older, and graduated high school, she worked for her uncle, chemist Dr. John Schotz, at his New Way Laboratories. She became fascinated with his beauty creams, lotions, fragrances and rouge.

In 1930 she married Joseph Lauter, but he changed it to Lauder, which had been its original spelling. Estee Lauder became quite the dedicated salesperson, selling her uncle's products to her friends and to beauty salons, especially "Super Rich All-Purpose Cream" and "Six-in-One Cold Cream." Her technique was "telephone, telegraph, tell-a-woman," and always with free samples. "When I thought I couldn't go on, I forced myself to keep going. My success is based on persistence."

In 1946 she co-founded with her husband, who died in 1982, Estee Lauder Cosmetics, with headquarters in Manhattan, New York City. Among her first products were skin lotion, cleansing oil, and a creme pack. Two years later an arrangement was made with New York City's Saks Fifth Avenue to carry her products. In 1953 came her "Youth-Dew" bath oil and perfume, a marvelous mixture of spices, flowers, and woods. It became the sexiest fragrance, according to women, and to men, as well. In the first year she sold fifty thousand, and by 1984 it was up to one hundred and fifty million.

By 1960 Estee Lauder was international, introducing her products in world famous London department store, Harrods. The next year she was in Hong Kong, and eventually even to the Soviet Union. "Aramis" men's scent arrived in 1964. Since then Estee Lauder collection includes Clinique, Tom Ford Beauty, Aveda, Bobbi Brown Cosmetics, Jo Malone, La Mer, Origins and many more. Clinique became the first dermatologist tested, allergy-free cosmetic. She now not only became associated with fashion designers such as Tommy Hilfiger and

Donna Karan, but also used well-known personalities such as model Paula Porizkova, actresses Gwyneth Paltrow and Elizabeth Hurley, and actor Bruce Boxleitner to promote her brands.

The Albert Einstein College of Yeshiva University honored her in 1968 with the Spirit of Achievement Award. Estee Lauder: The Sweet Smell of Success was a 1985 documentary about her. In 1998 Time magazine listed her as the only woman in their list of "20 Most Influential Business Geniuses of the Twentieth Century." A few years later she was inducted into the United States Business Hall of Fame, and was presented with both the Presidential Medal of Freedom, and France's Legion of Honor.

"If you have a goal, if you want to be successful, if you really want to do it, and become another Estee Lauder, you've got to work hard, you've got to stick to it and, you've got to believe in what you're doing."

She passed away in New York City on April 24, 2004 of heart failure. Her son Ronald went on to become a deputy Secretary of Defense and ambassador to Austria. Her little 1946 company's 2016 total assets were approximately nine billion dollars. Since the early 1990s, the Estee Lauder Companies have successfully promoted the Breast Cancer Campaign.

#73- *Emma Lazarus* (1849-1887)

Statue of Liberty

Dark-haired Emma Lazarus was born in New York City on July 22, 1849. On her mother's side she could trace her ancestry back to colonial times. Her father, Moses, was a sugar refiner. Emma was a precocious child, fluent in German, French and Italian, and while still in her teens had her poems published in such leading periodicals of the day such as Lippincott's Magazine. In 1867 Poems and Translations appeared, a collection of her work written before she was sixteen. It attracted the attention of Henry Wadsworth Longfellow, and Ralph Waldo Emerson, who was to become her close friend.

In 1871 her Admetus and Other Poems, dedicated to Emerson, was published, and three years later a prose romance, Alide: An Episode of Goethe's Life, appeared. In 1876. The Spagnoletto, a tragic verse historical drama, and in 1881, Poems and Ballads of Heinrich Heine were published and very well received, especially in London. She also wrote the multi-part poem "Epochs."

At this juncture of her life, possibly because of the Russian persecution of the Jews, Emma Lazarus became more aware and involved in her Sephardic and Jewish heritage. Her purely artistic literature, up to this time delicate, soft and smooth, turned passionate in the defense of her religion and against the prejudices always facing it. Songs of a Semite in 1882 displayed this indignation best, as well as demonstrating her enormous faith in America as a refuge for all. Examples of this are "The New Ezekiel," "By the Waters of Babylon," "The Crowing of the Red Cock," "Hanukah" and "The Banner of the Jews." "The Dance of Death" dramatized the burning of the Jews at Nordhausen. She was a Zionist even before the term was coined: her "An Epistle to the Hebrews" called for a return of the Jewish nation to Palastine. That is the Zionist belief. She also translated works of the Spanish Jews.

She also helped establish the Hebrew Technical Institute of New York for vocational training.

These are the lines of Emma Lazarus' 1883 sonnet, "The New Colossus" that are engraved on the Statue of Liberty:

"Not like the barren giant of Greek fame,

With conqueing limbs astride from land to land;

Here at our sea-washed, sunset gates shall stand

A mighty woman with torch, whose flame

Is the imprisoned lightning, and her name

Mother of Exiles. From her beacon-hand,

Glows world-wide welcome; her mild eyes command

The air-bridged harbor that twin cities frame.

'Keep ancient lands, your storied pomp!' cries she

With silent lips. 'GIVE ME YOUR TIRED, YOUR POOR,

YOUR HUDDLED MASSES YEARNING TO BREATHE FREE,

THE WRETCHED REFUSE OF YOUR TEEMING SHORE.

SEND THESE, THE HOMELESS, TEMPEST-TOST TO ME,

I LIFT MY LAMP BESIDE THE GOLDEN DOOR!'"

The poem was written to help raise funds for the pedestal of the statue. A few months after returning home from Europe, Lazarus died of Hodgkins lyphoma in New York City on November 19, 1887, at only thirty-eight years of age, and just a little over a year after President Grover Cleveland dedicated that famous statue. However, her immortal words were not engraved on a bronze plaque on the pedestal until 1903. Her home in New York City is on the map of Women's Rights Historic Sites, and the Museum of Jewish Heritage had an Emma Lazarus exhibition in 2012. She has been inducted into the National Women's Hall of Fame.

#74- *Lydia Liliuokakani (1838-1917)*

An American Queen

Lydia Liliu Loluka Kamakaeha Walania Wewehi Kamakaeha Kapaakea, eventually known as Liliuokalani, was born in Honolulu, Hawaii on September 2, 1838, daughter of a high priest (Konia Paki) and a chieftess (Kapaakea Keohokalole, a consultant to King Kamehemeha III), and a descendant of the Kamehameha dynasty, and was to become heir-apparent and crown princess in 1877. She attended the Royal School, which was for the children of the chiefs, and to other schools run by the missionaries. She was extremely intelligent with a passion for books and learning, and was adept at the piano, organ, guitar, ukelele and in voice.

In 1862 she married John Owen Dominis, who became governor of Oahu and Maui. They made their home at Washington Palace, a huge estate built by Dominis' father, a ship captain. In that same year she, in her capacity as a royal princess and governor's wife, gave what was probably the most spectacular luau in the history of Hawaii, on the occasion of a visit by the Duke of Edinburgh. A luau is an elaborate and traditional Hawaiian feast. After Lydia's brother, David Kalakaua, became king, she acted as regent as he went on a world tour. During the regency she played no small part in curtailing a devastating measles/smallpox epidemic, and in diverting the flow of lava from a volcano.

Even though the population of the islands was overwhelmingly Hawaiian, the one percent of outside businessmen had a great deal of influence. The various Hawaiian kings had appreciated the aid given by these people, but still wanted Hawaii controlled by Hawaiians. In 1887, while Princess Liliuokalani was visiting England on the occasion of Queen Victoria's golden jubilee, due to some very foolish political transgressions, King Kalakaua found himself at the mercy of anti-royalists. He was made to sign the "Bayonet Constitution," strongly damaging the chances of continued Hawaiian self-government, and permitted Europeans and Americans to vote in Hawaiian elections, even though not citizens of Hawaii.

In January 1891 Lydia Lilioukalani became Queen Liliuokalani, the first woman ruler of Hawaii, and the only true queen in American history, upon the death of her brother Kalakaua. The first thing she did was rid herself of any anti-royalist ministers, with the support of the Supreme Court. The politicians who had created a figurehead monarchy were at first unprepared to deal with a shrewd, intelligent and determined queen. What she wanted was Hawaii in control of Hawaiians, and she formed a new cabinet with like-minded ministers. In 1893 Lilioukalani informed her cabinet that a new constitution would allow only Hawaiian citizens to vote. Residents who were not citizens strongly objected.

Armed sailors from the American USS Boston surrounded her home, and the warship stood ready in the harbor. To prevent bloodshed, the queen stepped aside, and Sanford Dole became provisional president. This new government wanted Hawaii annexed to the United States. President of the United States Benjamin Harrison was leaning toward the annexation when he was voted out of office. His successor, Grover Cleveland, sent an impartial representative to report on the situation. His findings showed that the overwhelming majority wanted Queen Liliuokalani back, but she initially would not agree to amnesty, and when she did, it was too late. However, that provisional government now stated that the United States should not be interfering in Hawaiian affairs. President Cleveland then had the United States step aside. Royalists staged a poorly organized revolts against Dole. In three decisive battles, including one at Diamond Head, Dole's troops were completely victorious.

Liliuokalani had to renounce all claims to the throne, was tried and convicted of treason. She was kept a prisoner in a room at Iolani Palace for nine months. Later she came to live in Washington, D. C. for awhile, even attending William McKinley's inauguration, but eventually returned to Hawaii, where she died of a stroke on November 11, 1917 at Washington Palace, which has become the governor's executive mansion, and still contains her koa-wood piano and an enormous portrait of her. The funeral was one of the most impressive in Hawaiian history, with much of her will given to destitute and orphaned children in a trust she set up in 1909. This trust fund still exists and is on Lydia's mother's ancestral land.

Lydia Liliuokalani wrote Hawaii's Story by Hawaii's Queen, and one of Hawaii's most well-known songs, "Aloha Oe," (Farewell to You), which has becomes Hawaii's anthem, as well as another one hundred and fifty songs. This queen has naturally been inducted into Hawaii's Music Hall of Fame. She has always remained very much loved, with a school, college building, children's center, botanical garden, park, freeway and other places named in her honor. And even the annual Queen Liliuokalani Outrigger Canoe Race in Kona, the largest in the world, is named for her. "To gain the kingdom of heaven is to hear what is not said, to see what cannot be seen, and to know the unknowable-- that is Aloha."

#75- *Belva Lockwood (1830-1917)*

Many Firsts

Trail blazing attorney and educator Belva Ann Bennett Lockwood, daughter of farmer Lewis and Hannah Bennett, was the first woman to ever have her name on the ballot for the presidency of the United States. She was born in Niagara County's Royalton, New York on October 24, 1830. There is a plaque dedicated to her in front of this childhood home. She became a teacher in 1845, and married farmer Uriah McNall in 1848, and they moved to Gasport, New York.

In 1853 her husband died from tuberculosis, and Belva returned to teaching, but decided she wanted and needed a college education, which she did receive, with honors, from Genesee College in Lima, New York. She again taught for a while and even became principal of the Lockport Union School and then in 1861, the Gainesville Female Seminary in Oswego, New York, and even opened her own school.

After the Civil War she moved to Washington, D.C., opened her own co-educational school, unconventional at that time, and where she married older Dr. Ezekiel Lockwood in 1868, who was very supportive of his wife's work, but died in 1877, unable to see the successes of his wife. He had been invaluable in opening important doors for her and making needed connections. She was interested in the the law and politics, and was able to get private legal instructions from the professors at the newly found National University Law School (now George Washington School of Law). At graduation in 1873 she was refused a diploma because she was a woman, but she wrote to the "technical" head of the university, President Ulysses S. Grant. Grant did sign it, but probably failed to notice it was a female name. Belva Lockwood had become the United States' first female lawyer. This was done with the law being the realm of men, and with all of the social discrimination and practice working against her. Most jurisdictions did not accept her, but she made a name defending women's causes. In that same year she fought a landmark case: at this time a woman was subject to complete obedience to her husband. In this instance a wife shot someone at her husband's request. Lockwood argued successfully that the law could not punish a woman for obeying her husband.

In 1879 was a series of some "firsts." She became the first woman to argue before a federal court and obtained passage of a law permitting a woman to practice before the United States Supreme Court, and she became that woman lawyer in Kaiser v Stickney.

Lockwood had become friends with activist Susan B. Anthony, but because Anthony and associate Elizabeth Cady Stanton chose to support the Republican party candidates in 1884, even though they showed no signs of supporting women's rights, Belva Lockwood became incensed. She declared herself a candidate and campaigned on the National Equal Rights Party. She failed, garnering few votes. It was not too bad considering that women could not vote, and newspapers opposed her, warning men about "petticoat rule." But she tried again in 1888. She had become the first woman to have her name on a ballot for the presidency. Other women had tried to run, but none had ever gotten on an official ballot. She was now one of the most well-known women in America.

However, she became the State Department representative to the International Congress of Charities, Correction and Philanthropy in Geneva, Switzerland. In 1889 she was a delegate to the Universal Peace Congress in Paris, and became secretary of the American wing of the International Peace Bureau. From then on, Belva Lockwood traveled throughout Europe to peace conferences, and became a member of the nominating committee for the Nobel Peace Prize. She was even the co-editor of The Peacemaker. She also was published often in Cosmopolitan, Harper's Weekly, Lippincott's, and American Magazine of Civics. She was a member of the National American Women Suffrage Association. Into her seventies and eighties she continued her activist work with lecture tours.

In 1906 she became a lawyer of record presenting a bill before Congress to prevent government encroachment on Cherokee territory in North Carolina. The tribe gained five million dollars, the largest award ever given up to that time. Belva Lockwood is also the one responsible for the preparation that led to the admitting of Oklahoma, Arizona and New Mexico as states, granting woman suffrage. Syracuse University granted her an honorary doctorate.

She died in Washington, D.C. on May 19, 1917 and is buried in the Congressional Cemetery there. "Nothing was too daring for me to attempt." There are communities named in her honor in New York, West Virginia and California. A number of mastheads for ships were carved in her likeness, one of which is in Mystic Seaport in Mystic, Connecticut. And there was a merchant marine liberty ship, the U.S.S. Belva Lockwood during World War ll. She is in the National Women's Hall of Fame and has her portrait is in the National Portrait Gallery in Washington, D.C. In 1986 there was issued a postage stamp in her honor.

"After all, equality of rights and privileges is but simple justice."

#76- *Juliet Gordon Low (1860-1927)*

Girl Scouts of America

Juliette Magill Kinzie Gordon Low, nicknamed "Crazy Daisy," founder of the Girl Scouts of America, was born in Savannah, Georgia on October 31, 1860, and was privately educated. As a youth she loved writing poetry. Her father, William Gordon II, was a cotton broker and her mother's family, she was Nellie Kinzie, played a role in the founding of Chicago. After the Civil War, the family moved to Chicago for a period of time, and while there Juliet suffered from brain fever. She somewhat recovered and they moved back to Savannah. She was sent to New York and other places to the best "finishing" schools, schools that taught young ladies the social graces and prepared them for entrance into society. In 1880 she returned to Savannah to help her grieving mother take care of the home upon another daughter's death.

In 1886 she married William Mackay Low, a wealthy Englishman from Warwickshire. At the outset of the marriage she suffered any number of illnesses, and he was quite often absent hunting and gambling. As a result, she spent much of her life alone, in England and Scotland, as well as the United States. After a troubled marriage, leading toward a divorce, he died in 1905. She had become friendly with Sir Robert Baden-Powell, actively participating in his newly organized Girl Guides. At her estate at Glenlyon, she formed the first troop in Scotland in 1911, teaching the girls camp lore and how to take care of themselves. Back in Savannah in 1912 she started the Girl Guides of America with two patrols and a dozen or so young ladies. She composed a guide for the girls, How Girls Can Help Their Country. In 1915 the name was changed to Girl Scouts of the United States of America, now having 2400 members, and the headquarters moved to Washington, D. C. in 1913, and then to New York City in 1915. Low remained president until 1920, and then took on the title of Founder, and began promoting scouting on an international level.

Juliet Gordon Low developed breast cancer in 1923 and tried many "cures" but died in Savannah on January 17, 1927. She was buried in a Girl Scout uniform. By that time the enrollment had grown to one hundred and forty thousand, and by mid-century there were over one and a half million Girl Scouts, and in every state of the United States. In 1948 a postage stamp was issued in her honor. Her home in Savannah is open to public tours and is listed on the Register of Historic Landmarks. There are schools in Savannah, as well as a federal building, named in her honor. She is among the Georgia Women of Achievement and in 1979 was inducted into the National Women's Hall of Fame, and in 2012 was awarded the Presidential Medal of Freedom. Needless to say, she was also honored with the Silver Fish Award, the highest prize given by the Girl Scouts of America. Her birthday, October 31, is celebrated as Girl Scouts Founders Day. Edmund Nash was an early contributor, and a renter from Low. His son, poet Ogden Nash, wrote "Mrs. Low's House."

Even though Juliette Gordon Low was deaf and worked tirelessly for the Girl Scouts, she also organized and was a leader of the Savannah Art Club.

#77- Amy Lowell (1874-1925)

Imagist

Amy Lawrence Lowell, a very outspoken, early twentieth century poet and literary critic, and a cousin to poet James Russell Lowell, daughter to Augustus and Katherine, was born in Brookline, Massachusetts on February 9, 1874. Her Dream Drops, written as a teen, were fairy tales, privately printed and for the benefit of the Perkins Institution for the Blind, where Anne Sullivan, tutor of Helen Keller, had just graduated. In 1910, her first published poem was, "A Fixed Idea," in The Atlantic.

Later, after a study of poetry, her A Dome of Many-Colored Glass was published in 1912. It was a success, and conventional. This would soon change. The next year she went to England and joined poet Ezra Pound and a group of international poet radicals, and her poem, "In a Garden," was printed in the anthology, Des Imagistes, published by Pound and Hilda Doolittle in 1914. She also wrote Sword Blades and Poppy Seeds, her first volume of free verse. It was called "polyphonic verse" which was very rhythmic prose. And Amy Lowell became America's leading Imagist. Imagist poetry was simply a reaction to romantic poetry, and demanded precision of wording, and simplicity. She was a polyphonic imagist.

She returned home, lecturing at Harvard, Yale, Columbia and other universities throughout the United States, and began editing Some Imagist Poets, a three volume anthology, raising imagist poetry from a cult following of Ezra Pound to a literary form of worldwide recognition. Her poetic works, as well as critiques and articles on poetry, only enhanced her reputation, and also of some of her contemporaries. Amy Lowell's 1916 Men, Women and Ghosts, along with her critique, Tendencies in Modern American Poetry, established her as one of America's greatest poets. Amy Lowell also replaced Ezra Pound as the leading Imagist, prompting him in a derisive manner, to call them "Amygists" due to her domination. 1918 and 1919 brought Can Grande's Castle and Pictures of the Floating World. The latter showed her new pre-occupation with Oriental poetry. She kept on a hectic lecturing pace, reading hers and the poetry of others to audiences. She was very popular, due mainly to this unconventional poetry, her witty and opinionated reponses to welcomed criticism, and her cigar smoking, as well. She actually made headlines. She even made the cover of Time magazine.

In 1921 she co-authored Fir-Flower Tablets: Poems Translated from the Chinese, and wrote Legends. The next year came the anonymous A Critical Fable, again witty and pungent. In 1925 her What O'Clock, which included the poem, "Lilacs," was awarded the Pulitzer Prize for poetry, posthumously. Amy Lowell was still working on her monumental biography of John Keats when she died of a cerebral hemorrhage in Brookline on May 12, 1925. She was only fifty-one. East Wind was published the next year. Other posthumous works are Ballads For Sale, Poetry and Poets, and Selected Poems. Amy Lowell was a radical thinker, even taking personification to a new level, such as in "The Green Bowl" and "The Red Lacquer Music Stand." However, as time progressed she did become a bit more conventional. Her "polyphonic verse" was a marriage of poetry and prose. It was her belief that a poet could pick the method and the manner in order to create new impressions. Her own best examples of this are the shorter poems such that "Lilacs," the anti-war "Patterns," "Two Speak Together" and "Sisters."

Amy Lowell also published two literary critiques, Six French Poets: Studies in Contemporary Literature, as well as the aforementioned Tendencies in Modern American Poetry.

#78- *Clare Boothe Luce (1903-1987)*

Diplomat and So Much More

Clare Boothe Luce had a career of many successful facets. She was a playwright, a novelist, a short story writer, a reporter, an editor, a critic, a politician, a diplomat, and a presidential advisor. In 1983 President Ronald Reagan presented her with the Presidential Medal of Freedom. She was born on April 10, 1903 in New York City, to violinist and salesman William F. Boothe and Ann Snyder Murphy.

In 1923 she married George T. Brokaw, who turned out to be an alcoholic, and they divorced in 1928. But due to her wit, creativity and beauty, she thrived in everything else she did. By 1930 she had become editorial assistant for Vogue, and the next year associate editor for Vanity Fair. But she quit the next year and turned to writing, and in 1933 her short story collection, Stuffed Shirts, was published. Then a play, Abide With Me, in 1935, which failed. However, her next play a year later, The Women, ran for six hundred fifty-seven satirical performances, and then became a successful film with major movie stars (Joan Crawford, Rosalind Russell, Norma Shearer, Joan Fontaine and Paulette Goddard). Also successful were her Kiss the Boys Goodbye and Margin For Error, which also made it to the screen, and was an attack on Nazism. Child of the Morning and Slam the Door Softly were additional works. Europe in the Spring was a result of her being a war correspondent for Life magazine. She also managed to get interviews with Douglas MacArthur, Jawaharlal Nehru, Chiang Kai-shek and other major world figures.

In 1935 she had married Henry Luce, publisher of Time, Life, Fortune and Sports Illustrated, and they became the "power couple" of the time. She also began getting interested in conservative politics. She supported Wendell Willkie for president in 1940, disagreeing heartily with President Franklin D. Roosevelt's policies, and decided to run for congress herself in Connecticut in 1942. Of course, she won, and was appointed to the House Military Affairs Committee. In office she continued her attacks on Roosevelt, and then Harry Truman, especially on foreign policy, which she called "globaloney," and became a strong anti-communist. While there, she co-introduced a bill that became the forerunner of the Marshall Plan. Clare Boothe Luce retired from Congress in 1947, and went back to writing.

In 1944 her daughter was killed in an automobile accident, causing her to seek counsel from Catholic Bishop Fulton J. Sheen. She converted to Catholicism in 1946, and became an essayist and lecturer for her new faith, including editing Saints for Now. The Catholic Church named her a Dame of Malta. In 1949 her Come To The Stable was nominated as "Best Picture of the Year."

Keeping her hand in politics, she worked for the Thomas Dewey and Dwight Eisenhower presidential campaigns, and was rewarded with an appointment as ambassador to Italy, where she worked to reduce the influence of communism there. Luce also helped create a truce between Italy and Yogoslavia over Trieste. Luce was the first American woman to be named to a major ambassadorial post. She resigned in 1956 due to ill health, but was appointed ambassador to Brazil in 1959, but declined the appointment due to a feud with Senator Wayne Morse. He felt she was too conservative. She did campaign again in the 1964 failed presidential election bid of Barry Goldwater. From 1973 to 1977 and again from 1981 to 1983 Clare Boothe Luce served on the President's Foreign Intelligence Advisory Board.

For a while she and her husband retired to Hawaii. He died in 1967, but she stayed on for a bit, and then moved to Washington, D. C. 1972 saw Clare Boothe Luce given a special award from the Freedom Foundation. In 1979 she became the first female recipient of the Sylvanus Thayer Award from the United States Military Academy at West Point. Her philosophy, in her own words: "Statistics are mirrors held up to the face of the people. If we do not like the image we see reflected in them, we cannot change it merely by accusing the mirrors of distortion...The image will change only if, somehow we can re-establish the belief that this nation, in Abraham Lincoln's word, is truly 'the last best hope of earth.'" She was awarded the Laetare Medal from the University of Notre Dame. Other noted recipients have been Martin Sheen, Alfred E. Smith, John F. Kennedy, Helen Hayes, and Joe Biden. Luce had the knack of letting out some of the wittiest, pithiest, comments. Among them: "Widowhood is a fringe benefit of marriage.

"War" is a world where men decided to die together because they are unable live together."
"No good deed goes unpunished."
"A hospital is no place to be sick."

She died of brain cancer in Washington, D.C. on October 9, 1987 and is buried at Mephem Abbey in South Carolina. She bequeathed fifty million dollars to the Clare Boothe Luce Program which has become a source of aid for women's education in science, mathematics and engineering, as long as it is done in the United States. The Clare Boothe Luce Policy Institute, named in her honor in 1993, is a think tank dedicated to the advancement of American women of conservative ideals. The Heritage Foundation established the Clare Boothe Luce Award, given to those aiding the conservative movement. She has been inducted into the National Women's Hall of Fame.

#79- *Mary Lyon (1797-1849)*

Mount Holyoke

Mary Mason Lyon, born on the one hundred-acre family farm on February 28, 1797 in Buckland, Massachusetts, was one of the first great educators to espouse the cause of higher education for women. Her father, Aaron, a Revolutionary War veteran, died when she was five years old, and her mother, Jemima, remarried and moved away. Mary stayed at the family farm with her older brother, and attended Sanderson Academy in Ashfield, and was an outstanding student, although teased unmercifully by the more affluent students. A prosperous family helped this rustic young lady learn some things she might need to know to succeed in that school. Mary claimed that at Sanderson her "intellect was stirred, the taste refined, and intensity given to the desire for knowledge."

In 1821 she attended Byfield Academy briefly, but returned to Sanderson as its first female teacher. She also worked at Adams Female Academy in Londonderry, New Hampshire and in 1828 she relocated to the Ipswitch Female Seminary in Massachusetts. Here she even taught sex education. In the early 1830s she made an unsuccessful attempt to start the New England Female Seminary for Teachers. After that it was the Wheaton Female Seminary (now college) in Norton, Massachusetts, where she created the curriculum.

Lyon was energetically determined to start a school of higher learning for females, and available to everyone, regardless of means. That was the key. Her aim was to widen the availability, to admit those who were not necessarily rich. She worked hard, campaigning for this goal, raising funds any way she could, reaching out to the affluent, giving lectures, even knocking on doors. This was all in defiance of what was expected. At last, on November 8, 1837, in South Hadley, Massachusetts, she opened Mount Holyoke Female Seminary, later named Mount Holyoke College (1895). In the beginning it was but one building, on rather barren land. There were about eighty enrollees that first year, but grew to over one hundred students by the end of that first year, and they had to clean, cook, do chores, in addition to studying. The next year four hundred had to be turned away. It was the beginning of education for women equal to what was available for men, and science and mathematics were heavily stressed. In 1843 she wrote A Missionary Offering.

Mary Lyon's Mount Holyoke prospered, and became the inspiration for other female colleges that came later, such as Vassar and Wellesley. Lyon inspired women of all means to go beyond what was expected of them. Her school, along with Vassar, Wellesley, and also Barnard, Radcliffe, Smith and Bryn Mawr became the "Seven Sisters," known for outstanding educational opportunities for women.

Mary Lyon continued as president, and as an excellent administrator, until her death in South Hadley, on March 4, 1849, brought on by a rare acute bacterial infection, erysipelas or "red skin", and is buried on the school grounds. During her tenure as president Mount Holyoke gained a national reputation, with Mary Lyon becoming a legendary figure, empowering women. "Go where no one else will go, do what no one else will do." Among those who attended Mount Holyoke were Emily Dickinson, Lucy Stone, Virginia Apgar and Frances Perkins. She has been inducted into the Hall of Fame of Great Americans and the National Women's Hall of Fame. A United States postage stamp was issued in her likeness.

Group Seven

Krista McAuliffe- Lucretia Mott

80- Astronauts Christa McAuliffe, Judith Resnik, Laurel Clark & Kalpana Chawla

Astronauts Who Gave Their Lives

80 A. Christa McAuliffe (1948-1986)

The Teacher

Sharon Christa Corrigan McAuliffe, who was always called by her middle name, was born on September 2, 1948 in Boston, Massachusetts to Edward and Grace Corrigan. From the time she was a child she was mesmerized by the space program, and wished she could fly in space.

She graduated Framingham State College in 1970, soon married Virginia Military Institute graduate Steven J. McAuliffe, and moved to Maryland to be near his work. For most of the 1970s she taught middle school in Maryland. When her husband got the position of attorney general in New Hampshire, she relocated there and got a Master's degree in educational supervision from Bowie State University. For a while she taught middle school, but in 1983 began teaching at Concord High School in Concord, New Hampshire. She taught various courses, even one she created entitled, "The American Woman."

In 1985 NASA started its "Teacher in Space Project." McAuliffe was one of eleven thousand applicants. The applicants were narrowed down to one hundred and fourteen, and she was one. Then it was down to ten, and she was still in it. Then she was selected to be a member of Space Shuttle Challenger's STS-51-L mission. She took a year-long leave of absence from her teaching position to prepare. During this time she became extremely popular on numerous talk shows, explaining what her role would be. It would be her job to conduct experiments in such areas as hydroponics, magnetism and Newton's laws, and teach two classes to students back on earth. She was also to take them on a tour of the Challenger, calling it the "Ultimate Field Trip."

On January 28, 1986, due to a failure of o-rings, Space Shuttle Challenger exploded seventy-three seconds after take-off, killing all on board, including Christa McAuliffe. Christa McAuliffe, and the other members of the Challenger shuttle, as well as those of the Columbia shuttle disaster, was awarded the Congressional Space Medal of Honor. There are over forty schools named in her honor, as well as any number of scolarships. In 1990 actress Karen

Allen portrayed McAuliffe in a television film, Challenger. In 2006 there was a documentary narrated by Susan Sarandon, entitled Christa McAuliffe: Reach for the Stars, with an original theme song by Carly Simon.

80B. Judith Resnik (1949-1986)

The Engineer

Judith Arlene Resnik was born in Akron, Ohio on April 5, 1949 to optometrist Marvin and Sarah Resnik. As a youngster she played classical piano, and did get a perfect score on her SAT test. She became a mission specialist on both the Discovery and Challenger space shuttles. She graduated with a degree in electrical engineering in 1970 from Carnegie Mellon University, and marrying that same year to Michael Oldak, but they divorced in 1975. She went to work at the Laboratory of Neurophysiology at the National Institutes for Health. Later in 1977 she received a doctorate in the same field from the University of Maryland.

Resnik began work with RCA, first in Moorestown, New Jersey and then in Springfield, Virginia, as a circuit design engineer and working with radar control systems. In 1978 actress Nichelle Nichols, a regular on the Star Trek series, now working as a recruiter for NASA, approached Resnik. As a result she became a mission specialist on the maiden voyage of the Space Shuttle Discovery in August and September, 1984, logging six days and fifty-six minutes in space. She also became the first Jewish American woman in space. She was very popular due to her sense of humor and her doing weightless acrobatics.

She was then selected as mission specialist on the Space Shuttle Challenger, launching on January 28, 1986. She was killed in the explosion, due to faulty o-rings, but there is the possibility she survived the initial explosion after the cockpit separated from the shuttle. Judith Resnik was a member of the American Association for the Advancement of Science, the American Association of University Women, the Society of Women Engineers, the American Institute of Aeronautics and Astronautics. The International Electrical and Electronic Engineers presents an annual Judith Resnik Award to those who display excellence in space engineering. In the 1990 television film, Challenger, Resnik is portrayed by actress Julie Fulton. There are a number of buildings and schools named in her honor, and she has been inducted into the Ohio Women's Hall of Fame and been awarded the NASA Space Flight Medal and the Congressional Space Medal of Honor. In Seabrook, Texas there is a memorial to the entire Challenger crew.

80C. Laurel Clark (1961-2003)

The Bio-scientist

Laurel Blair Salton Clark was born on March 10, 1961 in Ames, Iowa, but was raised in Racine, Wisconsin. She received her college degree in 1983 from the University of Wisconsin at Madison in zoology. She received her medical doctorate from the same school.

During medical school she studied with the Diving Medicine Department of the United States Naval Experimental Diving Unit. Clark went on to study at the National Naval Medical Center Naval Undersea Medical Institute in Groton, Connecticut, and at the Naval Diving and Salvage Training Center in Panama City, Florida. She even dove with Navy SEALs performing medical evacuations from submarines off the coast of Scotland, where she met her husband, Jonathan Clark, and was designated a Naval Submarine Medical Officer and Diving Medical Officer. She went on to the Naval Aerospace Medical Institute in Pensacola, Florida and became a Naval Flight Surgeon, going on several deployments. She was also a member of the Aerospace Medical Association and the Society of Medical Flight Surgeons.

In 1996 she joined NASA and for two years prepared at the Johnson Space Center in Houston, Texas. Already, by this time, Laurel Clark was a navy captain; a Wisconsin licensed medical doctor; a radiation health officer; an undersea medical officer; a diving medical officer; a submarine medical officer; a naval flight surgeon; and an advanced cardiac life support provider, and had received the Navy and Marine Commendation with two gold stars, a National Defense Service Medal and an Overseas Service Ribbon.

She was assigned to the STS-107 Space Shuttle Columbia. She was to conduct bioscience experiments, including gardening. Clark successfully spent fifteen days, twenty-two hours, and twenty minutes in space, before the Columbia disintegrated with sixteen minutes to landing on re-entry on February 1, 2003.

On February 3, 2003 there was a memorial service at the Johnson Space Center, with a eulogy by President George W. Bush. There are a number of buildings and schools named in her honor, and there is a Laurel Salton Clark Memorial Fountain in Racine, Wisconsin. Posthumously, she has been awarded the Defense Distinguished Service Medal, the NASA Distinguished Service Medal, and the Congressional Space Medal of Honor.

80 D. Kalpana Chawla (1962-2003)

The Doctor

Kalpana Chawla was born in what was Karnal Punjab, India on March 17, 1962 to Banarasi Lal and Sanjyothi Chawla. As a child she loved to draw airplanes. Eventually she graduated from Punjab Engineering College, and in 1982 emigrated to the United States. She became a Certified Flight Instructor and got her pilot's license for both airplanes and gliders in 1982. In 1983 she married flying instructor Jean-Pierre Harrison. She went on to a get a master's degree in aerospace engineering at the University of Texas at Arlington in 1984, and a doctorate in the same area at the University of Colorado at Boulder in 1988.

She began working for NASA at the Ames Research Center dealing with vertical and short lift-off and landing concepts and computational fluid dynamics. In 1991 Kalpana Chawla became an American citizen, and in 1993 became vice president at Overset Methods in Los Altos, California, specializing in the simulation of problems with moving multiple bodies. In 1995 she joined the NASA Astronaut Corps. On November 19, 1997 she became the first Indian-born woman in space on the Space Shuttle Columbia, flight STS-87. She went two hundred and fifty-two times around the earth, and for over three hundred seventy-six hours, as a mission specialist and robotic arm operator, and deploying the Spartan satellite. It malfunctioned, but it was determined it was a software problem.

Chawla went on her second mission, again with the Space Shuttle Columbia, flight STS-107. It finally took off on January 16, 2003, after numerous technical and scheduling delays. Her duties involved microgravity and astronaut health and safety. However a piece of aluminum and foam insulation had broken off, and upon re-entry on February 1, 2003 this allowed hot atmospheric gases to penetrate and destroy the left wing structure, and Columbia slowly broke apart and burned up, killing all on board, sixteen minutes before the scheduled landing.

Kalpana Chawla has been awarded the Congressional Space Medal of Honor, the NASA Space Flight Medal and the NASA Distinguished Service Medal. There are numerous streets and buildings named in her honor, both here in the United States and in India. The prime minister of India named an Indian satellite after her, the "Kalpana." The International Space University at the University of Texas at El Paso now has a Kalpana Chawla Memorial Scholarship and the University of Colorado renamed its alumni award the Kalpana Chawla Outstanding Recent Alumni Award.

#81- *Carson McCullers (1917-1967)*

Southern Gothic

Born Lula Carson Smith, Carson McCullers, was born in Columbus, Georgia to jeweler Lamar and Marguerite Smith, on February 19, 1917. All her life she was plagued with ailments. She had rheumatic fever as a teen, had a series of strokes, and by thirty-one her left side was paralyzed. But she was not to be stopped, and went on to write some of the most memorable works of the mid-twentieth century. Carson left Georgia to study at the Juilliard School of Music in New York City, but became ill and returned home. Eventually she returned to New York to study at both Columbia and New York universities. In 1937, however, she married Reeves McCullers and they moved to Charlotte, North Carolina for a while. They divorced in 1941 and remarried in 1945.

In 1940 she wrote The Heart Is A Lonely Hunter. This first novel was an immediate success. It was the story of a Southern town and the outcasts and misfits of its society, the first of many of her works to have portrayed rather eccentric characters. It was made into a film starring Alan Arkin. 1941 saw Reflections in a Golden Eye published. This also was made into a film. Reflections had quite the cast with Elizabeth Taylor and Marlon Brando. In 1942 she was honored by the American Academy of Arts and Letters. After World War II she lived in Paris for a while, striking up a friendship with other southern writers, Tennessee Williams and Truman Capote.

Her greatest triumph, A Member of the Wedding, was written in 1946, and again she was honored by the American Academy of Arts and Letters. It is the heart-wrenching story of a motherless teenage girl, showing McCullers continued abilty to see into the adolecsent being. It opened as a play on Broadway in 1950 and won the New York Drama Critics Award as Best American play, and went on to become a successful film. Ethel Waters appeared in both the stage and film versions. All her works were set in the Deep South even though she had no longer lived there.

The Ballad of Sad Cafe in 1951 was a collection: a novella and six short stories, including "Wunderkind," one of the first things she wrote. A play, The Square Root of Wonderful in 1957, told of the dark period of her life when she attempted suicide, and then later when her husband succeeded at it. Other works by Carson McCullers are a novel, A Clock Without Hands in 1961, and poetry collection, Sweet as a Pickle and Clean as a Pig in 1964. The Mortgaged Heart, published in 1972 contained, among other works, "Sucker," a classic tale of adolescence, which was written when she was seventeen. Illumination and Night Glare, an unfinished autobiography, was published in 1999. In 1958 she had recorded The Member of the Wedding and Other of Her Works.

Throughout her life Carson McCullers suffered from numerous maladies, not the least was alcoholism, and died of a brain hemorrhage at age fifty, on September 29, 1967, in South Nyack, New York, where she had lived the last twenty years or so. Columbus State University has the Carson McCullers Center for Writers and Musicians, which is located in her childhood home. She was inducted into the Great Women of Georgia. In 2016 singer/songwriter, and admirer, Suzanne Vega recorded Lover, Beloved: Songs from an Evening with Carson McCullers.

#82- *Dolley Madison (1768-1849)*

White House Heroine

Dolley Payne was born on May 20, 1768 in Scotchtown, North Carolina, and a cousin to Patrick Henry. Her wealthy Quaker parents, John and Mary, moved the family first to a plantation in Virginia in 1769 and then to Philadelphia in 1783. In 1790 she married John Todd, a Quaker lawyer, and had two sons, one dying young during a yellow fever epidemic in Philadelphia, as did her husband. Dolley was now a widow with a young son at the age of twenty-five. John Payne's business had failed and he died in 1792.

Mary Payne opened a boarding house to make ends meet, and Aaron Burr had become a tenant, and a romance might have bloomed, until Burr introduced her to his more serious friend, congressman James Madison. In September 1794 she married Madison, forty-three years old and seventeen years her senior. However, she was excommunicated from the Quakers because she married outside the faith. From that moment on, Dolley Madison stopped wearing the "plain" Quaker clothing, and she now delightfully dressed in such a manner to bring out her vivacity. Even though she was no longer a Quaker, she always hold on to and believe in the Quaker ways.

They remained in Philadelphia while Madison was in office, but then moved to his home in Virginia. Thomas Jefferson selected Madison as his Secretary of Stae, and so they moved to Washington, D. C. She was wonderful in Washington, where she sometimes acted as hostess for Jefferson, who was a widower. She was friends with Martha Washington, with her sister having married Washington's nephew, George Steptoe Washington. Her own reputation grew as a great hostess, having many a social affair in her own home. When James Madison became president, Dolley was a fantastic help. He was such a somber, serious man, and her bouyant personality and hospitality were true assets. She made the White House lively and her very charm and social graces made her home a place of grace and wit.

Soon the War of 1812 came, placing Madison in dire straits, even moreso when it became apparent that Washington itself would be captured. The city was evacuated, with Madison instructing his wife to gather up important papers, and depart. She did pack up the documents and sent them away, but she remained. She now really became a grand part of history. The famous portrait of George Washington was screwed to the wall, and seemingly could not be taken down. Only after having the portrait of Washington cut from its frame, and taking it and a copy of the Declaration of Independence, and some other material, did she finally flee. She did not make it to her husband immediately. She disguised herself as a old woman in a soldier's camp, nursing them and family members. She then joined Madison in Virginia. When the British left, she returned to the White House. That Washington portrait she saved is the only original piece belonging to the mansion.

Her heroism, daring and personality helped her husband who had been losing support. They lived at Octagon House while the presidential mansion was repaired. Now is when it started being called the White House because they painted it white. Around this time James Madison thought it a better idea to move the capital back to Philadelphia, but Dolley argued against that choice. She is the only First Lady to be given an honorary seat in Congress. After Madison's terms ended they returned to Montpelier, his home in Virginia. He died in 1836, and Dolley Madison returned to Washington, leaving Montpelier in the not-so-capable hands of her son. She again became a popular hostess, especially with close friend Daniel Webster. Dolley also was sought out for advice from Angelica Singleton Van Buren, her own cousin, and daughter-in-law/hostess to widowed Martin Van Buren.

As time went on Dolley Madison began enduring hard times. Her son had become not only an alcoholic disappointment to her, but also a huge drain on her finances. Montpelier had to be sold, as did many of Madison's papers. She would not seek aid, but at the urging of Daniel Webster, people helped her without her ever knowing it.

In 1848 she was a chief guest at the laying of the cornerstone of the Washington Monument. The next year she became the guest of honor at President James Knox Polk's final reception as president. It was also Dolley Madison's last public appearance. She died in Washington on July 12, 1849. Initially she was buried there, but later moved to Virginia to rest alongside her husband.

#83- Helene Madison (1913-1970)

Queen Helene

Extraordinary record-breaking swimmer Helene Emma Madison, born on June 19, 1913, moved to Seattle, Washington as a youngster. She began her amazing swimming career at nearby Green Lake where, eventually, her abilities were noticed. As a fifteen-year old high schooler she broke the state record for the 100-yard freestyle. Then went on to break the record for the Pacific Coast. She became associated with the Washington Athletic Club and began competing nationally.

From 1930 to 1931 Helene Madison broke sixteen world records, completely dominating the world of female competitive swimming. She won every freestyle race in which she competed, and winning the United States Women's Nationals in 1930, 1931, 1932. In the 1930 nationals alone she set six records, and was given a homecoming greeting by thousands of fans, and given a luncheon on Boeing Field. She became the first woman to swim the 100-yard freestyle in under one minute. The Associated Press named her Female Athlete of the Year in 1931.

In 1932 Madison went to the Olympic Games being held in Los Angeles, California. She got the gold medal in the 100-meter freestyle, got the gold in the 400-meter freestyle, and got the gold in the 4 x 100-meter freestyle relay, breaking records in all three, even in the preliminary races. She was the most decorated woman and American at these Olympics, and tied for the most overall. In Madison's victory in the 400-meter freestyle she defeated another American, Lenore Kight, by less than one-tenth of a second. It is still considered one of the most thrilling races in Olympic history. When she returned to Seattle she was given a ticker-tape parade and hailed as "Queen Helene." However as great as Helene Madison was, this was the end of her glory. She went to Hollywood to be a star, and made three films, The Human Fish, It's Good to Be Alive, and The Warrior's Husband. All three failed badly and by 1933 Helene Madison's movie career was over, although she did make a documentary, Sports Slants, in 1934. Due to her professional movie "career" she was now ineligible to participate in the 1936 Olympics in Berlin, Germany.

She approached the Seattle Parks Department for a position as a swimming instructor, but was turned down because they would not hire a woman as a swim instructor. It did not matter that she was "Queen Helene," an Olympic swimming champion and breaker of twenty-six world records. She wound up with a job at the concession stand. It is ironic that Seattle has two pools named after Madison, one at her Washington Athletic Club, and the other with the Seattle Department of Parks and Recreation.

Eventually she did manage to open a swimming school at the Moore Hotel, but by the late 1950's she was suffering from a number of medical problems, including two strokes and a back surgery. She had to close the school. In the meantime, she had married and divorced three times.

In 1966 Madison was inducted into the International Swimming Hall of Fame in Florida, but was so destitute she could not afford to go. The Washington Athletic Club came to her aid and paid for the trip.

But by 1965 she had already been diagnosed with diabetes and then with throat cancer. Helene Madison died in Seattle on November 27, 1970, and has also been inducted into the United States Olympic Hall of Fame.

#84- *Wilma Mankiller (1945-2010)*

First Female Chief of the Cherokee Nation

Wilma Pearl Mankiller, first female chief of the Cherokee Nation, was born to Charley and Clara Mankiller on November 18, 1945 in Tahlequah, Oklahoma. The name "Mankiller" was derived from a Cherokee rank. She grew up very poor and the family, as well as forty-five other Cherokee families, was forced by a United States Army's decree of eminent doman to move from their ancestral home to Tahlequah in 1942 because the Army needed to expand the size of a nearby army camp. They were relocated by the Bureau of Indian Affairs to San Francisco in 1956, but then to Daly City, California.

In the 1960s she became an activist with the San Francisco Indian Center, and in 1963 Wilma married Hector Hugo Olaya de Bardi and moved to nearby Oakland, California. She attended Skyline Community College in San Bruno, California and San Francisco State University. Mankiller became involved with the IOAT (Indians of All Tribes) and took part in the 1969 occupation of Alcatraz, the former island prison in San Francisco Bay that had once been Indian land. The treaties had stated that lands taken away from Indians, and if no longer in use, must be then returned to the Indians, thus the occupation. She also did volunteer work for the various members of the Pit River Tribe in northern California.

She and Olaya de Bardi divorced in 1977 and Mankiller returned to Oklahoma and eventually got involved with Cherokee politics, working as a program developer and planner. She was elected deputy chief in 1983 and became Chief of the Cherokee Nation in 1985. She was elected and re-elected, remaining chief until 1995, winning her last election with eighty-three per cent of the vote.

Her administration faced hard problems, beginning with dealing with a Cherokee culture that was very male-oriented, but she showed them all. She got things going by instigating community developement projects and forming a Cherokee Nation Community Developement Department. She worked with the Bureau of Indian Affairs to get funding for self-help programs. Mankiller helped to establish tribally-owned businesses, improving the infrastructure, working on tribal and federal negotiations, improving both health care and educational facilities, and building a hydroelectric facility. During her tenure the Cherokee population rose from fifty-five thousand to one hundred and fifty-six thousand. In the meantime, she received her social science B. A. from Flaming Rainbow University in Stilwell, Oklahoma, and got a graduate degree from the University of Arkansas, and married again, to Charlie Soap, a Cherokee lecturer.

Wilma Mankiller declined to run again because of ill health. Back in 1979 she had been in a horrific car accident that required many surgeries. But she also suffered from myasthenia gravis, breast cancer, lymphoma, and had a kidney transplant. But she kept going. She became a guest lecturer at Dartmouth College, and was even given an honorary degree from there. She wrote a national bestselling autobiography, Mankiller: A Chief and Her People, and co-wrote and compiled Every Day Is a Good Day: Reflections by Indigenous Women with a forward by Gloria Steinem.

As time passed Wilma Mankiller was not only inducted into the National Women's Hall of Fame, but also inducted into the Oklahoma Women's Hall of Fame and the National Cowgirl Hall of Fame, was Ms. Magazine's Woman of the Year, given the John W. Gardner Leadership Award, the Elizabeth Blackwell Award, and the American Association of University Women's Achievement Award.

In 1998 President Bill Clinton presented Wilma Mankiller the Presidential Medal of Freedom. She passed away in Oklahoma due to pancreatic cancer on April 6, 2010. On her passing President Barack Obama "recognized her for her vision and commitment to a brighter future for all Americans." She was, indeed, a role model for girls. In 2013 a film, The Cherokee Word for Water, was released with actress Kimberly Norris Guerrero portraying Wilma Mankiller. In Stilwell there is a Wilma Mankiller Health Clinic.

#85- Julia Marlowe (1865-1950)

Juliet

Julia Marlowe was born Sarah Frances Frost to John and Sarah Frost in Cumberland, England on August 17, 1865, but the her shoemaker father fled to Kansas in America in the early 1870s on the mistaken belief that he had harmed someone with a whip. With Sarah, and her mother they moved to Ohio. He changed their name to Brough, and his daughter eventually joined the Juvenile Opera Company, acting under the name of Fanny Brough, under the direction of Robert E. J. Mills and one of her first performances was in H.M.S. Pinafore, and then appeared in Pygmalion and Galatea. She went on tour throughout the midwestern United States. In 1882 she began playing youthful roles in Shakespearean plays, such as Balthazar in Romeo and Juliet and Marco in Twelfth Night.

In the early 1880s she left for New York City where she studied singing and acting for three years, and then taking the name Julia Marlowe, but still finding it difficult to find work. Mills had become manager of the New York Bijou Opera House and offered her some work. In 1887 she debuted in Ingomar the Barbarian and became an overnight success and a star. The critics raved over her performance, and she went on tour for the next two years. In 1895 she made her Broadway debut, and eventually appearing in over seventy productions there. In 1896 she portrayed Juliet for the first time, and from then on she had been considered one of the greatest "Juliets" of all time. She also went on to appear in For Bonnie Prince Charlie, Barbara Frietchie, The Hunchback, and The Cavalier over the next few years. In 1900 she opened as Mary Tudor in When Knighthood Was in Flower and was quite again a smashing success. At this point in her career she became financially independent. Julia Marlowe was one of the greatest leading ladies of her day, and a great romantic actress.

In the early 1900s she presented Shakespeare at The Academy of Music in New York at affordable prices, and even did special performances for school children. Julia Marlowe revived her Ingomar in 1904, and in that same year joined up with actor Edward Hugh Sothern. They went on to become a harmoniously wonderful and very successful Shakespearean couple earning a great sum of money, on Broadway, touring America, and in England, appearing in Romeo and Juliet, Hamlet, Macbeth, Taming of the Shrew, The Merchant of Venice, Much Ado About Nothing, Twelfth Night, Antony and Cleopatra, and also in Jeanne d'Arc, John the Baptist, Gloria, The Goddess of Reason, and The Sunken Bell. Their Shakespearian productions were considered the best ever done. Marlowe had married and divorced Robert Tabor, and in 1911 she married Sothern, and then retired in 1914. In 1919 she was given an honorary doctorate from George Washington University, the first time an American actress was so honored, and was similarly honored by Columbia University in 1943. She made a bit of a comeback in 1919, but retired again in 1924. In 1929 the American Academy of Arts and Letters awarded her with a gold medal.

Edward Sothern died in 1933, and Julia Marlowe became mostly a recluse for the rest of her life. She died in New York City on November 12, 1950, but had become an inspiration for many upcoming actresses.

#86- *Maria Mayer (1906-1972)*

First AmericanWoman Nobel Laureate in Physics

Maria Goeppert was born in Kattowitz, Germany (now Poland), the daughter of professor of pediatrics at the University of Gottingen, Friedrich and his music teacher wife Maria, on June 28, 1906. She received her doctorate in 1930 from the University of Gottengin, where she was known as "the beauty of Gottengin." Her graduate thesis was on the possible two-photon absorption by atoms. It was a masterpiece, but at the time proving her thesis was not possible, but decades later it was. This was the sign that this was a most brilliant physicist.

In that same year she married American Joseph Edward Mayer, a student who boarded with her family, and they moved to Baltimore, Maryland. And the now Maria Mayer took a teaching position at Johns Hopkins University and became a citizen in the early 1930s. For a portion of her career, Maria Mayer could not work with her husband and expect full pay or full professorship. It was considered nepotism. In 1940, in collaboration with her husband, while they were at Columbia University in New York City, they published Statistical Mechanics. With the rise of Nazism in Germany she got involved with refugee relief efforts. She also took a position at Sarah Lawrence College in 1941 and during World War ll she worked for the Manhattan Project at Columbia University on separation of the isotopes of uranium, and at the Los Alamos Laboratory in New Mexico on the development of the atomic bomb, working with the brilliant Enrico Fermi, Niels Bohr and Edward Teller.

From 1946 until 1960 she worked at the University of Chicago and her attention was devoted to nuclear physics, and again working with those three brilliant minds. She discovered signs of closed shells in nuclei, and concluded that protons and neutrons move independent of each other, and made a model for the structure of nuclear shells. She also worked at the Argonne National Laboratory, beginning in 1946. In the 1950s she collaborated with J.H. D. Jensen on Elementary Theory of Nuclear Shell Structure.

By 1960 she became a full professor of physics at the University of California at San Diego, along with her husband. She suffered a stroke, had heart problems, but kept on teaching. She was the winner of the Nobel Prize in Physics in 1963 for proposing the nuclear shell model of the atomic nucleus. She was the first American woman so honored. Upon winning this prestigious award, she said, "Winning the prize wasn't half as exciting as doing the work itself." She was, too, elected a fellow of the American Academy of Arts and Sciences in 1965. Both the Argonne National Laboratory and the University of California at San Diego honor Mayer by giving awards to outstanding young women scientists, engineers and researchers.

Maria Goeppert Mayer died in San Diego on February 20, 1972. She was an outstanding physicist on many levels, and a giant role model for young women of science. A 2011 postage stamp was issued in her honor. And she has been inducted into the National Women's Hall of Fame.

#87- *Margaret Mead* (1901-1978)

Cultural Anthropologist

Edward Mead was a professor of finance at the prestigious Wharton School of Economics of the University of Pennsylvania and Emily Mead was a sociologist. They were the parents of cultural anthropologist Margaret Mead, considered by many to be one of the most outstanding Americans of all time, born on December 16, 1901 in Philadelphia, Pennsylvania, and grew up in nearby Doylestown. She went on to graduate from Barnard College in 1923, and received her master's degree a year later from Columbia University, changing her area of study from English to sociology. This was done primarily due to the influence of her professors, including Dr. Ruth F. Benedict.

In 1925 the Social Science Research Council of the United States and the American Museum of Natural History rewarded her with fellowships, enabling her to take an extensive sojourn among the Samoan people. Coming of Age in Samoa, her masterpiece and a best seller, was the result. She explained how the young Samoans go through puberty without all the conflicts that are deemed normal in western civilization. Margaret Mead now became assistant curator of ethnology at the American Museum of Natural History, later becoming associate curator. She became curator emeritus later on in life, in 1969. In 1929 she received her doctorate from Columbia, and another fellowship, allowing her to leave for the Admiralty Islands for six months. Growing Up in New Guinea in 1930 was the result. She continued her writing with Balinese Character: A Photographic Analysis, written with her third husband, anthropologist Gregory Bateson. Mead had been married twice before, both times also to anthropologists, Luther Cressman and Reo Fortune. Dr. Benjamin Spock, who become a world famous pediatric author, was Mead's pediatrician, and he adopted many of her proposals, such as the timing of breastfeeding. Other writings were Sex and Temperament in Three Primitive Societies, The Mountain Arapesh, Male and Female: A Study of the Sexes in a Changing World, and And Keep Your Powder Dry, and a memoir about her parents, With A Daughter's Eye.

During World War ll she became executive secretary of a committee of the National Research Council studying food habits. After the war she became director of research studies on contemporary cultures at Columbia, and did the same for the American Museum of Natural History in 1951. In the 1950s Margaret Mead was elected president of the World Federation of Mental Health, was awarded the Viking Fund Medal, edited An Anthropologist At Work: Writings of Ruth Benedict, started teaching both at Columbia and the New School, and went back to the sites of her earlier field trips, reporting on the children of the children she had met and studied. Margaret Mead became quite the controversial figure and became very outspoken on the cause of equality for women, child rearing, population control, and world hunger, among other topics, even contributing magazine articles, including "A Proposal: We Need Taboos on Sex at Work" in Redbook magazine. Her detailed accounts of the attitudes toward sex in the South Pacific and Southeast Asia are considered partially responsible for the sexual revolution of the 1960s.

Margaret Mead became president of the American Anthropological Association in 1960, as well as vice president of the New York Academy of Sciences in the later 1960s, and president of the American Association for the Advancement of Science in 1975. She taught at Fordham University from 1968 to 1970 and became the Distinguished Professor of Sociology and Anthropology at the University of Rhode Island. In 1970 she was awarded UNESCO's Kalinga Prize, given to one who popularizes and expresses skills in presenting science to lay people.

Additional writings from the pen of Margaret Mead were the autobiography of her early life, Blackberry Winter, New Lives For Old, People and Places and Soviet Attitudes Toward Authority. She even wrote, "A Talk With Santa Claus," published posthumously in the December 1978 issue of Redbook. She passed away on November 15, 1978 from pancreatic cancer, and is buried in the Trinity Cemetery in Buckingham, Pennsylvania. In January 1979 she was posthumously awarded the Presidential Medal of Freedom.

She was also inducted into the National Women's Hall of Fame, and a 1998 postage stamp was issued in her likeness. One famous line of hers is often quoted: "Never doubt that a small group of committed people can change the world. Indeed, it is the only thing that has."

#88- Edna St. Vincent Millay (1892-1950)

First Female Pulitzer Prize Winner

Edna St. Vincent Millay, daughter of Henry (who left the family in 1899) and Cora Millay, a nurse, and one of the most popular poets (and playwrights) in American history, was born on February 22, 1892 in Rockland, Maine. She was given her middle name because a maternal uncle was saved from near death at St. Vincent's Hospital in New York City. Edna actually wanted to be called "Vincent" when she was young.

She began writing poetry very young, and she won the St. Nicholas Gold Badge and a fifteen dollar prize from St. Nicholas Magazine. Then she was published in the Camden Herald and Current Literature.

At the age of nineteen, Millay did a reading of her poem, "Renascence." It attracted a member of her audience who was so impressed she arranged a scholarship to Vassar College. She had entered into a contest that had ten thousand entrants, and it came in fourth place, but many were shocked. The winner said Millay should have won, and the second place contestant offered her the prize money earned. As it turned out, it is one of the best American philosophical poems. Millay graduated Vassar in 1917, being almost a legendary student, writing school plays, acting in them, and always being involved in spirited free-wheeling activities. Her Renascence and Other Poems was published. After the war, her pacifist, anti-war verse play Aria da Capo was published. It was televised much later in 1949. The light and fun A Few Figs From Thistles appeared in 1920, exploring female sexuality and feminism, and in 1921 Second April. Two other verse plays, Two Slatterns and a King and The Lamp and the Bell (1921), also appeared the same year.

Edna St. Vincent Millay went on to live the true bohemian artist's life in Greenwich Village in New York City, and even wrote short stories under the pseudonym Nancy Boyd. She did some acting and writing with the Provincetown Players and the Theater Guild. In 1924, along with some others, she founded the Cherry Lane Theater which put on experimental drama.

Earlier she went to Paris and Europe, working for Vanity Fair magazine. In 1923, even though Millay was an avowed bisexual, Millay married Dutchman Eugen J. Boissevain, and in 1925 they bought over six hundred acres of property in upstate New York, eventually moving there. Boissevain became her manager, and arranged readings and radio and public appearances for Millay, many of them sold out, and she did, indeed, become very popular. Their life at the estate was at times reflective and productive, and at times with lively, unconventional, wild parties and huge gatherings with lots of drinking.

"My candle burns at both ends;
It will not last the night;
But oh, my foes, and oh, my friends-
It gives a lovely light!

1923 also brought The Harp Weaver and Other Poems, for which she won the Pulitzer Prize, the first woman to do so. Her work had matured and her reputation and popularity soared. Her poetry was conventional in many ways, but demanded to be seen as individualism, and filled with passion, rebellion and romance. Her verse play, The King's Henchman was transformed into a libretto for an opera, becoming the greatest success of an American opera. Soon after came The Buck in the Snow and Other Poems (1928) and, in 1931, her very praiseworthy Fatal Interview love sonnets.

In the 1940's Edna St. Vincent Millay wrote Collected Sonnets, and the verse political commentary, The Murder of Lidice which dealt with the Nazi massacre at a village. It also served as an introduction to her screenplay Hitler's Madman. The Poetry Society of America awarded her the Robert Frost Medal for her lifetime of contributions. She had also become a member of the American Academy of Arts and Letters.

Millay did not belong to any particular school of poetry, and did not conform to traditional poetry, nor to any "modern" style. It seems her poetry was an innovative reflection of social consciousness. Other works by her are: Poems (1923), Huntsman, What Quarry? (1939), Flowers of Evil (1936), Conversation at Midnight (1937), Make Bright the Arrows (1940), and Prayer for an Invading Army (1944).

In the 1930s she was involved in a car accident that left her with a sore back and right arm. And in 1944 she had a nervous breakdown, and then Boissevain died in 1949, and Millay was desolate for a while. Edna St. Vincent Millay died at her estate, Steepletop, in upstate Austerlitz, New York on October 19, 1950. She had a heart attack and slipped on a flight of stairs. Steepletop is now the Edna St. Vincent Millay Museum and on the list of National Historic Landmarks.

#89- *Patsy Mink (1927-2002)*

Title IX

Patsy Matsu Takemoto was born on the island of Maui in Hawaii, on December 6, 1927, to civil engineer Suematsu Takemoto and his wife Mityama. While in Maui High School, soon after the bombing of Pearl Harbor in Hawaii, Patsy was able to overcome the absolute distrust of Japanese-Americans by her gift of effective consensus building, and was elected class president. She also was valedictorian.

After being passed over for promotions on numerous occasions due to prejudice, following World War II, her father moved the family to Honolulu on the island of Oahu, and opened his own business.

Patsy enrolled in the University of Nebraska and here she faced very strong segregation policies. Sororities and fraternities were segregated, and so were dormitories. Patsy stood up against the university and the student body as a whole, and formed the Unaffiliated Students of the University of Nebraska, and she succeeded in changing policy. However, she came down with typhoid fever, and returned to Hawaii, where she enrolled in the University of Hawaii and graduated.

When she found that twenty of the medical schools to which she applied still did not admit women, she decided to apply to law schools so that eventually she could make changes. She went to and graduated from the University of Chicago Law School, where she met, and married, fellow student John Mink. After a while they moved back to Hawaii, where Patsy Mink became the first woman to practice law.

Wanting to see change, she attained the chair of the Young Democrats. In 1956 she was elected to the Hawaii Territorial Legislature, and two years later to the territorial senate. The next year, 1959, Hawaii attained statehood, and Patsy Mink became a Hawaii State senator. Her prestige had grown to the extent that she was asked to be a speaker at the Democratic National Convention in 1960. In 1965 she became the first ethnic minority elected to the United States House of Representatives, where she served six consecutive terms. Mink was also honored with being requested to give the 1970 Democratic Party Response to the State of the Union Address. During this time she was a leader against gender discrimination, and was the main force behind the Title IX Amendment to the Women's Educational Equity Act. Although Title IX was only part of the whole package, it was this that opened much greater opportunities for women in athletics. She was, as well, a strong advocate behind the Early Childhood Education Act. Also in 1972 she became the first Asian American to seek the nomination for President of the United States, although it made little headway. 1977-1978 saw Patsy Mink as Assistant Secretary of State, and then president of Americans for Democratic Action. She returned home where she was elected and served on the Honolulu City Council from 1983 to 1987.From 1990 until her death in 2002 she was back in Congress, a passionate proponent of universal health care, and becoming a leader of the Democratic Women's Caucus.

In 2002 Patsy Mink ran for re-election and won handily. However in August of that year she was admitted to the hospital for complications from chicken pox, and on September 28, 2002 she died of viral pneumonia. Her husband John tried to run for her vacant seat, but failed. There was a grand Hawaii state funeral for her in the Hawaii State Capitol Rotunda, and burial at the National Cemetery of the Pacific. She has been inducted into the National Women's Hall of Fame, and in 2014 Patsy Mink was posthumously awarded the Presidential Medal of Freedom. There are documentaries on her life: Rise of the Wahine and Patsy Mink: Ahead of the Majority. The Patsy Takemoto Mink Educational Foundation is an extension of Mink's ideals and gives opportunities and support to women, especially mothers and low income earners.

#90- *Margaret Mitchell (1900-1949)*

Gone With the Wind

Margaret Munnerlyn Mitchell was born on November 8, 1900 in Atlanta, Georgia, to a family that had included men who had fought in the American Revolution, the War of 1812, and the Civil War. Her parents were the rather wealthy and prominent attorney Eugene and woman suffrage advocate May Belle Mitchell. She attended finishing school at Washington Seminary and was active in the drama club and literary editor of the yearbook.

While at the seminary, during World War I, it was expected that the young ladies would entertain soldiers at the nearby army camps. There she met New Yorker Clifford Henry, a captain stationed at Camp Gordon. They fell in love, became engaged, and he was shipped off, and subsequently killed in France.

She then attended Smith College in Massachusetts for a year, but dropped out to help care for her newly widowed father. Upon returning to Atlanta she began working for the Atlanta Journal Sunday Magazine, under the name of Peggy Mitchell, did interviews, wrote sketches of Georgia life, and did proof reading. She also became a debutante, and although Mitchell had the reputation of being quite the flirt, she did meet and marry North Carolina bootlegger Berrien Kinnard Upshaw in 1922. The marriage was short-lived, but she did in 1925 marry publicist Kentuckian John Robert Marsh, and they remained married until her death. She stayed with the Journal until 1926 when a broken ankle forced her to retire.

Throughout her life, even in her earliest years, she heard stories of the Civil War, reconstruction, and the Old South from her relatives. She began to research the Civil War and this reconstruction period. All this work, which fascinated her, led to her writing the outstanding bestselling novel, Gone With the Wind, published in 1936. It was awarded the Pulitzer Prize, the National Book Award as the Most Distinguished Novel, and the American Booksellers also selected it as the best novel of 1936. During the Great Depression this novel amazingly managed to sell a million copies in the first six months. She became an instant celebrity, making many speaking engagements and giving interviews. But after a while, it was too much for her, and she stopped. Indeed, it was the bestselling book in American history, and translated into twenty-seven languages in thirty-eight countries. A fact that is sometimes forgotten is that the original name for Scarlet O'Hara was Pansy.

Mitchell struggled to find a title, even considering Tomorrow Is Another Day. However, lines from a poem by Englishman Ernest Christopher Dowson solved the problem:

"When I awoke and found the dawn was gray: I have been faithful to thee Cynara! in my fashion. I have forgot much, Cynara! gone with the wind"

Margaret Mitchell's novel became possibly the best-known film ever made, released in 1939. It won eight Academy Award Oscars, especially as Best Picture of the Year. Vivian Leigh's portrayal of Scarlett O'Hara won her the Best Actress award, and Hattie McDaniel won the Best Supporting Actress award. Clark Gable was nominated for his portrayal of Rhett Butler, and Olivia deHavilland was also nominated. It had an all-star cast with Leslie Howard, Thomas Mitchell, Ward Bond, Eddie "Rochester" Anderson, Victor Jory, and a brief appearance by George Reeves, who would gain fame later on as Superman on television.

She did write a novella, Lost Laysen, but it was not published until 1996, and another book, The Big Four, but it had been lost and never published.

During World War ll she volunteered with the American Red Cross, and also sold war bonds. Margaret Mitchell was hit by a car in Atlanta on August 11, 1949, and died five days later on August 16. She was recognized in 1994 by the Georgia Women of Achievement and is in the Georgia Writers Hall of Fame.

#91- *Maria Mitchell (1818-1889)*

Astronomer

Maria Mitchell was America's first outstanding female scientist and astronomer. She was born on Nantucket in Massachusetts to William and Lydia Mitchell, on August 1, 1818, and as a child, became her father's telescope observation assistant. They were distant descendants of Benjamin Franklin. He was a United States Coast Survey astronomical observer and a school principal.

She worked for a while as a teaching assistant, but in 1835, at sixteen years of age, she opened her own integrated school on Nantucket, something unheard of at the time. A year later she became librarian at the Nantucket Athenaeum, and remained librarian for over twenty years.

In her spare time and in the evenings she read, and Maria and her father built a small observatory for a telescope atop the Pacific Bank, where her father was an officer. This was for the United States Coast Survey and the United States Military Academy.

On October 1, 1847, at 10:30 in the evening, Maria Mitchell discovered a new comet, C/1847 T1 (which now bears her name, "Miss Mitchell's Comet"). Her observation was seconded by Professor William Bond of Harvard University. As a result of her find, she was awarded the

King Frederic VI of Denmark Cometary Prize gold medal in 1848, and was the first woman elected to the American Academy of Arts and Sciences. In 1850 she was unanimously elected to the American Association for the Advancement of Science. Her telescope is on display at the Smithsonian Institution in Washington, D.C. In the later 1850s Maria Mitchell traveled to Europe where she met with other scientists and astronomers. When Vassar College opened in 1865 she became the very first appointment, as a professor of astronomy, and then director of the college observatory, with a twelve-inch telescope, third largest in the nation. She discovered, however, that her male counterparts were being paid at a higher rate. She objected and fought for pay equality, and got it. She studied Jupiter and Saturn and also began work on the Nautical Almanac, calculating positions of the planet Venus. With her students she tracked Venus traversing the sun, a rarity, only occurring eight times from 1608 to 2012. She sometimes even invited suffrage speakers, such as Julia Ward Howe, to her observatory. In 1869 she was elected into the American Philosophical Society. One of her best thoughts was "Question Everything." She had, indeed, achieved worldwide fame.

Mitchell began a crusade against all prejudice, but particularly against gender discrimination. Because she attained an international reputation, her efforts were applauded for the certain degree of success reached for the education of women. She had become friends with Elizabeth Cady Stanton, and even help found the American Association for the Advancement of Women, and became its president in 1873. This organization later became the American Association of University Women.

Mitchell retired from Vassar in 1888, and died the next year, on June 28, 1889 in Lynn, Massachusetts, and is buried in Prospect Hill Cemetery on Nantucket. She was posthumously elected to the National Women's Hall of Fame and New York University's Hall of Great Americans. The observatory on Nantucket is now the Maria Mitchell Observatory, and her home a memorial. During World War II they named a liberty ship the SS Maria Mitchell.

"The best that can be said of my life so far is that it has been industrious, and the best thing that can be said of me is that I never pretended to be what I was not."

#92- *Marianne Moore (1887-1972)*

The First Lady of Poetry

Marianne Craig Moore, first lady of poetry, the "bard of baseball," avid Brooklyn Dodger fan (who wrote "Hometown Piece for Messrs. Alston and Reese) and then a New York Yankees fan, who, at age eighty, threw out the first pitch of the Yankees 1968 season, was born on

November 15, 1887 in Kirkwood, Missouri. Moore was such a fan of those strong Yankee teams of the 1960s that she managed in one poem to name Roger Maris, Mickey Mantle, Bobby Richardson, Tony Kubek, Whitey Ford, Yogi Berra, Elston Howard and Clete Boyer, all regulars of those championship years. Also a fan of boxer Muhammed Ali, she wrote the liner notes for his spoken-word album, I Am the Greatest!

She was the daughter of John and Mary Moore, but her father left the family before she was born. The family first moved to St, Louis, then the Pittsburgh area, and finally, in 1896, to Carlisle, Pennsylvania, where her mother taught school. She graduated Bryn Mawr College in 1909, after publishing poems in its literary magazine, Tipyn O'Bob. Moore then decided to become a writer, but first she became a teacher of commercial subjects at the Indian School at Carlisle, Pennsylvania from 1911 to 1914.

In 1915 her first poems appeared in Egoist magazine. She moved to New Jersey and then in 1918 to Greenwich Village, in New York City, where she socialized with the avante-garde likes of Ezra Pound, T. S. Eliot, Wallace Stevens and William Carlos Williams, with her Poems being published without her permission in 1921. The influence of the Imagists, such as Pound, had a great deal of influence.

In 1924 her Observations appeared, and was given an award by Dial magazine, the foremost and most respected literary journal at that time. Moore then quit teaching to become editor of Dial, from 1925 to 1929, and this capacity exerted much influence on young poets such as Allen Ginsburg.

In 1929 she moved again, this time to the Fort Greene neighborhood in Brooklyn, New York, where she would live for the next thirty-six years, and continue to work, but as an assistant in the New York City Public Library. Marianne Moore continued to write a number of volumes of poetry, and in 1933 was awarded the Helen Haire Levinson Prize from Poetry magazine, and, also, her 1935 Selected Poems, for which she was awarded the Ernest Hartsock Memorial Prize, was published. The next year Pangolin and Other Verse was published. Some other volumes were What Are Years, Like A Bulwark, and The Arctic Ox.

She spent much time in seclusion for a number of years before her Collected Poems appeared. She was then given just about every award for poetry that there was, including Guggenheim Fellowship. These Collected Poems won the Pulitzer Prize, the National Medal for Literature and the Bollinger Prize in 1951. She actually became quite the celebrity and character, even becoming a desired college campus speaker. She even became the subject of photo essays in both Look and Life magazines. In 1955 she became a member of the American Academy of Arts and Letters and in 1962, a fellow of the American Academy of Arts and Sciences. Moore's poems were published in The Nation, The New Yorker, The New Republic and other magazines. A Marianne Moore Reader was published in 1961. In 1965 she moved back to Greenwich Village. She also translated, in 1954, the Fables of La Fontaine. Her

1967 Complete Poems of Marianne Moore saw her revise many of her poems. In 2017 New Collected Poems was introduced.

Marianne Moore suffered a series of strokes and passed away in New York City on February 5, 1972, and is buried in Gettysburg, Pennsylvania. She was a modernist poet whose poetry was innovative and witty, filled with irony, and was musical, and influential, but, in truth was much about adversity and faith, but a gifted editor, translator and critic as well. Her entire library and other of Moore's possessions are at the Rosenbach Museum and Library in Philadelphia (including a personally autographed Mickey Mantle baseball), and she is on the St. Louis Walk of Fame and was given numerous honorary degrees. In addition, she is in the New York State Writers Hall of Fame.

"If you will tell me why the fen appears impassible I then will tell you why I think that I can cross it if I try."

#93- Mary Tyler Moore (1936-2017)

The Girl With Three Names

Mary Tyler Moore was born in Brooklyn, New York on December 29, 1936 to Marjorie and George Tyler Moore. At eight years of age the family moved to Los Angeles, California. Moore managed to get work both in television commercials and some modeling. From 1955 to 1961 she was married to Dick Meeker. And from 1962 to 1981 was married to television executive Grant Tinker.

Her first notable work was in Richard Diamond, Private Detective, where mysteriously all you heard was the voice of Sam, and all you saw were her legs. She did get guest appearances on such shows as Bachelor Father, 77 Sunset Strip, Wanted: Dead or Alive, Hawaiian Eye and Surfside Six, and auditioned for the role of comedian Danny Thomas' daughter in his show, Make Room for Daddy.

Danny Thomas' production company put on The Dick Van Dyke Show, and he remembered "the girl with three names" from her audition with him, and he recommended her for the Emmy-winning role of Laura Petrie on the show that ran from 1961 to 1966, and made her extremely popular and well-known.

Now making use of her celebrity, she delved into film. In 1967 she co-starred with Julie Andrews in Thoroughly Modern Millie and in 1969 in A Change of Habit with Elvis Presley.

In 1970 she returned to television with a show that stretched the gender roles. The Mary Tyler Moore Show ran from 1970 to 1977, and the character of Mary Richards, working at television station WJM in Minneapolis, demonstrated to the world the unmarried professional woman's life, at work, at home, with friends. Over the years the show garnered twenty-nine Emmy awards, a record at the time. It truly was one of the best television series ever. It was so successful, that when it ended, three of Mary's co-stars, Ed Asner, Cloris Leachman and Valerie Harper, all went on to their own shows, staying in their characters from The Mary Tyler Moore Show. Three others, Gavin McLeod (The Love Boat), Ted Knight (Too Close For Comfort) and Betty White (The Betty White Show and others) also used Mary's show as a springboard. In 1978 received another Emmy nomination, appearing as Betty Rollins in First You Cry.

With husband Grant Tinker, they created MTM Productions which went to produce such successes as WKRP in Cincinnati, Remington Steele, St. Elsewhere, Rhoda, The Bob Newhart Show, Hill Street Blues, Lou Grant and The White Shadow.

In a complete turnaround of character portrayal, she received an Oscar nomination for her role as the resentful mother in Ordinary People, and a Tony award for Whose Life Is It Anyway?. She also hosted the Tony Awards ceremonies in 1980. The rest of the early 1980s proved difficult for Mary Tyler Moore. She and Grant Tinker divorced in 1981. Also her son Richard Meeker, Jr. was killed in a gunshot accident in 1980. She attempted Broadway, but without much luck at all. She somewhat bounced back with a marriage to Dr. Robert Levine in 1983 and an Emmy nomination in Heart Sounds with James Garner and one for the role of Mary Todd Lincoln in 1988. In the mid-1980s she was twice nominated for awards in Noises Off and Benefactors. In 1993 she portrayed a baby smuggler in Stolen Babies, and garnered another Emmy. In 2003 she appeared again with Dick Van Dyke in The Gin Game on television.

Much of her life was plagued with diabetes and alcoholism, and wrote two memoirs, After All in 1995 and Growing Up Again: Life, Loves, and Oh, Yeah, Diabetes in 2009. Mary got very active in diabetes research, becoming chair of the Juvenile Diabetes Foundation, and animal rights, being a big promoter of "Broadway Barks," urging pet adoption.

Mary Tyler Moore was awarded seven Emmy awards, two Tony awards, and Oscar nomination, and a slew of other Emmy and Tony nominations. In 1986 she was inducted into the Television Hall of Fame, and 2011 given a Lifetime Achievement Award from the Screen Actors Guild.

Also in 2011 she had brain surgery to remove a benign meningioma. She passed away on January 25, 2017 from cardiopulmonary arrest, in Greenwich, Connecticut, and is buried there.

#94- Julia Morgan (1872-1957)

Hearst Castle

Julia Morgan, who designed over seven hundred buildings in California alone, was born in San Francisco, California on January 20, 1872. Her father was mining engineer Charles Bill Morgan of a very prominent family. Her mother was Eliza Parmelee Morgan of a fabulously wealthy New York family. Her family settled in San Francisco, but when Julia was two years old, they moved to nearby Oakland.

On a family trip back east she met architect Pierre LeBrun, a relative through marriage. He encouraged her to seek higher education, which she did. She graduated from the University of California at Berkeley in 1894, as the only woman with a civil engineering degree. Upon graduation she joined the Association of Collegiate Alumnae, later called the American Association of University Women.

Having decided to become an architect, she applied to L'ecole nationale superiere des Beaux Arts in Paris. All sorts of reasons were used to deny her acceptance, but by her third try they agreed to accept her. She returned to San Francisco with her certificate, and in 1904 became the first woman licensed architect in California, and began working with noted architect John Galen Howard. One of Howard's primary clients was the Hearst family and their interest in the Berkeley campus. She helped him with the university's master building plan. She also designed and built El Campanil, a bell tower for Mills College, which withstood the earthquake of 1906.

In 1906 she opened her own firm, and due to her already growing reputation for sturdy buildings, became quite in demand after that San Francisco earthquake. The Hearst family was especially interested in her designs and construction ideas. She did the Phoebe Hearst Hacienda del Pozo and William Randolph Hearst's Los Angeles Examiner building.

The biggest job, and most prestigious, was on La Cuesta Encantada, which under her guidance would become the iconic Hearst Castle in San Simeon, California. It was done in the Mission Revival style, and she worked on it from 1919 until 1947, twenty-eight years. She designed and built the well-known façade, the indoor pool, the outdoor Neptune pool, and Morgan decorated the castle with antiquities, and even brought in animals for William Randolph Hearst's own zoo there.

But although the Hearst family was her main concern, she did much more. She redesigned the historic Fairmont Hotel, the Riverside Art Museum, Merrill Hall of the Asilomar Conference Grounds, many Y.M.C.A. structures, the North Star House, the Margaret Carnegie Library, the Ming Quong Home for Chinese Girls, which later became the Julia Morgan School for Girls. She also did do work outside of California, primarily in Utah and Hawaii.

Julia Morgan lived modestly, almost reclusively. She never married, she never wrote an autobiography, and only worked, worked, worked. There have been numerous biographies about Morgan, but not much as ever been learned of her life outside of her work. Belinda Taylor, being curious about Morgan, wrote an imaginative play, *Being Julia Morgan*, and it was very successful.

Julia Morgan died on February 2, 1957 and is buried in Oakland, California. Her innovative use of local materials got her inducted into the California Hall of Fame, and was a recipient of the AIA (American Institute of Architects) gold medal posthumously in 2013.

She was granted an honorary doctorate as a from her own University of California at Berkeley; "Julia Morgan, Distinguished alumna of the University of California; Artist and Engineer; Designer of Simple dwellings and stately homes, of great buildings nobly planned...; Architect in whose work harmony and admirable proportions bring pleasure to the eye and peace to the mind."

#95- "Grandma" Moses (1860-1961)
The Grand Old Lady of American Art

Anna Mary Robertson Moses, better known as "Grandma" Moses, was born in Greenwich, New York on September 7, 1860. She left home at the age of twelve and took on jobs such as housekeeping, sewing and cooking. She eventually married Thomas Salmon Moses and they moved to the Shenandoah Valley of the Blue Ridge Mountains of Virginia, in the Staunton/Verona area. Their home there is on the Register of Historic Places. Over her marriage she gave birth to ten children, although only five lived to maturity. But a number of years later they moved back to a farm in New York near Eagle Bridge. This is where she quietly resided until the death of her husband in 1927, when "Grandma" was in her sixties. And it was not until after that, that she began to paint!

And paint she did, with no training whatsoever, just imitating the prints of Currier and Ives. Then, with a bit of confidence, she painted from scenes in her vast memory. She entered contests in fairs, but never won. So she put them up for sale in a local drug store in Hoosick Falls, New York, from three to five dollars each. An art collector, Louis J. Caldor, happened by, bought a slew of them, and voila! "Grandma" Moses was about to be famous, and rich.

The next year, in 1939, New York City's Museum of Modern Art showed Moses' work in its exhibit of "Contemporary Unknown Artists." In 1940 nearly forty of her paintings were put on display at the Galerie St. Etienne, also in New York City. Her reviews were outstanding. Next she was shown in the Whyte Gallery in Washington, D.C. By the early 1950s she was successfully touring the United States and Europe. As time went on reproductions of her works appeared on everything, from greeting cards to towels.

Her folk art of simple farm life and the rural countryside had a depth of feeling for color. The art was considered to be authentic "primitive," were very individualistic and showed the world optimistically as it used to be. "Grandma" Moses, a nickname created by the press, created over fifteen hundred paintings. Some of the more well-known are: "The Old Checkered Inn in Summer," "Going to Church," "Bringing in the Christmas Tree," "Catching the Thanksgiving Turkey," "Wash Day," "Our Barn," "Over the River to Grandma's House," and "The Old Oaken Bucket." "Sugaring Off" was sold in 2006 for one point two million dollars. "Fourth of July" was made into a six cent stamp in 1969, and the painting itself has hung in the White House. The largest collection of her work is in the Bennington Museum in Bennington, Vermont.

However, such museums as the Metropolitan Museum of Art and the Brooklyn Museum of Art in New York and the National Museum of Women in the Arts also have collections, as do many other museums. And to think that before she became an artist Grandma Moses was quite adept at both embroidery and quilting. She only quit these endeavors because painting was easier on her arthritis.

She became the "grand old lady of American art." In 1949 President Harry S Truman presented her with the Women's Press Club trophy as outstanding artist and Moses was presented with the award from the National Press Club, as one of the five most newsworthy women. At the age of eighty-eight she was Madamoisele magazine's "Woman of the Year." She received two honorary degrees, one from Russell Sage College and another from the Moore College of Art and Design, wrote her autobiography, My Life's History in 1952, and had a documentary of her life nominated for an Academy Award. On her ninetieth birthday in 1950, the capital city of New York, Albany, declared it to be "Grandma Moses Day". On her one hundredth birthday, Governor of New York Nelson Rockefeller declared it "Grandma Moses Day" throughout the whole state. The humorous The Beverly Hillbillies television program's "Granny" character was named "Daisy Moses" in a tribute to "Grandma" Moses.

At the age of one hundred and one, Anna Mary Robertson Moses passed away in Hoosick Falls on December 13, 1961. On her passing, President John F. Kennedy said, "The directness and vividness of her paintings restored a primitive freshness to our perception of the American scene...All Americans mourn her loss."

I "paint it so people will know how we used to live."

#96- *Lucretia Mott (1793-1880)*

Lioness

Lucretia Coffin, a descendant of Benjamin Franklin, who later married James Mott, was born to Quaker sea captain Thomas and Anna Coffin, on Nantucket, Massachusetts on January 3, 1793. Lucretia would go on to become one of the great leaders, and one of the finest speakers, of both the women's rights movement, for the abolition of slavery and for religious freedom. She was among the truest and most complete of the social reformers.

She was sent to a Quaker school in Millbrook, New York in the Hudson Valley area, and taught there after she graduated. This experience led her to begin her lifelong battle for equal economic opportunities for women, since she found that male teachers were being paid triple women's salary. The family moved to Philadelphia, Pennsylvania, and in 1811, she married Mott, who had been a fellow teacher. In 1821 she became a Quaker minister with her fine and eloquent voice being quite helpful. As did most Quakers, Lucretia Mott believed in "free produce." This meant that she would not enjoy anything gotten from slave labor, including cotton products. She helped organize anti-slavery fairs that were meant to raise funds and awareness. She attended anti-slavery conventions in 1837, 1838 and 1839.

But in 1840 she attended a world anti-slavery convention in London, but, even though a delegate, was not allowed to speak because she was a woman. It was felt that if a woman were allowed to speak, it would detract from the sole purpose, opposition to slavery. She simply went outside the hall and preached with that great voice about feminine equality. She was called the "lioness of the convention," and it was here that she met and became friends with Elizabeth Cady Stanton. Back home, she traveled extensively, speaking all along the east coast, and even met with President John Tyler. In 1848 Lucretia Mott and Elizabeth Cady Stanton organized the first women's rights convention in Seneca Falls, New York. At first Mott objected to the demand for the "vote" but eventually agreed. In her influential Discourse on Woman in 1850 she advocated equal economic opportunity for women, and called for the right to vote.

In 1864, with other Quakers, she helped found Swarthmore College, and after the Civil War she, with others such as Ralph Waldo Emerson, founded the Free Religious Association and was elected president of the Equal Rights Association, again advocating universal suffrage. In the later 1860s Stanton and Susan B. Anthony got involved with eccentric, presidential hopeful, millionaire George Francis Train, and Mott did not care for the situation and broke from these women. The women's movement suffered a blow when various groups disagreed on tactics. Lucretia Mott tried unsuccessfully to be a peacemaker. Stanton and Anthony formed the National Woman Suffrage Association, while Julia Ward Howe and Lucy Stone formed the American Woman Suffrage Association. Eventually they did join together.

At one time or another she was a member of the New England Non-Resistance Society, the Pennsylvania Anti-Slavery Society, the American Free Produce Association, the American Anti-Slavery Society and the Philadelphia Female Anti-Slavery Society (and its president). At the time of her death of pneumonia on November 11, 1880 near Philadelphia, she was considered to be the greatest woman of the nineteenth century, and a mentor to Elizabeth Cady Stanton. A Picasso sculpture of her sits in the Carrier Dome in Syracuse, New York. A 1948 postage stamp, on the one hundredth anniversary of the Seneca Falls convention, honored Mott, Stanton and Carrie Chapman Catt. In the United States Capitol in Washington, D. C. there is a large sculpture of Mott, Stanton, and Anthony. In 2020 a new ten dollar bill will also feature Mott, Stanton, Anthony, Alice Paul and Sojourner Truth. Lucretia Mott is in the National Women's Hall of Fame.

Group Eight

Louise Nevelson- Rosa Ponselle

#97- Louise Nevelson (1899- 1988)

Unconventional

Leah Berliawsky was born on September 23, 1899 in Kiev, the Ukraine, which was part of the Russian Empire. Her parents, lumber businessman Isaac and Mina brought her to Rockland, Maine in 1905. She graduated Rockland High School in 1918, and married wealthy Charles Nevelson two years later. They moved first to Boston, and then to Mount Vernon, New York, where she began studying painting, and changed her name to Louise.

Much has been made of the eclectic works of the flamboyant, eccentric sculptor Louise Nevelson, with her use of "found objects" which less complimentary folk called "junk," calling herself the "original recycler," and her use of monochromatic "coloring," using only one color. But it was her innate gift of expressionist vision and innovative composition that gained her worldwide fame. And what did she do? She made walls, she made collages, she made reliefs, she made boxes and compartments. And she did it with wood, with plaster, with aluminum, with metal, with terra cotta. And she loved working in black, at least up to the 1960s. For Louise Nevelson black was "the total color."

In 1929 and 1930 she studied at the Art Students League. She was making no money and was quite destitute, and separated from her husband. But then, probably the best of her art education came, from her time with Hans Hofmann in Munich with collages and Picasso-inspired cubism and surrealism. She also traveled to Italy and France. In 1933 she became an assistant to the famous Diego Rivera, and the next year continued her studies at the Educational Alliance Art School. Nevelson had her first one-woman show in 1941 at Nierendorf Gallery. Two years later she had another solo show, at the Norlyst Gallery, but it was a dismal failure. But this was the beginning of her fame.

In the early 1950s she took some trips to Mexico and Guatamala, and came away with a feeling for, and influenced by, pre-Columbian art. From 1951 to 1958 Louise Nevelson was president of the New York chapter of Artists Equity, and in 1955 she had a one-woman show at Collette Roberts' Grand Central Modern Gallery. In 1958 she began an alliance with the Martha Jackson Gallery, and for the first time became financially solvent. She even made the cover, and was featured in LIFE magazine. In 1959 she won First Prize with her "Art U.S.A." at the New York Coliseum. Now her reputation was secure.

In 1960 she had her first one-woman European show, at the Galerie Daniel Cordier in Paris. Now she began adding white and gold, making art in boxes, and started getting even more noticed, and in 1962 left for Los Angeles with a fellowship from the Tamarind Institute and now she began working now with lithographs. This helped her through a very rough financial patch. Arriving back in New York she began an alliance with the Pace Gallery, and had showings with them until the end of her career.

In 1967 the Whitney Museum did the first retrospective of Louise Nevelson's work, even showing material from the 1930s. She had one-woman shows every year until 1964 and from 1969 to 1971, from 1973 to 1977, from 1979 to 1981, 1983, and from 1985 to 1986. Throughout the 1970s and 1980s she had constant traveling exhibitions going on throughout the United States, especially a two-year one curated by Minneapolis' Walker Art Center, and in 1975 designed the chapel of St. Peter's Lutheran Church in New York City.

Among the most well-known works of this prolific artist are; Black Majesty, Bride of the Black Moon, Sixteen Americans, Young Shadows, Homage to 6,000,000 1 and 11, The Clown is the Center of the World, First Personage, Atmosphere and Environment, Sky Cathedral, Sky Tree, Sky Gate New York, Sky Gates and Collages, Dawn's Wedding Feast, Bicentennial Dawn, Windows to the West, Trilogy, The Forest, Keeping Time with Fashion. A large collection of Louise Nevelson's works can be found in the Farnsworth Art Museum in Rockland, Maine Louise Nevelson won and received such a vast number of awards of honor that it would seem impossible to list them all. However some are: National Medal of Art, National Society of Arts and Letters Gold Medal, the New York State Governor's Art Award, the Presidential Medal of the Municipal Art Society of New York, the New York City Citizenship Award, the Skowhegan Medal for Sculpture, the George Friedrich Handel Award, the Logan Award, the Edward MacDowell Medal, and both the Communication Award and the Creative Arts Award from Brandeis University. Her works are shown in at least twenty-five states and a dozen countries. She received honorary degrees from Harvard, New York, Columbia, Boston and Rutgers universities, Smith and Hebrew Union colleges, Western College for Women and the Art School of Chicago. In 2000 a five-part series of postage stamps were issued in her honor.

Nevelson died in New York City on April 17, 1988. In 2005 her granddaughter, Maria Nevelson, began the Louise Nevelson Foundation. There is in New York City a Louise Nevelson Plaza, a sculpture garden.

#98- *Georgia O'Keeffe (1887-1986)*
Mother of American Modernism

Georgia Totto O'Keeffe was born in Sun Prairie, Wisconsin on November 15, 1887, to dairy farmers Francis and Ida O'Keeffe, and went on to become an extraordinary painter of the American Southwest's natural beauty. As a teen she moved to Williamsburg, Virginia, graduating from Chatham Institute in 1904. She also studied at the Art Studio of Chicago and the Art Students League in New York, where she won the William Merritt Chase Prize for her "Rabbit With Copper Pot.".

For a while she gave up on her creative art and became a commercial artist from 1908 to 1912 and then became a teacher and art supervisor in the Amarillo, Texas schools from 1912 to 1914, and taught art in summers at a college. In 1916 Alfred Stieglitz successfully displayed her charcoal abstractions in his gallery 291. She went on to head the art department at West Texas A & M University until 1918, but quit teaching to devote full time to her art, and based on Stieglitz urging, moved to New York City, and in 1924 married him. Her art began appearing in the Anderson Galleries, the Museum of Modern Art, the Brooklyn Museum of Art, the Whitney Museum and the Art Institute of Chicago. She has had one-woman retrospectives at both the Art Institute of Chicago and the Museum of Modern Art in New York. By the mid-1920s she was one of the most important American artists. In 1927 O'Keeffe had her first retrospective at the Brooklyn Museum. In 1939 she went to Hawaii to do some commercial art for the Dole company, loved the islands' beauty, but did not complete the commission. When Stieglitz died in 1945, Georgia O'Keeffe permanently moved to New Mexico, where she had vacationed in summers past. She began painting the beauty she found there: the mountains, the flowers, the desert, showing a deep appreciation for the natural world. Her work could not be put into any standard classification. It seemed almost photographic, and was very harshly criticized, but still remained very successful and popular.

She was awarded honorary degrees from the University of Wisconsin, William and Mary College and Mills College, and the recipient of the Brandeis University Creative Arts Award and Clarion Award. At the 1939 World's Fair Georgia O'Keeffe was declared as one of the dozen outstanding women of the past fifty years. She was also an awarded membership of the American Academy of Arts and Letters and the American Academy of Arts and Sciences. She has also been inducted into the National Women's Hall of Fame. In 1977 President Gerald Ford awarded her the "Presidential Medal of Freedom" and in 1985 was given the National Medal of Arts. Practically every major museum and art gallery possess her paintings. "Cow's Skull: Red, White and Blue" is probably her most well-known painting. Other of her paintings are: "Ram's Head White Hollyhock and Little Hills," "Blue and Green Music," "Black Iris lll," "Ladder to the Moon," Summer Days," "Above the Clouds," "The Lawrence Tree," Petunia No. 2," "The Green Apple," "No. 13 Special," and her calla liliy collection. In 2014 her "Jimsin Weed/White Flower No.1" sold for over forty-four million dollars.

In 1961, at seventy-three, and very active, she rode a raft down the Colorado River in Utah. She was, indeed, a daring woman. Alfred Stieglitz had taken many, many photographs of her, some very risqué, and some forty-five of them were put on display in his gallery. At seventy-two she was diagnosed with macular degeneration, and it was the end of her painting. On her ninetieth birthday a film portrait of her life was presented on television. In addition in 1991 A Marriage: Georgia O'Keeffe and Alfred Stieglitz was on PBS television. In 2009 yet another biography came out on Lifetime Television. On March 6, 1986 the "Mother of American Modernism" died in Santa Fe, New Mexico at the age of 98. In tribute to her love of New Mexico, arcosaur dinosaur fossils were found near her home and named "effigia okeeffeae."

Appropriately the Georgia O'Keeffe Museum is in her old home in Santa Fe. In 1996 a postage stamp bearing her image was issued and in 2013 another one displaying her artwork, "Black Mesa Landscape." She has been inducted into the National Women's Hall of Fame. The Brooklyn Museum had "Living Modern" about her.

#99- Annie Oakley (1860-1926)

Little Sure Shot

One of the most unusual and successful performing artists was Annie Oakley. Born in poverty in Patterson Township, Darke County, Ohio on August 13, 1860, and named Phoebe Anne Mosey (although there have been various spellings of the name). She was an excellent shot by the age of nine. She began shooting rabbits and quail, first for food, and then to ship to local restaurants and to Cincinnati for money. By the age of fifteen she had paid off most of the mortgage on the family farm. For a while she was placed in an orphanage and worked as a servant in abusive and wretched conditions, eventually running away and back home.

She entered a Thanksgiving shooting contest against famed sharpshooter Frank E. Butler, and defeated him! Afterward, they corresponded, with Butler eventually proposing, and they were married in 1876, and by this time she had started calling herself Annie Oakley. She joined his act, but he stepped aside to promote her as the attraction. In 1885 they joined Buffalo Bill's Wild West Show, with Butler as her assistant and manager. Fellow cast member, Sitting Bull, called the five foot Annie "Watanya Cicilla," translated and publicized as "Little Sure Shot." For seventeen years this markswoman traveled the world with the show, gaining a worldwide reputation, becoming a favorite, even of Queen Victoria. She once supposedly shot a cigarette from the mouth of Kaiser Wilhelm II. Her accuracy, speed and endurance were amazing. She could hit a dime in the air, hit a playing card held sideways at ninety feet, hitting a card at least five times before it hit the ground, creating a term, "an Annie Oakley," which was the term for a hole-punched railroad or theater ticket. Once, out of 5000, she hit 4772 glass balls tossed in the air.

In 1901 she became partially paralyzed in a railroad accident, but continued performing for another twenty years. In 1922 she and Butler were in a car accident. after which she had five spinal operations and had to have a steel brace on her right leg. For a while she became an stage actress in "The Western Girl."

Annie Oakley became an advocate for women learning to shoot, and proposed women be allowed in combat. She had volunteered, but was rejected. So, instead, she began putting on shooting exhibitions to raise money for the Red Cross. At one point she was accused of cocaine use, but fought the accusation and was cleared. But at this time, cocaine was being used legally for medicinal purposes.

Annie Oakley died of pernicious anemia in Greenville, Ohio on November 3, 1926. Frank Butler died eighteen days later. Many of her personal possessions can be found in the Garst Museum & the National Annie Oakley Museum in Greenville, Ohio. For a while in the 1890s, they lived in Nutley, New Jersey, but the home she lived in from 1913-1917 in Cambridge, Maryland is the one known as the Annie Oakley House, and is on the National Register of Historic Places. She has been inducted into the National Women's Hall of Fame, the Ohio Women's Hall of Fame, the National Cowgirl Hall of Fame and the Trapshooting Hall of Fame, among others.

The play "Annie Get Your Gun," is based on her life, and had such outstanding performers as Ethel Merman, Reba McEntire and Bernadette Peters playing her part. In the film version Betty Hutton played Annie. And there even was a very fictionalized "Annie Oakley" television series.

#100- Antonia Pantoja (1922-2002)

Nuyorican

Educator, social and civil rights activist, and feminist Antonia Pantoja was born on September 13, 1922 in San Juan, Puerto Rico to unwed mother Alejandrina Pantoja y Acosta. For a while she lived with her mother and grandparents in Santurce. With some financial help she managed to get a teaching certificate in 1942 from the University of Puerto Rico, and taught school there for two years.

In 1944 she was doing welding "Rosie the Riveter" work in New York City. This was the title given to women who did men's work during World War II while the men were away in combat. However, by 1952 she had gotten her degree from Hunter College in social work. Two years later was a master's degree from Columbia University. Much later, in 1973, she obtained her doctorate from Union Graduate School.

By 1953 the no-nonsense Pantoja had already had enough of racism and prejudice against Puerto Ricans and founded the Hispanic Youth Adult Association, later becoming the Puerto Rican Association for Community Affairs. A few years later came the Puerto Rican Forum, an organization for diverse groups to come together to assist in Hispanics gaining economic self-sufficiency.

This led in 1961 to the creation of ASPIRA, one of whose aims was to curtail the alarming school drop-out rate of Puerto Rican children and to introduce bilingual education to the education system. ASPIRA also promoted a positive self-image in communities, and stressed the importance of education, and made career and college counseling available. Talented actors Jimmy Smits and Luis Guzman benefited from it. And so did other accomplishments made by such as Aida Alvarez as director of the Small Business Administration, and Fernando Ferrer as Bronx Borough president of New York City.

And then there was her assistance in the 1970 establishment of Universidad Boricua, now Boricua College, a post-secondary institution for the benefit of Puerto Ricans and others of Hispanic descent.

As if these efforts were not enough, the charismatic, but unapologetic Antonia Pantoja fought successfully for the decentralization of New York City schools, and attracted funds from President Lyndon Johnson's War on Poverty and created the Puerto Rican Community Development Project. She also helped found and fund the Puerto Rican Research Center in Washington, D. C.

In 1978 Antonia Pantoja left New York for California. There she joined the faculty of the San Diego State University School of Social Work, becoming director of Graduate School for Community Development. For health reasons she later returned to Puerto Rico, and while there established both Producer and Provivienda, both to benefit small businesses and housing. By 1998 she was back in New York City, declaring that she resigned herself that she was a "nuyorican," (New York Puerto Rican).

In Latinas in the United States: An Historical Encyclopedia, Antonia Pantoja is cited as "one of the foremost figures in community activism." She has been given honorary doctorates from the University of Connecticut, the University of Massachusetts and the University of Puerto Rico. Pantoja has been inducted into the Hunter College Hall of Fame, been given the Hispanic Heritage Award, the Julia de Burgos Award from Yale University, Lifetime Achievement Award from the New York State Board of Regents, and is on the Legacy Walk. In 2002 in her Memoir of a Visionary: Antonia Pantoja, she alludes to, but not confirms, her lesbianism. She is also the subject of Lillian Jimenez' documentary, Antonia Pantoja! Presente!

In 1996 Antonia Pantoja was presented the Presidential Medal of Freedom. She passed away from cancer on May 24, 2002 in New York City.

"One cannot live a lukewarm life. You have to live life with passion."

#101- Dorothy Parker (1893-1967)

The Algonquin Round Table

Dorothy Rothschild, later known as Dorothy Parker, was born in her parent's summer cottage in New Jersey on August 22, 1893 to Jacob and Eliza. She had a rather unpleasant childhood, but did graduate from an elite finishing school in New Jersey. Her father died in 1913 and she left home and earned money teaching dance.

In 1916 some of her poems were accepted by Vogue, and then she started working for them. The next year she moved to the rival, Vanity Fair, as a theater critic, and she married Edwin P. Parker. Edwin Parker began armed service during World War I and Dorothy Parker began the career that would mark her as one of the wittiest and most urbane women in America. Each day she would lunch at the Algonquin Hotel with some of her fun-loving, witty and intellectual Vanity Fair co-workers. This lively group's spirit caught on and they became known as the "Round Table" of the Algonquin. They became the heart of New York City's intellectual life, as well as that of the entire nation. Parker ruled as queen over this coterie that included Robert Benchley, Robert Sherwood, Alexander Woolcott, and Franklin Pierce Adams. Sometimes they would be joined by Moss Hart, George Kaufman, Edna Ferber, Douglas Fairbanks, Jascha Heifitz, Charles MacArthur and even Harpo Marx. What made their reputations was Adams' newspaper column, "The Conning Tower," that reported on all the witticisms uttered at their table. This included the wise-cracking queen, Dorothy Parker, so bittersweet and disillusioned. This was to remain a well-known spot of satirical and intellectual discussion in the 1920s and 1930s. From 1927 to 1933 she worked for The New Yorker with her "Constant Reader" book reviews. She had become the consummate New Yorker, and when her husband returned from World War l, it was clear that they were no longer the same people as before. They tried for a while, but in 1928 they divorced.

She also got herself fired from Vanity Fair, and went out on her own as a writer. The 1920s began with her Women I'm Not Married To; Men I'm Not Married To, co-written with Adams, and her appearance in a one-act play, No Siree, later titled 49ers. Close Harmony, co-written with Elmer Rice did not do well. However when she turned away from plays and periodicals in 1926 with Enough Rope, her satirical and flippant verse made her a success as a poet. The 1920s saw three hundred or so of Parker's poems in Vanity Fair, Vogue, The New Yorker, Life, McCall's and The New Republic. "For A Sad Lady" and "Resume" are included in Enough Rope. However during this time she did not take care of herself, drinking excessively, smoking heavily, having affairs, and suicide attempts. She left New York for a while and went to Paris. There Dorothy Parker met F. Scott Fitzgerald, John Dos Passos and Ernest Hemingway.

Back in New York she went to work for the New Yorker, new at the time. She successfully increased its circulation as a contributor and a reviewer for two years. In 1929 she was awarded the O. Henry Memorial Prize for her story, "Big Blonde." More poetry followed with Sunset Gun and Death and Taxes in the early 1930s, and marrying actor Alan Campbell.

With her husband she moved to California and for five years was very successful and very well-paid as a script writer and lyricist. She received Oscar screenwriting nominations for A Star Is Born and Smash Up. While there she also published a short story collection, After Such Pleasures, and a book of poems, Not So Deep As A Well, possibly her best. After a stint as a royalist-leaning reporter in Spain during their civil war, in 1939 published Here Lies, another short story collection. Dorothy Parker divorced Alan Campbell. Then she re-married him. She separated from him and so on. Meanwhie she had helped to found the Hollywood Anti-Nazi League and as such as, therefore, was suspected of being a communist. As a result she was denied a job as a World War ll foreign correspondent. She tried a comeback with the semi-autobiographical play, Ladies of the Corridor, written with Arnaud d'Usseau. It did not do well. New York State, following the example of the Washington House on UnAmerican Activities lead, called upon her as a suspected communist. She was again blacklisted (denied employment because of suspicion) and returned to Hollywood in hopes of gaining employment there. Campbell died in 1963 and Parker returned to New York City. But by this time she had reverted to old habits, deserted by everyone and almost blind. She died of a heart attack on June 7, 1967. Lillian Hellman, who had befriended her, read her eulogy. Sadly, no one claimed her ashes until 1988 when the N.A.A.C.P. claimed them and buried them outside their Baltimore headquarters, honoring her commitment to civil rights.

She had always seen the funny things life threw at you, became the greatest of the great wits, wrote some really wonderful verse and stories, particularly in the 1920s and 1930s. Laments for the Living, Star Light, Star Bright and The Portable Dorothy Parker were hers. "The first thing I do in the morning is brush my teeth and sharpen my tongue."

Singer/songwriter Prince had a song, "The Ballad of Dorothy Parker," and she has been portrayed in countless stories, film and on television. The United States issued a stamp in her honor in 1992. She has been inducted into the New Jersey Hall of Fame.

#102- *Rosa Parks* (1913-2005)

The Symbol of Resistance

Rosa Louise McCauley Parks, granddaughter of slaves, and a civil rights activist, the "mother of the freedom movement," was born in Tuskeegee, Alalbama on February 4, 1913, to James and Leona McCauley. One of her earliest memories was of her maternal grandfather standing in front of his home with a shotgun while the KKK (Ku Klux Klan) marched by in a parade. She attended the schools in Tuskeegee for a while and the Industrial School for Girls, but dropped out to earn money. She worked as a domestic helper and a hospital aide. In 1932 she married barber Raymond Parks, a marriage that lasted until his death in 1977. At his urging, she completed high school. In the 1940s she became a secretary for the NAACP in Montgomery, a post she held until 1957. In the summer of 1955 she attended the Highlander Folk School in Monteagle, Tennessee, for the purpose of learning how to be an activist.

On December 1, 1955, Rosa Parks was sitting in the designated "colored" section of a Montgomery bus. Since it was crowded, with any number of white people standing, the bus driver asked her and three others to get up and give the seats to the white people. While the others complied, Rosa did not give up her seat. The bus driver warned her and then called the police. She was removed and charged with civil disobedience and disorderly conduct, put in jail, but bailed out. Her trial was on December 5 and she was fined ten dollars and a four-dollar court fee.

She appealed the decision, but it was realized this would languish in the courts, probably for years. Now she was not the first to do this, but the NAACP (National Association for the Advancement of Colored People) thought she was the best candidate for them to see it all the way through the courts, if necessary. As they stated, "she was a responsible, mature woman with a good reputation. She was securely married and employed, was regarded as possessing a quiet and dignified demeanor." Realizing that this one incident could become the symbol of resistance, the same day as the trial, civil rights activist Ralph Abernethy and others decided on a one-day bus boycott in support of Rosa Parks' dilemma. Then they formed the Montgomery Improvement Association, and newcomer Dr. Martin Luther King, Jr. became its president. 35,000 handbills were printed announcing this boycott. It was successful and completely supported.

The group decided a one-day boycott would not meet their needs, and they continued it. The Montgomery bus boycott lasted 381 days, until December 20, 1956, and when it was over, laws were changed and there was no bus segregation. It was a great blow to the "Jim Crow" laws that had perpetuated segregation in public and retail places.

Parks' actions really started the nationwide efforts to stem segregation in public places, but after her action, she suffered. She was fired from her job and received death threats. In 1957 she left Alabama for financial and employment reasons, stayed briefly in Virginia, and then, at the invitation of relatives, moved to Detroit. Eventually she became the secretary and receptionist for Congressman John Conyers of Detroit from 1965 to 1988. She got involved with the struggle for fair housing and schools, also began to take a harder stance, lining up with Malcom X, the Black Panthers, and espousing "black power." In the 1970s she spent time working for prison reform.

In 1980 she was given the Martin Luther King Award, and initiated the Rosa L. Parks Scholarship Foundation, and in 1987 the Rosa and Raymond Parks Institute for Self-Improvement, which ran "Pathways to Freedom" tours, visiting important sites in the battle for civil rights. In 1984 the National Coalition of 100 Black Women presented her with their Candace Award and in 1992 was presented with the Peace Abbey Courage of Conscience Award at the Kennedy Library and Museum in Boston. Time magazine named her as one of the twenty most influential persons of the twentieth century. In 1994, when the Ku Klux Klan volunteered to be the clean-up organization for a highway in Missouri, the state could not legally refuse them, so they decided to name the road the Rosa Parks Highway. In 1996 President Clinton awarded her the Presidential Medal of Freedom and she was later awarded the Congressional Gold Medal. She wrote her autobiography, Rosa Parks: My Story in 1994 and the next year a memoir, Quiet Strength, about her faith. In 2002, The Rosa Parks Story, starring Angela Bassett was released, and in the same year, Mighty Times: The Legacy of Rosa Parks was nominated at the Academy Awards in the short documentary category. In 1994, while in her eighties, a man broke into her home and robbed her. She was so frightened that she moved out and into a high-rise apartment. But she really had no funds, and could not pay the rent, and at the age of 91 the "First Lady of the Civil Rights Movement" faced eviction. At the last moment the ownership of the apartment backed down, and permitted her to live rent free for the rest of her life, which would only be a year or so.

Rosa Parks died in Detroit on October 24, 2005 from complications from dementia. Her body was flown to Montgomery, where Condoleeza Rice spoke. Then by bus she was brought to Washington, D. C., where she would lie in Capitol Rotunda, the first woman so honored. In Congress' Statuary Hall there is now a statue of Rosa Parks. Flags were ordered flown half-staff on October 30 in her honor.

There are streets, roads and highways all over America named in her honor, and in 2006 Nassau County (NY) Executive Tom Suozzi renamed the transit (bus) hub the Rosa Parks Hempstead Transit Center. Troy University in Montgomery now has a Rosa Parks Library and Museum. In various states, "Rosa Parks Day" is celebrated on either February 4th, her birthday, or December 1st, the day of her arrest.

She is in the National Women's Hall of Fame, the Alabama Academy of Honor and the recipient of the Governor's Medal of Honor, and the Michigan Hall of Fame, and has been awarded the Springarn Medal, listed as one of the 100 Greatest African Americans. There is even a United States postage stamp honoring her, and that famous bus she was on. It is in the Henry Ford Museum!.

#103- *Alice Paul (1885-1977)*

Mother of the E. R. A

Alice Stokes Paul, "Mother of the E.R.A.," and one of the most prominent and effective persons in the fight for women's equality, was born to Quaker parents, businessman William and Tacie, in Moorestown, Mount Laurel Township, New Jersey on January 11, 1885. Their 265-acre farm, Paulsdale, and her Quaker roots, taught her the need for perseverance and hard work, which stood her well in her long, long fight for gender equality. Paul was a descendent of both William Penn and one of the founders of Swarthmore College. She must be considered the architect and main force of the 1910s movement leading to the passage of the Nineteenth Amendment, giving women the right to vote. Her mother was a member of the National Woman Suffrage Association, and Alice attended some of the meeting with her mother. Alice graduated from the Swarthmore College in 1905, did some graduate work at the New School for Social Research, and eventually got her master's degree from the University of Pennsylvania. She had decided to go to England to attend a Quaker school and do social work there, but met Emmeline and Cristobel Pankhurst, two of the most outspoken feminists. From them she garnered the feeling that direct and visible measures must be taken to get the job done to assure any success for women, and not social work.

She was transformed there from a quiet Quaker young lady to a militant one. After all her activities in England, she had become well-known. She had joined the Women's Social and Political Union, and was arrested numerous times, and jailed three while there. She was treated badly, but it brought out sympathy for the cause. She then returned home, sorely convinced that equal legal status was mandatory for women.

After getting her doctorate from the University of Pennsylvania (her doctoral dissertation was "The Legal Position of Women in Pennsylvania"), she became active in the National Woman Suffrage Association, and appointed chair of the Congressional Committee, and called for a campaign for obtaining an amendment giving women the right to vote. In 1913 she organized the Woman Suffrage Procession at Woodrow Wilson's inauguration, with a band, floats and chariots and eighty-thousand participants. Their lead banner read, "We Demand an Amendment to the United States Constitution Enfranchising the Women of the Country." These very well-organized large protest parades were what she felt would get the job done.

The National Woman Suffrage Association thought her methods too aggressive. Paul wanted the fight on a national level while the NWSA wanted the fight on state levels. Paul resigned, feeling the others were too timid. She briefly formed the Congressional Union for Woman Suffrage, which became the National Woman's Party in 1916. Alice Paul picketed the White House carrying more banners, and continued with her group to picket the White House during World War l. Many were arrested and sent to jail, either in Virginia or Washington, D. C. They became what was known as "Silent Sentinels," acting in a non-argumentative civil disobedience mode, but non-violent themselves. As a result they were harassed by males, who thought them disloyal during the war, and the police did nothing to stop it. Only college students and boy scouts aided them. Some women who were arrested were then pardoned. Later on none were pardoned. She actually wanted to be put in jail to stir up both sympathy and support. She spent seven months in jail with poor sanitation and rat-infested food. She went on a hunger strike, but they force-fed her raw eggs. These horrible events brought about a public outcry, especially about the police mistreatment, and what was needed to be done for women.

In 1918 Wilson gave in and urged Congress to approve the nineteenth amendment. The House of Representatives approved, but the Senate did not, but the next year they did, and the states approved and it became law in 1920.

In 1923 it was Paul who submitted the first Equal Rights Amendment proposal before Congress. Even though it failed, it did not deter her. From the 1920s through the 1950s she traveled throughout Europe and South America, and with the League of Nations, promoting women's rights. In 1938 she help found the World Woman's Party. She also got herself a law degree from American University. In the 2004 film, Iron-Jawed Angels, based on the 1910s fight for the passage of the nineteenth amendment, actress Hillary Swank portrayed Alice Paul.

Until the end of her life Alice Paul fought for the Equal Rights Amendment, which had been nicknamed the "Alice Paul Amendment." It eventually passed Congress, but did not get the necessary approval from the states. It needed thirty-eight states to approve, but only thirty-five did. She remained chair of the National Woman's Party until 1970, and was very instrumental in having the cause of women's protections included in the Civil Rights Act of 1964. This was the work of six decades of her life.

Alice Paul had a stroke in 1974, and she died on July 9, 1977, just a very short distance from her birthplace in New Jersey. The Alice Paul Institute, within the housing of Paulsdale, has many of Paul's papers housed there, while many more are at Radcliffe Institute. Paulsdale is now a National Historic Landmark. The 2012 United States ten dollar gold coin was minted in her likeness. In 2020 Alice Paul will be joined with Susan B. Anthony, Elizabeth Cady Stanton, Sojourner Truth and Lucretia Mott on the new twenty-dollar bill. She is in the National Women's Hall of Fame, as well as the New Jersey Hall of Fame and the Connecticut Hall of Fame.

#104- Annie Smith Peck (1850-1935)

Mountaineer

Adventurous Annie Smith Peck, daughter of well-to-do lawyer, merchant and one-time congressman George Peck and his wife Ann, was one of the greatest mountain climbers in American history. She was born in Providence, Rhode Island on October 19, 1850, and after being gender-rejected at Brown University, attended and graduated from the University of Michigan with honors in classical languages in 1878, and her masters in 1881. Peck did this while also teaching in Michigan. She also taught Latin at Purdue University from 1881 to 1883. She then studied music in Germany, and in 1885 became the first woman to study at the American School of Classical Studies in Athens, Greece, specializing in archeology. While in Europe she became enthralled with mountain climbing, first up relatively small ones, and then the 10,000-foot Theodul Pass in Switzerland. She returned to the United States where she became a teacher and preceptress in Rhode Island, Ohio and New Jersey, and a professor of Latin at Smith College from 1886 to 1887. In 1888 she climbed the 14, 160-foot Mount Shasta in California's Cascade range.

In the 1890s it was Switzerland's Matterhorn, which made her a celebrity, as she was possibly the first woman to climb it. "A precipice cannot hurt you. Lions and tigers can. The streets of New York I consider more dangerous than the Matterhorn to a thoroughly competent and careful climber." She dressed in her own unconventional manner, including knickers. The Singer Sewing Machine Company provided purchasers a photograph of Peck with each sale.

1897 saw the determined Peck climb Mexico's Popocatepetl and Pico de Orizaba, both over 18, 500 feet. In 1906 on an expedition to find the source of the Amazon River she climbed to 18,000 feet in the Raura Range in Peru. In 1908, now in her late fifties, Annie Smith Peck, admittedly after three attempts, ascended Nevado Huascaran in west central Peru, at 22, 205 feet, the highest peak reached by an American at that time. Now she received international recognition. Its northern peak was named "Cumbre Ana Peck" in her honor in 1928. Beginning back in 1892 she gave lectures and made speaking engagements to accumulate funds she needed for her expeditions, and she was an unexpectedly captivating speaker.

She was a founding member of the American Alpine Club in 1902, and was also a suffragist, and a president of the Joan of Arc Suffrage League, and after climbing atop Mount Coropuna, also in Peru, at over sixty years of age, she placed their banner that read "Women's Vote." At the age of eighty-two she climbed Mount Madison in New Hampshire. In addition, she constantly promoted pan-Americanism.

Peru awarded her a gold medal, the Lima Geographic Society a silver slipper, and when she reached eighty years old, Chile awarded her its Decoration Al Merito. Annie Smith Peck was also an author of many very popular books, among them are: The Search for the Apex of America: High Mountain Climbing in Peru and Bolivia including the Conquest of Huascaran, with Some Observations on the Country and People Below, The South American Tour: A Descriptive Guide, Industrial and Commercial South America and Flying Over South America. She was a member of the Society of Women Geographers and the Royal Geographic Society.

She died in New York City on July 18, 1935 from bronchial pneumonia, and her ashes were buried in Providence. She was inducted into the Rhode Island Hall of Fame.

#105- *Frances Perkins* (1882-1965)

Secretary of Labor

Fannie Coralie Perkins, who later changed her name to Frances, the first woman ever appointed to a presidential cabinet position, was born in Boston, Massachusetts on April 10, 1882 to Frederick and Susan Perkins, and grew up in Worcester. Her American heritage dated back to pre-Revolutionary War. She graduated first in her class from Mount Holyoke College in 1902 with degrees in physics and chemistry, and became a social worker. Then she was off to Chicago where she became a teacher and worked in Jane Addams' Hull House.

She came back to the east and earned a political science master's degree from Columbia University in 1910, taught for a while at Adelphi University on Long Island, New York, and went to work for the Consumers' League. She investigated factory conditions and lobbied for worker protection. She happened to be in this situation when the awful tragic Triangle Shirtwaist Factory fire occurred. Because of this horror, the New York Committee on Safety was formed with Frances Perkins as executive secretary. Beyond this she was instrumental in getting the New York State Factory Commission formed, with her as Director of Investigation. And during this time she married Paul Wilson, and they had a daughter, Susanna.

Expanding her roles, during most of World War 1 she was executive director of the New York Council of Organization for War Service. In 1918 she enrolled in the Wharton School of Economics of the University of Pennsylvania to study economics and sociology. In the early 1920s she was appointed to the New York State Industrial Commission and Industrial Board. Governor Alfred E. Smith, realizing her abilities, appointed her as president of the board in 1926. When Franklin D. Roosevelt, whom she had gotten to know back when she was investigating factory problems, became governor, knowing full well her talents, named her Commissioner of the New York State Department of Labor, where she expanded factory investigations fought for a unemployment insurance, a minimum wage, and child labor laws. She also reduced a woman's work week to forty-eight hours.

When Roosevelt became president he gave her the same position in his presidential cabinet. As Secretary of Labor during the Great Depression and World War II, she showed her worth. She got the Civilian Conservation Corps (C.C.C.) going, easing the burgeoning unemployment problem, and abetted the efforts to form the United States Employment Service, the Works Projects Administration, and eventually the Federal Works Agency. And while she was doing all this, she reorganized the Department of Labor Statistics and continued to work for minimum and hourly work laws. Probably her great accomplishment was tirelessly and successfully working to get the Social Security bill passed and along with it the gaining of unemployment benefits, pensions and welfare. Frances Perkins was one of only two cabinet members to stay with FDR throughout his long presidency. She remained Secretary of Labor until shortly after his passing, resigning in June, 1945. In a less stressful arena, she became a member of the Civil Service Commission, and did the rounds of the lecture circuit speaking on labor relations, as well as becoming associated with Cornell University, where they founded a Frances Perkins Memorial Fellowship.

There have been a number of biographies written about Frances Perkins, but she also wrote extensively. Some of her works are: Women As Employers, People at Work, A Social Experiment Under the Workmen's Compensation Jurisdiction, and The Roosevelt I Knew. Her home in Washington has been declared a United States National Landmark and the Department of Labor headquarters has been named the Frances Perkins Building. She has been inducted into the National Women's Hall of Fame.

Frances Perkins died in New York City on May 14, 1965, and is buried in Maine, the home of her ancestors. The Frances Perkins Center in Damariscotta, Maine educates visitors on her life and work.

106- Molly Pitcher (Mary Hays and Margaret Corbin)

106A- Mary Hays (1754-1832)

"Molly" was often used for women named "Mary." She was born in October, 1754 near Trenton, New Jersey, to her parents, Johann and Maria Ludwig. She married a barber, William Hays in 1769, becoming Mary (Molly) Hays.

Mary Hays became a heroine at the Revolutionary War Battle of Monmouth, New Jersey. At the outbreak of the war her husband enlisted, and Mary went along with him as a "camp follower." These "followers," including Martha Washington, would wash and mend clothes, cook, and care for the sick and injured. Some even went out onto the battlefield to help bring back wounded men. She was with Hays at Valley Forge in that horrible winter of 1777.

During the battle at Monmouth, Mary was a water carrier. The "pitchers" of water were used both to cool down the soldiers and the overheating cannon. William Hays collapsed, or was injured, at his cannon, and was carried off the field. Mary immediately took his place at the cannon and continued there until the end of the battle. A shot came so close that it went right between her legs and ripped off part of her dress. And she commented, "Well that could have been worse." There is enough eyewitness documentation that all this took place, with soldiers commenting that Molly was quite a character, one that smoked and chewed tobacco. She received praise from General Nathaniel Greene, and George Washington made her a non-commissioned officer, and from then on was referred to as "Sergeant Molly."

After the war, in 1783, they moved to Carlisle, Pennsylvania. William Hays died in 1786 and Mary later married John McCauley, a stone cutter, but he eventually deserted her. She went on to become a servant.

In 1822 Pennsylvania awarded her a pension. She died near Carlisle on January 22, 1832,

In 1928 the United States issued a postage stamp with her name printed over the portrait of George Washington, but she did get her own stamp in 1978, the two hundredth anniversary of the battle at Monmouth. During World War ll a liberty ship was christened the "SS Molly Pitcher." The Field Artillery and Air Defense Artillery branches of the United States Army created the Honorable Order of Molly Pitcher given to the wives of servicemen who voluntarily contribute in a significant way to the field artillery community. The United States army base at Fort Bragg celebrates Molly Pitcher Day every year. In 1884 sculptor James E. Kelley created at Freehold, New Jersey, the Monmouth Battle Monument at the battle site, and Molly Pitcher is pictured on one of the bronze reliefs depicting scenes from the battle.

106B- Margaret Corbin (1751-1800)

As has been seen, it does not necessarily take a lifetime of accomplishment to inspire people. Sometimes it takes just a brief moment in time, as was the case with Mary Hays, but also with Margaret Corbin. Margaret Cochran was born in Franklin County, Pennsylvania on November 12, 1751. In 1756 her father was killed by the Native Americans, and her mother taken captive. Margaret was then raised by an uncle.

In 1772 she married John Corbin, a farmer, who joined the First Company of Pennsylvania Artillery at the start of the American Revolution. Margaret Corbin accompanied her husband. On November 16, 1776 at the Battle of Fort Washington, also known as Fort Tryon, in northern New York City, John Corbin was killed at his cannon during a four- thousand Hessian soldier attack.

Margaret, who has also been designated "Molly Pitcher," simply took his place at the cannon and continued discharging her husband's duties for the American cause until she was badly wounded in the arm, the chest and the jaw with grapeshot. Grapeshot was a group of small iron balls fired from a cannon altogether. She was also captured, and later released, and then assigned to a unit of other disabled soldiers at West Point, New York. She did guard duty for a while, but eventually returned to Pennsylvania, and in 1779 was awarded half of a soldier's pension, the first woman ever to get a military pension. "Captain" Margaret Corbin spent the latter part of her life in Highland Falls, New York, where she died on January 16, 1800.

In 1909 a memorial to her was dedicated in Fort Tryon Park, and in 1977 the City Council of the City of New York voted to put her name on street signs at Fort Tryon Plaza, such as Margaret Corbin Circle and Margaret Corbin Drive. In 1916 her remains were moved to the United States Military Academy at West Point, and a memorial was erected to her by the Daughters of the American Revolution.

#107- *Rosa Ponselle (1897-1981)*

The Most Beautiful Voice of the Century

Operatic soprano Rosa Ponzillo (later Ponselle) was born in Meriden, Connecticut to Neapolitan Italian immigrants Bernadino and Maddalena Ponzillo on January 22, 1897. She was a gifted piano player and got a job as a silent movie accompaniest. Her sister Carmela was already making a living as a singer, and Rosa decided that while the projectionist was changing reels in the theater, she would sing ballads to the audience. Her beautiful voice attracted attention, and soon she was doing the singing at one of New Haven, Connecticut's larger theaters, the San Carlos. In 1915 she auditioned for vaudeville with her sister and were hired as either "The Ponzillo Sisiers" or "Those Tailored Italian Girls." Eventually they became the headliners. However, when they demanded a raise in 1918, their act was dropped.

As luck would have it, their agent, William Thorner, managed to get an audition for them with the legendary Enrico Caruso. Unexpectedly Caruso was greatly impressed with Rosa's opulent soprano voice, even though most thought Carmella would garner more attention. He arranged another audition, this time with the general manager of the Metroplitan Opera, Giulio Gatti-Casazza. Rosa Ponselle was given a one-year contract, and starred at the Metropolitan Opera for almost the next twenty years. Rosa's debut was as Leonore opposite Caruso in La forza del destino, and she was a phenomenal success. The natural beauty of her voice was critically acclaimed. She went on that season performing in such operas as Cavalleria rusticana and Oberon. Over the next few decades Ponselle performed in and thrilled audiences in such other operas as William Tell, Aida, La Giaconda, Il trovatore, Don Carlos and La Juive. Her 1927 performance in Bellini's Norma is not only considered one of her best, but is also considered one of the best performances of the century. She also enhanced her reputation by singing in concert halls.

For a while she traveled and performed outside of the United States. She spent three seasons at the Royal Opera House at Covent Garden in London, performing, among others Norma, La traviata, La forza del destino and La Giaconda. She had promised her mother she would sing in Italy, and she did, in La vestale in Florence. She would not sing again in Italy because she feared the fanatical Italian opera fans.

She returned to the United States and continued her career, adding to her repertoire Carmen. By 1937 she was having disagreements with the Metropolitan Opera over salary and selection of operas, as well as the fact that not only was she physically and mentally exhausted, but realized she was beginning to lose some of her voice range, and so Rosa Ponselle decided to retire. In 1936 she had married Carle Jackson and they moved to a home outside of Baltimore, Maryland. However, they divorced in the 1940s, and she had a nervous breakdown in 1949.

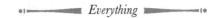

After retirement Rosa Ponselle spent efforts getting the fledgling Baltimore Civic Opera Company going, and opening a voice coaching school. Among her students were Beverly Sills and Placido Domingo. In the 1950s RCA Victor wanted to make recordings of the great soprano, and traveled to her home in Maryland to do so.

Rosa Ponselle died in Green Spring Valley, near Baltimore, Maryland of bone marrow cancer on May 25, 1981, and is buried nearby, and has been considered one of the greatest sopranos over the past one hundred years. She has been inducted into the Connecticut Women's Hall of Fame, and is on a 1997 postage stamp series, honoring opera.

Group Nine

Ma Rainey- Lillian Russell

#108- *Ma Rainey (1886-1939)*

Mother of the Blues

The date and place of Gertrude Nix Pridgett's birth are unclear, but most likely she was born on April 26, 1886, in Russell County, Alabama, but raised in Columbus Georgia, the daughter of Thomas and Ella Pridgett.

By 1900 she was already singing and dancing at the Springer Opera House, and in 1904 she married Will Rainey and, although she had started using her powerful vocals as a teen with the Alabama Fun Makers Company, they then toured the South in tent shows for a number of years with Rabbit Foot Minstrels. Now they were Pa and Ma Rainey. For a while the future legendary Bessie Smith traveled with them. By 1914 they were Rainey and Rainey-Assassinators of the Blues. Ma and Pa separated in 1916 and she formed Madam Gertrude Ma Rainey and Her Georgia Smart Sets.

African American female blues singers had already made recordings, but Ma Rainey, the "Songbird of the South," started her recording history from 1923 to 1928 with Paramount Records. Among songs recorded were: "Bo-weevil Blues," "Soon This Morning," Moonshine Blues," "Countin' the Blues," "Yonder Comes the Blues," "See See Rider Blues" and "Bad Luck Blues." By 1928 she had made over one hundred recordings, but unfortunately the rather poor equipment at Paramount records does not allow listeners to hear Ma Rainey's true voice quality and feel her energy. "Black Bottom" was Ma Rainey's allusion to the fad dance of the same name, that was such a craze that it replaced the Charleston.

She toured the South, Chicago and Midwest with Louis Armstrong and her Georgia Jazz Band. She would appear wearing long gowns, sometimes covered in diamonds, sometimes with a necklace with gold pieces, hence, one of her nicknames, "Gold-necked Woman of the Blues." Rainey would oftentimes be downright bawdy, and defiantly dropping clues of lesbianism.

When Ma Rainey's style of blues started becoming out of fashion, she retired to Columbus, Georgia, opening theaters there, such as the Lyric and the Airdome. There is a Ma Rainey Blues Festival in Columbus.

According to her arranger, Thomas A. Dorsey, Rainey's listeners "swayed, they rocked, they moaned and groaned, as they felt the blues with her." W. K. McNeil stated, "Her artistry brings life to what is essentially would be a dull elementary piece."

Ma Rainey has been inducted into the Blues Foundation Hall of Fame, the Rock and Roll Hall of Fame and the Georgia Women of Achievement. Her performance of "See See Rider" has been selected in the Grammy Hall of Fame. Long after she was gone, she was an inspiration to poets such as Langston Hughes. Bob Dylan references her in his "Tombstone Blues." In the 2015 film, Bessie, the actress Mo'Nique portrayed Rainey. In 1994 a postage stamp was issued in her honor. August Wilson's play, Black Bottom, is more about Ma Rainey than the dance.

Gertrude (Ma) Rainey, Mother of the Blues, died on December 22, 1939 in Rome, Georgia, from heart disease.

#109 Jeannette Rankin (1880-1973)

"I won't be the last"

Outspoken Jeannette Pickering Rankin was born on June 11, 1880, near Missoula, in what was then the Territory of Montana, to immigrant rancher John and schoolteacher Olive Rankin. She graduated from the University of Montana with a degree in biology in 1902, and lived for a while in Boston where her brother Wellington was in college. Then it was off to San Francisco where she found an interest in social work, and returned east to a get a degree from Columbia University. Now she was back in the west at Spokane, Washington, where she again enrolled in college, and became very interested in the suffrage movement.

In 1911 she became the first woman to address the Montana legislature, and did so lobbying for suffrage. In 1916, Montana had its first congressional race, and Rankin entered. Her brother Wellington had become a force in Montana politics and he managed and arranged financing for his sister, and she did win one of the congressional seats. When approached about her historical victory, being the first woman ever elected to the House of Representatives and the first to hold a national office, she replied, "I may be the first woman member of Congress, but I won't be the last." As it so happens that since her election, over three hundred women have been elected to Congress.

Two things were uppermost in Rankin's agenda, suffrage and peace. Inside congress she was the main force for universal suffrage, voting rights for women, but shortly after her election, President Woodrow Wilson called for a declaration of war against Germany in World War I. She was not the only member to oppose the majority vote, but she did stand and declare, "I wish to stand for my country, but I cannot vote for war."

At the next congressional election, the Montana seats were changed and she chose not to run. She made an attempt to run for the senate, but failed.

Rankin moved to Georgia where she bought a farm, but continued lecturing around the country on the topic of pacifism, forming the Georgia Peace Society and becoming the field secretary for the National Consumers League and a member of the National Council for the Prevention of War. She seemed to be at home both in Georgia and in Montana.

In 1940 she again decided to run for congress, and again the United States was on the precipice of war, this time, World War II. She won the election, and again when Congress was asked by President Franklin D. Roosevelt to declare war on Japan after the attack on Pearl Harbor, she voted in the negative. "As a woman I can't go to war and I refuse to send anyone else." This time she was the lone dissenting vote, three hundred and eighty-eight to one. She became extremely unpopular, and did not run for re-election.

Jeannette Rankin did a lot of traveling around the country and the world, particularly to India. In 1968 during the Vietnam War she formed the Jeannette Rankin Brigade and led five thousand protesters to the Capitol Building in Washington, D. C. delivering a peace petition.

Rankin passed away on May 18, 1973 in Carmel, California. There is a Jeannette Rankin Women's Scholarship Fund for educational scholarships for low-income women over the age of thirty-five. A Single Woman is a one-act play based on her life. It was also made into a film biography, narrated by actor Martin Sheen, with music by Joni Mitchell. She has been inducted into the Georgia Women of Achievement and the National Women's Hall of Fame. A statue of Jeannette Rankin, the first woman elected to the House of Representatives stands in Congress' Statuary Hall with the inscription, "I Cannot Vote For War." A replica stands in the Montana capitol building in Helena.

#110- Janet Reno (1938-2016)

Attorney General

Janet Wood Reno was born on July 21, 1938 in Miami, Florida to newspaper reporters Jane and Henry Reno. Henry's birth name in Denmark was Rasmussen, but his family changed the name to Reno because they thought it sounded American. By eight years of age her family had moved to the edge of Florida's Everglades, in a home built by her mother.

Janet graduated Cornell University with a degree in chemistry, and having been president of the Women's Self-Governing Association. In 1963 she received her law degree from Harvard Law, and from then until 1971 she practised private law in her home state of Florida. She did try an ill-fated run for Florida's state legislature, but found success with Judiciary Committee of the Florida House of Representatives and the Dade County State's attorney general office.

She was appointed Attorney General of the State of Florida 1978, and was elected to that position four more times, the first woman attorney general in the state's history. Much of her efforts in this role was fighting child abuse.

In 1993 President Bill Clinton selected her as the Attorney General of the United States, the first woman to hold that position, as well. She would serve eight years, becoming the second longest in American history. To find the the longest, one had to go back to 1829.

During Janet Reno's tenure and under her lead, in the attorney general position, a good number of noteworthy events took place. Among them were: the capture and conviction of Ted Kaczynski, the infamous Unibomber; the capture and convictions of Timothy McVeigh and Terry Nichols, the terrorists who blew up the office building in Oklahoma City; the capture and conviction of Omar Abdel-Rahma and other conspirators for the initial 1993 World Trade Center bombing; the very controversial return of six-year old Elian Gonzalez in 2000 to his Cuban father; the identifying of Eric Rudolph as the Centennial Park bombing in Atlanta (after first mistakenly identifying Richard Jewell); prosecuting CIA spy/mole Aldrich Ames; and the controversial decision to storm the Waco, Texas Branch Davidian compound of David Koresh in 1993, resulting in approximately eighty deaths. All the deaths were attributed to the sect itself.

It turns out that the Branch Davidians were an offshoot of Seventh Day Adventists. Vernon Howell, who later changed his name to what he felt was a religious name, David Koresh, after an armed conflict, took control of the group, and claimed to be the Prophet, also the "sinful messiah," and had a loyal following, and had been in defiance of federal authorities for a while. They were suspected of both child abuse and weapons violations. A court order was ignored and an initial battle took place, leading to a fifty-one day stand-off.

After her service as attorney general, Janet Reno sought the Democratic Party nomination for governor of Florida, but partially due to her unpopularity among Cuban-Americans over the Elian Gonzalez return to Cuba, she was unsuccessful. She became a popular and much sought-after speaker, where she concentrated on criminal justice, juvenile courts and education. She was a founding member of the Innocence Project, which helped prisoners to be exonerated through DNA, later becoming Director Emeritus. Reno was given the Professionalism Award from the Council on Litigation, and the Justice Award from the American Judicature Society for "commitment to improving our system of justice, and educating Americans about our

great common enterprise- to insure equality under the law." She also "voiced" herself on The Simpsons.

Janet Reno died from complication from Parkinson's Disease on November 7, 2016 in Miami, Florida. She has been inducted into the Florida Women's Hall of Fame and the National Women's Hall of Fame.

"My mother always told me to do my best, to think my best, and to do right."

#111- *Sally Ride (1951-2012)*

First Woman and Youngest Astronaut

Sally Kristen Ride, astronaut, physicist and educator, was born in southern California on May 26, 1951. Both her parents, Dale and Carol, were elders in the Presbyterian church. She attended Swarthmore College, where she became a nationally-ranked amateur tennis player, actually becoming the Eastern Intercollegiate Women's Champion twice, but transferred back to California where she briefly attended UCLA (University of California at Los Angeles), and then on to Stanford University where she not only double-majored, went on to get a master's degree in 1975 and a doctorate in 1978.

While at Stanford she saw an article in the college newspaper asking for astronaut applicants. Eight thousand applied and she was one of the few accepted. Upon this acceptance she had to go through rigorous training exercises, including weightlessness, navigation, water survival, parachute jumping and radio communications, among others. Her first jobs with NASA (National Aerospace and Space Administration) were on the ground as a communications officer and as a conductor of special scientific experiments. In 1982 she married fellow astronaut Steven Hawley, but they divorced in 1987.

But with her becoming a mission specialist on the Challenger shuttle in 1983, she became the first female American astronaut, and the youngest, as well. She deployed communication satellites and did pharmaceutical experiments. She returned to the Challenger for another mission in 1984.

Sally Ride was scheduled to go on a third mission when the Challenger shuttle disaster ended that plan. After the explosion occurred, Sally Ride was assigned to the investigation, and it was not until after her death that it was learned that she was the one who determined it was an

"O" ring malfunction. She was also on the investigative committee on the Columbia shuttle disaster in 2003.

After her astronaut endeavors, Ride spent time working at NASA headquarters in Washington, D. C. as the first director of the Office of Exploration, and in 1987 worked for Stanford University's Center for International Security and Arms Control. Two years later she became a professor of physics at the University of California at San Diego, and became director of the California Space Institute. From the 1990s until her death Sally Ride constantly promoted public outreach programs for NASA, aimed primarily at middle school students.

And with her partner, Tam O'Shaugnessy, she became a champion of science education, and they wrote a half dozen books aimed at those same middle school students. The main thrust of these books was "STEM" (science, technology, engineering and mathematics). Sally Ride Science created entertaining science programs and publications, for all students, but primarily aimed at girls.

Having achieved a great deal of respect, Sally Ride was asked to be on numerous boards of directors, including NCAA Foundation, the President's Commission of Advisors on Science and Technology, the Congressional Office of Technical Assessment, the Pacific Council on International Policy, the Aerospace Corporation, California Institute of Technology, and Carnegie Institute of Washington.

She was also awarded many honors, among them the National Space Agency von Braun Award, the Lindbergh Eagle, the NCAA Theodore Roosevelt Award, the Samuel S. Beard Award for Greatest Public Service by an Individual Under 35 Years of Age. Flying Magazine listed her as one of the "51 Heroes of Aviation."

In 2013 she was awarded the Presidential Medal of Freedom, posthumously, presented to her partner, Tam O'Shaugnessy, and also awarded the prestigious General James E. Hill Space Achievement Award from the Space Foundation, and was declared "An Engineering Hero" by Stanford University. Sally Ride had died on July 23, 2012 of pancreatic cancer in La Jolla, California. Of course, Sally Ride is in the National Women's Hall of Fame, as well as the Astronaut Hall of Fame, California Hall of Fame, the Texas Women's Hall of Fame, and the International Pioneer Hall of Fame.

#112- *Felisa Rincon de Gautier (1897-1994)*

Dona Fela

Felisa Rincon Marrero de Gautier was born in Ceiba, Puerto Rico on January 9, 1897 to an attorney, Enrique Rincon Plumey, whose ancestor had been a mayor of San Juan. Her mother, Rita Marrero Rivera, died when Felisa was eleven years old, and she quit school at fifteen to help the family in any way she could.

She first was a pharmacist, something she learned from an uncle. But she was also an excellent seamstress, and spent two ambitious years up in New York City to learn something about the business. When she returned to Puerto Rico she opened a clothing factory and Felisa's Style Shop in Old San Juan.

At the same time she began her activist and political life, particularly seeking suffrage for Puerto Rican women, which they finally achieved in 1932. She joined the Liberal Party of Puerto Rico, becoming its executive director, but 1938 abandoned it and helped Luis Munoz Marin found the Popular Democratic Party of Puerto Rico. In 1940 she married Genaro Gautier, an assistant attorney-general, and secretary general of that Popular Democratic Party of Puerto Rico.

In 1946 Felisa Rincon de Gautier became the first woman mayor of an American capital city, when she became mayor of San Juan. She was also the first woman anywhere in the Americas to be a mayor of a capital city.

She remained mayor from 1947 until 1969, with San Juan growing from 180,000 inhabitants to 450,000. During her tenure she turned San Juan into an urban center, a center for tourism and finance in the Caribbean, improved the schools, sanitation, and housing, restored and renovated many historical structures in Old San Juan, formed pre-school centers which were the inspiration for Head Start programs on the mainland, and founded centers for the elderly. Rincon renovated the San Juan Municipal Hospital and soon established a School of Medicine. Ricon became "Dona Fela" to her constituents, and started the tradition of distributing gifts and treats to the needy on Three Kings Day, also known as the Feast of the Epiphany, on January 6. She even had much land cleared for Little League baseball teams in San Juan. In 1959 San Juan, Puerto Rico was given the All American City Award.

Once out of office she became a goodwill ambassador for four American presidents. Her efforts in this position earned her the Joan of Arc Medal from France, the Gold Medal of Honor from Ecuador, and one from Spain. Also from Spain she received the Medal of Isabella and the Don Quixote Medal. Francis Cardinal Spellman of New York City bestowed upon her the Medal of the Holy Sepulcher, the Union of American Women of New York named her "Woman of the Americas." In addition, Eleanor Roosevelt presented her with the Hebrew Philanthropic Award.

Rincon passed away on September 16, 1994, and was eulogized by many important figures, and is buried in Rio Piedras. She was a woman of great perseverance and had been the oldest delegate at 1992's National Democratic Convention in New York City. There is a museum named after her and in 2014 was honored at La Plaza en Honor a la Mujer Puertoriqueno. There is a school in Brooklyn, New York named in her honor.

#113- *Mary Roberts Rinehart (1876-1958)*

America's Agatha Christie

Mary Roberts Rinehart, "America's Agatha Christie," was born in the Pittsburgh suburbs on August 12, 1876, to failed and suicidal inventor Thomas Roberts and his wife Cornelia. Mary graduated the Pittsburgh Training School for Nurses in 1896, and married Dr. Stanley M. Rinehart soon after.

To ease her family's financial woes from a stock market crash of 1903, she began writing, and had stories published in newspapers and magazines. The first novel was The Man in Lower Ten in 1906 and her first detective story, The Circular Staircase, was published in 1908, the first of her "had I but known plots," followed by The White Cat. These novels propelled her to national fame and popularity.

In 1909 she co-wrote a comedic play, Seven Days for Broadway, and it was a hit. Soon after came the serialization of The Amazing Adventures of Letitia Carberry in the Saturday Evening Post. These "Tish" stories were fun and entertaining, and continued on for years. In 1955 they were collected in The Best of Tish.

During World War I she worked as a correspondent in Belgium for the Saturday Evening Post, and the experience led to Kings, Queens and Pawns and The Altar of Freedom. The Bat, a play based on The Circular Staircase, came in the 1920s, and later into a film. It was also co-written with Avery Hopwood, with whom she would collaborate many times. It is considered one of the inspirations of the creation of "Batman." The Door, written in 1930, created the phrase, "the butler did it." No one says that in the book, but, in fact, the butler did do it.

Mary Roberts Rinehart's autobiography, My Story, was published in 1931, but she kept writing for many years after. Her husband died while they were living in Washington, D.C. in 1932, and a few years later she moved to New York City. Some other stories are Where There's A Will and The Breaking Point. Most of her stories were light-hearted and humorous, and those "had I but known" mystery stories were particularly excellent. Many, many of her stories were adapted into films, plays and talking books. Once, while vacationing in Maine, a chef attempted to kill her, first with a gun, and then with a knife, but she survived, and he committed suicide. She also had a radical mastectomy for breast cancer. In a Ladies Home Journal, "I Had Cancer" interview in 1947, she openly discussed this, at a time when such topics as this were not discussed openly, encouraging women to go for examinations.

She died on September 22, 1958 in New York City, after also having helped her sons found the Rinehart Publishing Company, of which she became director. Mary Roberts Rinehart Nature Park in Glen Osborne, Pennsylvania, where she lived for a while, is dedicated to her. She was also honored with the Mystery Writers of America Special Award, and given an honorary doctorate from George Washington University.

#114- Lola Rodriguez de Tio (1842-1924)

Daughter of the Isles

Poet, feminist, activist, and revolutionary, Dolores Rodriguez de Astudillo y Ponce de Leon was born in San German, Puerto Rico on September 14, 1843, but the family soon moved to Mayaguez. Her father was Sebastian Rodriguez de Astudillo, a founder of Illustre Colegio de Abrogados de Puerto Rico (Illustrious College of Attorneys), a sort of legal bar association. Her mother was Carmen de Ponce de Leon, a descendant of the famous explorer, seeker of the "Fountain of Youth," and first governor of Puerto Rico.

In 1863 Dolores married revolutionary activist writer Bonocio Tio Segarra, and she became Lola Rodriguez de Tio. She soon published her first book, Mis Cantares (My Songs), and it was a huge success.

In the meanwhile a great deal of unrest was happening in Puerto Rico, with resentment against the mother country of Spain, due to a lack of economic and political freedom, and a good deal of repression. On September 23, 1868 a group of about five hundred rebels, primarily led by Ramon Betances and Segundo Ruiz Belvis, began the first major revolt, coming to be known as Gritos de Lares (Cries of Lares), which quickly spread throughout Puerto Rico. However, in the end it failed miserably, and many of the rebels were imprisoned, humiliated, and tortured. Some were exiled. Lola Rodriguez de Tio was among the exiled due to her patriotic, but fiery lyrics written to the tune of "La Borinquena." "Awaken,PuertoRican! The signal to fight has been made! Arise from your sleepiness for it is time to fight!....The Cries of Lares must be repeated and then we will know victory or death."

This became the national anthem of Puerto Rico, although some of lyrics have been modified.

She and her husband went to Caracas, Venezuela in their banishment, where they became very close with Puerto Rican patriot, Eugenio Maria de Hostos. They were allowed to come home in 1885. Upon returning they established a magazine, La almajabana, and Lola Rodriguez de Tio wrote "Nochebuena," which was a tribute to political prisoners. Again she was exiled in 1889. This time she went to New York City where she met with Jose Marti, and decided to help his cause in Cuba. She went to Cuba, remaining in exile there for many years, where her home became a haven for other Puerto Rican exiles.

In 1919 she was honored back in Puerto Rico at Ateneo Puertorrueno, one of San Juan's cultural institutions, and recited her Cantos de Puerto Rico.

Lola Rodriquez de Tio, who was one of the most influential nineteenth century poets, and referred to as the "Daughter of the Isles," passed away on November 10, 1924. In 2014 she was honored at La Plaza en Honor a la Mujer Puertorrequeno (Plaza in Honor of Puerto Rican Women).

Other writings by Lola Rodriguez de Tio are Claros y Nieblos (Bright Interval and Mist) and Mi Libra de Cuba (My Book on Cuba). Her "Cuba y Puerto Rico son de un pajardo" compared Puerto Rico and Cuba as the two wings of the same bird. She not only expressed the spirit of Puerto Rico, but also of Cuba, and of the disparity of opportunity for women, as well, as well as the abolishment of slavery.

#115- *Eleanor Roosevelt (1884-1962)*

A Most Admired Woman

Born in New York City on October 11, 1884, Anna Eleanor Roosevelt was a daughter of wealth and a member of one of America's prestigious families, including the colonial Livingstons. She could have sat back and let the world come to her, but instead, she became a tireless worker for the rights of people, and in doing so, became one of the most outstanding women in America.

Her mother, Anna, died of diphtheria when Eleanor was eight, and her father, Elliott, whom she adored, was an alcoholic and spent much time away in a sanitarium, dying when she was ten. She went to live with her unusually strict grandmother and was thought of as an ugly duckling, but once said, "No one can make you feel inferior without your consent." So, at fifteen she began attending London's Allenswood, where Marie Souvestre exposed Eleanor to the joys of life, taking her on holidays throughout Europe. When she returned home she worked for the Rivington Street Settlement House and the Consumer's League.

On March 17, 1905 she married her fifth cousin, Franklin Delano Roosevelt, and her father's brother, President of the United States Theodore Roosevelt, gave her away. She would give birth to six children.

The marriage, it turned out, became more of an agreeable political partnership. Soon her husband began his political climb, and in 1920, he was the unsuccessful vice presidential candidate, and she joined the New York State League of Women Voters. In 1921 Franklin came down with a tragic illness, debilitating polio, but she continued on, joining the Women's Division of the Democratic State Committee, becoming finance chair. She did this to keep Franklin's name in circulation, and in 1928 she was a member of an advisory committee on women's activities of the Democratic National Campaign Committee. She founded, taught at and was vice-principal of the Todhunter School for Girls.

Franklin became governor of New York (1929-1932), but Eleanor's first real area of achievement did not begin until her husband became president from 1933 until his death in 1945. She used this position of influence to its ultimate capacity, was very outspoken, including having her own press conferences. She wrote a daily syndicated column, "My Day," in Ladies Home Journal and McCall's magazine. She also was responsible for her husband's forming the National Youth Administration. In that capacity she arranged the appointment of Mary McLeod Bethune as director of its Division of Negro Affairs. She did the unheard of when she spoke at the 1940 Democratic Party National Convention.

Perhaps her most important act was her resignation from the Daughters of the American Revolution when they denied Marian Anderson the right to sing in their Constitution Hall because she was African American. She then helped make arrangements for Anderson's concert at the Lincoln Memorial. Eleanor also had Marian Anderson sing at the White House. Roosevelt had earlier resigned from the Colony Club of New York when Jewish Elinor Morgenthau was not admitted.

After Franklin Roosevelt's death she did not quietly retire. President Truman named her a delegate to the first seven sessions of the United Nations General Assembly. Having traveled widely and speaking out for world peace and human rights, from 1946 to 1952 she was the United States' representative to the Commission on Human Rights, under the United Nations Social and Economic Council, and eventually became the chair. In that capacity she drew up and had accepted the Declaration of Universal Rights, which was to be "a common standard for all peoples and all nations."

She remained an influential voice in politics and strongly supported Adlai Stevenson for the presidency. After 1953 she worked for the American Association for the United Nations, and in 1961 President John F. Kennedy appointed her to the Commission on the Status of Women, and again as delegate to the United Nations. She held that post until her death in New York City from cardiac arrest, brought on by tuberculosis, on November 7, 1962. At the time of her death she was also working on a plan for the Wiltwyck School for Boys. She worked tirelessly in so many difficult ways and situations, and came to symbolize her own words, "A woman is like a tea bag; you never know how strong it is until it's in hot water."

Eleanor Roosevelt received honorary degrees from all over the world; had a forest named for her in the Near East; has been placed on any number of stamps, and worked tirelessly all her life for social and educational improvement, women's recognition, and human rights. In 1948 the American Institute of Public Opinion declared her to be "the most admired woman living today," and her husband, FDR, had been already dead three years. In a Gallup poll she was ninth on the list of the Most Widely Admired People of the Twentieth Century. She is in the National Women's Hall of Fame. "Well behaved women rarely make history."

Among her writings were: This Is My Story, a very honest telling of her development, This I Remember, memoirs of the White House years, On My Own, another autobiography, and India and the Awakening East, It's Up to the Women, and This Troubled World. There numerous schools, colleges and other institutions named in her honor.

In 1972, Joseph P. Lash's bestselling book, Eleanor and Franklin, went on to win the Pulitzer Prize, National Book Award, and the source of several television movies. In 1977 her home, Val-Kill, was designated a National Historic Site, and in 1996 a monument was erected in her honor in Riverside Park in New York City.

#116- *Wilma Rudolph (1940-1994)*

La Chattanooga Choo Choo

Wilma Glodean Rudolph, nicknamed "Skeeter," was born on June 23, 1940 in St. Bethlehem, Tennessee, the twentieth of twenty-two children of her father, porter Ed and his second wife Blanche. When she was young, the family moved to Clarksville, Tennessee.

Wilma contracted infantile paralysis due to a polio virus at four years of age, got double pneumonia and scarlet fever, making her a very sickly child. She had to wear a brace on her foot, which, in turn twisted her leg, leaving her with a crooked leg. By the age of eight she was walking with a specially reinforced high top left shoe. At eleven all she had was a limp.

By the time she graduated from high school she had overcome her handicaps to such an extent that she had become both a track and basketball star athlete. She was an All-State basketball player, averaging thirty-two points per game, and never lost any track event she entered.

She was good enough to make the 1956 Australia Olympics, but was eliminated in the two hundred meter race, and only took a bronze medal as part of the relay team. She became determined to win some gold in the 1960 Olympics.

She returned home, had a baby daughter, but soon was running for Tennessee State University. She participated in the AAU (Amateur Athletic Union) Championships and the Pan Am Games. She won the 100 meter dash four years running at those games. She did extremely well, qualifying for the upcoming Rome Olympics.

In Rome her first event was the one hundred meter dash. She broke the record in the preliminary round, but it was discounted due to wind. In the final round she ran a record-tying time, won the race, and her first gold medal. In the two hundred meter race she broke the record, won the race, and picked up her second gold medal. In the four hundred meter relay she and her Tennessee State teammates tied the record, won the race, and Wilma Rudolph won her third gold medal. She had become the first American woman to win three gold medals, and was considered "the fastest woman in the world." She had elevated women's track in America to heights it had never had. The Italians called her "La Gazzella Nera" (Black Gazelle), and the French began calling her, "La Chattanooga Choo Choo" and the "Black Pearl." After the Olympics she continued running, touring Europe and winning just about everything. She broke the record for the sixty yard dash, the seventy yard dash and the hundred yard dash, and won the James E. Sullivan Sportsmanship Trophy, the first track athlete so honored, and only the third female. Even her likeness was put in Madame Tussaud's Wax Museum in London. She was the Associated Press Athlete of the Year in 1960, the Associate Press Woman Athlete of the Year in 1960 and 1961. At home she had a meeting with President John F. Kennedy.

In 1963 she graduated Tennessee State, and went on a tour of the Orient for the United States, and began teaching and coaching when she came home. After a while she began working with Job Corps and Operation Champ, but became disillusioned because of the lack of adequate funding. For a while she was a lecturer and a sports commentator. She moved to various locations and for a while lived in Indianapolis, Indiana before returning home to Tennessee.

Wilma Rudolph died in Brentwood, Tennessee on November 12, 1994 of a combination of a brain tumor and throat cancer. She married twice and had four children. In 1977 there was a docu-drama Wilma, with a young Denzel Washington in the cast. She is in the International Association of Athletics Federations (IAAF) Hall of Fame, the National Black Sports and Entertainment Hall of Fame, the National Track and Field Hall of Fame, and, of course in the National Women's Hall of Fame. There is a life-size bronze statue of Rudolph in Clarksville, Tennessee. The Woman's Sports Foundation presents a Wilma Rudolph Courage Award to worthy athletes. In 2004 a stamp was issued in her honor. The state of Tennessee has declared June 23 "Wilma Rudolph Day."

#117- *Maria Amparo Ruiz de Burton (1832-1895)*

Forerunner of Chicano Literature

Maria Amparo Ruiz was born in Loreto, Baja California in Mexico, and raised in LaPaz, on July 3, 1832 to Jesus Maitorena and Isabel Ruiz Maitorena. Hers was a life of privilege and she learned to speak French, and later English, as well as her native Spanish. As was the custom with some of the privileged, she chose to use her mother's surname. Her grandfather had been governor of part of Baja. She was a adolescent when the Mexican-American War broke out, and was present when the American troops took over her town. She met an army captain, Henry Burton, who later became a brigadier general, and they began a relationship. When Baja California remained in Mexican hands, Burton was able to move her and the family to Alta California (now just California), and they became American citizens. They were married in Monterey on July 7, 1849, just a few days after her seventeenth birthday.

In some ways Maria Amparo Ruiz de Burton was seen as a traitor, marrying a man who was part of her former country's defeat. The entire family moved to San Diego in 1852, when Burton took command of Mission San Diego de Alcala. They bought land and created Rancho Jamul.

Once the American Civil War broke out, Burton was called to the east coast, and Maria sailed there, following him. The next few years found her living in Washington, D.C., where she became friendly with Mary Todd Lincoln, and in New York, Delaware, Virginia and Rhode Island. While on assignment in Virginia, Burton contracted malaria, and was sickly the rest of his life. He died in Rhode Island in 1869.

Maria decided to return to her ranch in San Diego, but when she arrived, not only did she find it in ruins, but there were squatters, people who just moved in and stayed there. It became a lifetime battle waged by a Mexican American to attempt to get her land back, but the powers that be were against her, and by the time she died, all she could manage to get back was a small parcel.

This is when Maria Amparo Ruiz de Burton became the first Mexican American to write a novel, and in English. Who Would Have Thought? was the title, and it is the story of Lola, a Mexican-American girl captured by Indians, and as a result of all that, faces a life of racism and hypocrisy. Because Ruiz de Burton was Mexican American, and her book dared to criticize the view of history that the United States presented to the world, the book remained unknown until the late twentieth century. Her other novel, The Squatter and the Don in 1885, did better. This told the story of the Alamar family and the Darrell family, and how the Mexican Californians were pushed to the edges of society, economically deprived, had their land taken away, much of this occurring with the assistance of the railroad tycoons. A comedic play had been written in 1876, Don Quixote de la Mancha. Maria Amparo Ruiz de Burton died of gastric fever in Chicago, Illinois, always believing that she was "persuaded that we were born for something more, for the rest of our poor countrymen." She was buried in San Diego, California.

In her literature she brought out how power, class, dual nationality, ethnicity, gender, race and corruption were a part of American history, and challenged the traditional history that has always been put forth.

#118- Lillian Russell (1861-1922)

Queen of the Gay Nineties

Lillian Russell, called Nellie as a youngster, was born Helen Louise Leonard on December 4, 1861 in Clinton, Iowa. Her father was newspaper publisher Charles E. Leonard, and her mother was author and woman's suffrage fighter Cynthia Leonard. She moved to Chicago as a child. In the late 1870s she moved again with her divorced mother to New York. She would go on to become perhaps the most successful musical comedy and light opera star of all time. She studied opera, and at the age of seventeen appeared in the chorus of a production of H.M.S. Pinafore. Under the stage name of "Nellie Leonard" she also appeared in Evangeline. She was to become the most popular singer in musical theater.

She married young, to orchestra leader Henry Brahamin 1879, and then also to producer and bigamist Edward Solomon from 1885 to 1893, and to tenor John Haley Augustin Chatterton, professionally known as Signor Giovanni Perugini from 1994 to 1898.

Using her stage name, Lillian Russell appeared in Tony Pastor's Theatre as "The English Ballad Singer." Pastor is considered the "Father of Vaudeville." Vaudeville was an entertainment presentation that showcased a variety of acts: dancers, singers, magicians, comedians and even circus acts and animal acts. Its popularity went from the 1880s to the 1930s. Russell also joined the McCaull Opera Company and soon gained true success and acclaim. Her success was so extraordinary, due both to her beauty, stage presence and her lovely, if not great, operatic voice. By 1883 she was always in the news and her fame was so universal that she found herself with a good number of simultaneous commitments. She simply traveled with Edward Solomon and went to London, again achieving phenomenal success, in such productions as Paul and Virginia and Pocahontas. However, it was also learned Solomon was already married, and, therefore, a bigamist. She had the marriage annulled.

Lillian Russell became "Queen of the Gay Nineties," as she was the perfect entertainer for the time, with her beauty and flamboyance, her glamorous costumes and outrageous hats. She even made the first long distance call in history, from New York City to President Grover Cleveland in Washington. She was not only a legend, she had become the most well-known woman in America. For about five years she stayed with Weber and Fields Music Hall.

Just prior to the opening of 1902's Twirly-Whirly, composer John Stromberg committed suicide. They found sheet music to "Come Down Ma Evening Star." Lillian Russell made that her signature song.

More important to her than any of her marriages was her friendship with "Diamond Jim" Brady which lasted forty years, and included starting the fad of riding "bicycles built for two" and theirs was gold-plated by Tiffany and Co. But she did marry again to newspaper publisher Alexander P. Moore in 1912, and, for the most part, retired, but in the spirit of her mother, wrote articles advocating women's suffrage. In 1915 she made her last Broadway appearance in Hokey Pokey.

After the turn of the twentieth century her popularity and her voice had begun to fade. However, she made a number of short films from 1906 to 1913. Some of her more well-known shows were: Lady Teazle, Gasparone, The Queen of Brilliants, The Grand Duchess of Gerolstein, The Mountebanks, Pepita, Patience, Dorothy, The Brigands, Erminia and Wildfire, as well as its film version.

She went on to lecture and do social work, including with the Red Cross during World War I. Lillian Russell also became an active proponent of workers' rights. President Warren G. Harding requested she undertake a fact-finding trip to Europe to investigate immigration policies. Soon after returning home she died in Pittsburgh on June 6, 1922, and is buried there. Harding sent a floral wreath to her funeral. There exists a Lillian Russell Theatre for summer stock on the "City of Clinton" showboat at her birth place. In 1940 a very fictionalized film biography was released with Alice Faye as the star, and also starring Henry Fonda and Don Ameche.

Group Ten

Sacajawea - Harriet Beecher Stowe

#119- Sacajawea (1788-1884)

Bird Woman

Sacajawea, the irreplaceable and indispensable Shoshone guide and interpreter of the Lewis and Clark expedition (Meriwether Lewis, William Clark), was born in the Lemhi River Valley in the Rocky Mountains of Idaho in about 1788. The correct spelling of her name is a mystery since it was never written when given. This is the most accepted phonetic spelling, and she was known as "Bird Woman."

The purpose of Lewis and Clark's expedition was to explore and find out everything they could about what has come to be called the Louisiana Purchase.

Sacajawea's husband, French-Canadian trapper Toussaint Charbonneau, was actually hired as the guide, and he suggested his wife accompany them. As a pre-teen she had been captured by the Hidatsa, and they named her, and brought her to the Dakota territory. Here Charbonneau won her, and then married her at thirteen years of age. They were living with the Mandans when the expedition came upon them. Charbonneau convinced Lewis and Clark that, although his wife was pregnant, she would be a great asset not only as a guide, but also as a liaison and interpreter. She gave birth in February, 1805 to her son, Jean Baptiste Charbonneau, called "Pomp" by Captain William Clark. Clark also called Sacajawea "Janey."

Sacajawea turned out to be even more than an extraordinary guide and peacemaker, bringing them through to her own Shoshone country. She managed to arrange for food and horses, and protection, because Comeahwait, her brother, was now chief.

The Corps of Discovery, as it was actually called, reached the Pacific Ocean at Fort Clatsop, Oregon, with Sacajawea carrying Pomp on her back. Time and time again she salvaged important records and items important to the expedition, especially once, when a boat overturned, and she retrieved much material. Charbonneau was paid five hundred dollars for his work, and Sacajawea nothing!

However, Clark had become very fond of her and her son, and volunteered to educate him. Eventually she went down to St. Louis to see if Clark was true to his word, and he was, enrolling the boy in the St. Louis Academy. At one point Pomp was befriended by a German duke who brought him to Europe, where he stayed for six years. Upon returning home he became a guide and a miner, among other things. There is much conjecture as to whether he ever saw his mother again.

Sacajawea remained in St. Louis for a while, with Clark helping Charbonneau get work. She left Charbonneau and went back to her people in the north in about 1811. By 1843 she was in Wyoming when Jerk Meat, her new husband, was killed. By the 1850s she was on the Shoshone Wind River Reservation, also in Wyoming. She is given credit for preventing a war with the Shoshone tribe in 1868. She died there in 1884.

There have been numerous books and biographies written about Sacajawea and there has also been speculation that she died at an earlier date and different place. But what is clear is that there are more things dedicated to her than any other woman in American history: the USS Sacajawea is only one of many ships named in her honor; there are mountain peaks, a mountain, a lake and a river, and a state park. The Sacajawea Interpretive, Cultural and Educational Center is located in Salmon, Idaho. There are statues of her in at least Missouri, Wyoming, Oregon, Idaho, Montana, Washington, Texas, Virginia, Illinois, and North and South Dakota. There are monuments and memorials to her in at least four states. She has been inducted into both the National Cowgirl Hall of Fame and the National Women's Hall of Fame. The United States issued a one dollar coin in 2000, bearing what is thought to be the likeness of Sacajawea.

She became an inspiration in the women's movements, showing what a woman could achieve and contribute under very adverse conditions.

#120- *Margaret Sanger (1879-1966)*

Mother of the Birth Control Movement

Margaret Louise Higgins Sanger was born the sixth of eleven children to Michael and Anne Higgins, in Corning, New York on September 14, 1879. She attended Claverack College, the Hudson River Institute, the Nurses Training School of White Plains Hospital, and did post-graduate work at the Manhattan Eye and Ear Hospital. In 1902 she married William Sanger, and worked as a nurse until 1912. At that point she became disgusted with the lack of aid given to the mothers in poor families who were dying from self-induced, "back alley," abortions. Birth control and the giving of advice on birth control was federally illegal due to the Comstock Law. This law stated that birth control and any advice and discussions of birth control were obscene.

So Margaret Sanger went to France to learn and understand more about birth control. This mother of the birth control movement in the United States ran into many problems back home, which partially led to her divorce eventually. In 1914 she became editor and publisher of Woman Rebel, which advocated birth control. It received an overwhelming response, but was banned. She wrote a pamphlet, "Family Limitation," which was in direct violation of the Comstock Law. She fled to Canada and then to the Netherlands. There she became aware of the diaphragm. This device put a barrier in the vagina covering the cervix, thereby preventing pregnancy. She came home in 1915, and the country's mood had changed and all charges had been dropped. In 1916 she successfully opened her first birth control clinic in the Brownsville neighborhood of Brooklyn, New York. However, ten days later it was shut down. She re-opened it and when she did, Margaret Sanger was sent to jail for thirty days. She appealed her decision and was then permitted to give married women birth control advice, the initial victory.

She became editor of the Birth Control Review until 1928. It became the official publication of the Birth Control League. In 1921 Margaret Sanger called for the first National Birth Control Conference, which led to the American Birth Control League. She would be its first president until 1928. And with this she began worldwide tours becoming a global figure. In 1922 she had founded the Clinical Research Bureau in New York, and she re-married, this time to businessman, James Noah Slee, who, for a while, smuggled diaphragm's in from Canada. They lived in Westchester, New York. She went on to organize the World Population Conference in Geneva, opened her Sanger Clinic, and founded and became president of the National Commission for Federal Legislation for Birth Control. By 1930 there were fifty-five clinics within the United States. And the next year, Margaret Sanger, who had spent thirty days in jail and had been a wanted criminal, was awarded a medal by the American Women's Association.

She continued her international tours and had begun to see the end of most of the prohibitive birth control laws. In 1942 the Planned Parenthood Federation of America was organized, and Sanger was named honorary president. She went on to found the International Planned Parenthood Federation and become its first president, but by the late 1950's she retired to Tucson, Arizona. She died there of congestive heart failure on September 6, 1966. She is buried in Fishkill, New York. Among her books are What Every Woman Should Know, The Case For Birth Control, The Pivot of Civilization, Happiness in Marriage, and Margaret Sanger, An Autobiography. She has been inducted into both the Arizona Women's Hall of Fame and the Natinal Women's Hall of Fame.

#121- Selena (1971-1995)

Queen of Tejano Music

Singer, actress and fashion designer Selena Quintanilla was born in Lake Jackson, Texas on April 16, 1971 to musician and restauranteur Abraham Quintanilla, Jr. and Marcella Ofelia Samora. By 1980 Selena y Los Dinos were performing at her father's restaurant. But the restaurant failed, Quintanillo went bankrupt and they were evicted. They moved to Corpus Christie, Texas. To help make ends meet they would then go on to perform at street fairs, weddings and quinceaneras (big celebrations for a young lady's fifteenth birthday). Although Selena grew up only speaking English, her father taught her Spanish, which she learned to speak quite well after a while.

Selena went on to become one of the most celebrated Mexican-American performers of all time, making her first recording in 1982. 1984 arrived with Selena Y Los Dinos first LP on Freddie Records. Soon there was "Alpha," "And the Winner is...,", "Preciosa," and "Monequito de Trapo" ("Rag Doll"). In 1987 at the Tejano Music Awards, she was voted Female Vocalist of the Year. She would go on to win it it nine years in a row. She is credited with, for a while, bringing tejano music into the mainstream. Her debut album, Selena, came out in 1989. A Tejano is a Mexican-American born in Texas.

In 1990 this soprano released her second album, Ven Conmigo, (Come With Me) which went gold (over five hundred thousand copies sold). It included one of her most popular dance singles, "Baila Esta Cumbia."

Entre a Mi Mundo (Come Into My World) in 1992 sold over three hundred thousand records, and included what was to be her signature song, "Como la Flor" ("Like a Flower"). She was the first female tejano singer to have such success. In that same year Selena, over the strong objections of her father, and unbeknownst to him, eloped with fellow band member Chris Perez.

!Live! concert in Nuevo Leon on the Mexican/Texas border brought out more than seventy thousand people, and as a recording, again sold five hundred thousand copies. In 2005, on the tenth anniversary of Selena's death, a concert in her honor was televised. Selena !VIVE! became the highest rated, most watched Spanish-language telecast ever.

In 1994 came Amor Prohibido (Forbidden Love) which brought forth such singles as "Amor Prohibido" and "No Me Queda Mas" ("I Don't Have Anything Left"). It is still one of the best-selling Latin recordings (five hundred thousand copies), and considered one of the most important Latin records in the latter part of the twentieth century. It is among the Billboard top 100 albums of all time.

Selena's duet with Alvaro Torres hit the number one spot on Billboard's Top Latin songs with "Buenos Amigos." Her popularity soared and she began touring throughout the United States, wearing her very provocative outfits, including New York City, Puerto Rico, and Central and South America. She now was a rhythm and blues (r & b) singer, but also did techno pop, disco, urban pop, country and western, reggae, funk, and cumbia dance music.

Selena Quintanilla-Perez died of a gunshot wound on March 31, 1995 in Corpus Christie, Texas. She is buried there. She was shot by Yolanda Saldivar, a founder of Selena's fan club, a good friend, and a manager of Selena Etc. boutiques, who had been accused of the embezzlement of over thirty thousand dollars. Saldivar was convicted of first-degree murder and sentenced to life in prison. There were boutiques in Corpus Christie and San Antonio, with plans for another in Puerto Rico. The memorials and vigils for Selena were overwhelming. Such important performers as Gloria Estefan, Madonna, Julio Iglesias and Celia Cruz sent condolences. Selena's collaboration with MAC cosmetics just before her death, posthumously made her the bestselling celebrity cosmetics brand in history. When People magazine issued a posthumous Selena edition, it sold out and has become a collector's item.

In 1995, just before her death, Selena recorded her first crossover album, Dreaming of You. It was released after her death and debuted at number one on Billboard 200, over three hundred thousand sold in one week, and eventually three and one half million, the first Latin woman ever to accomplish that. She had also begun a hopeful movie career with a small part in Don Juan DeMarco, starring Johnny Depp, Marlon Brando and Faye Dunaway.

Billboard declared her the Best Selling Latin Female Singer of the 1990s and the Best Female Vocalist of the 1980s. The Albany Times-Union actually declared her one of the "100 Coolest Americans in History."

The governor of Texas at the time, George W. Bush, declared April 16 "Selena Day" in Texas. In Corpus Christie there is a museum and statue in her honor. In 1997 the very successful biographical film, Selena, was released, with Jennifer Lopez in the role and also with Edward James Olmos and Jon Seda. There have also been numerous biographical documentaries on her, as well as crime documentaries. Selena has been inducted into the Billboard Latin Music Hall of Fame, the South Texas Music Hall of Fame, the Tejano Music Hall of Fame and the Hard Rock Cafe Hall of Fame, and is enshrined in the Hollywood Walk of Fame. She has come to be regarded as one of the most influential Latin performers of the twentieth century. In 2011 she was honored with a United States postage stamp.

#122- *Elizabeth Ann Seton (1774-1821)*

First Native-born American Saint

Elizabeth Ann Bayley was born in New York City on August 28, 1774, an Episcopalian, and the daughter of an outstanding physician and Columbia professor, Dr. Richard Bayley and his wife Catherine. Her family was wealthy and she was a belle of society. However, her mother died when she a child and her father remarried to Charlotte Amelia Barclay. Even at this time of her life she was very devout, going about nursing he sick and dying. But when the parents separated and her father went to Europe to study. Her stepmother did not take her, and she went to live with relatives. This was a dark time in her life, feeling abandoned by all.

Marrying in 1794 to William Magee Seton, a wealthy shipping merchant, was a good change. In time they had three daughters and two sons. In 1797 Elizabeth Seton helped found the Society for the Relief of Poor Widows with Small Children, New York's first charitable society. At the end of the eighteenth century, France and the United States were at odds, and American shipping was greatly harmed. When William Seton's business was also harmed as a result, and his health declined, they went on a trip to Italy to try to recoup. It did not work. William Seton died in Italy in 1803. The kindness expressed by her Catholic friends in Italy and back home awed her and got her interested in the Catholic faith. When she returned to America she converted to Catholicism in 1805. Although the Catholics embraced her, her original friends ignored her, and her stepmother disinherited her. First she tried to open a school, but that did not succeed.

But things began to turn around when, at the request of Archbishop John Carroll, Father Louis William Valentine Dunbourg, a visiting priest and the president of St. Mary's College in Baltimore, asked her to start a school there. She opened the Paca Street School for girls. It was the first Catholic parochial school in the United States.

She decided to be become a Catholic nun in 1809 and moved to Emmitsburg, in Maryland, where she organized the Sisters of Charity of St. Joseph. They were nicknamed "God's Geese" due to their white winghead pieces. She was the first mother superior of the order and from then on was always referred to as "Mother Seton". She started with the St. Joseph's Academy and Free School for girls with a day school for orphans and the poor. In 1814 the Orphan Asylum of Philadelphia opened, the first Catholic orphanage. She is also given at least some of the credit the founding of the first Catholic hospital, maternity hospital and parish school.

The Sisters of Charity of St. Joseph grew to twenty communities by the time of her death due to tuberculosis on January 4, 1821 in Emmittsburg. The Roman Catholic Church beatified her in 1963 and canonized her as a saint on September 14, 1975. She is the first native-born American to be so honored. Her feast day is January 4, and she is the patron saint of seafarers.

In Emmittsburg, where she is buried, there is the National Shrine of St. Elizabeth Ann Seton. There is also the Shrine of St. Elizabeth Ann Bayley Seton in New York City at the site of her former residence and her statue in St. Raymond's Cemetery in the Bronx, New York. There is a Seton Hall University in New Jersey and a Seton Hill University in Pennsylvania, and schools named after her everywhere. And there are churches in at least three states in her honor. She has been inducted into both the Maryland and National Women's Hall of Fame.

#123- *Beverly Sills* (1929-2007)

America's Queen of Opera

American operatic soprano Belle Miriam Silverman, nicknamed "Bubbles," was born in Brooklyn, New York on May 25, 1929 to Jewish immigrants Morris Silverman, an insurance broker, and Sonia Markovna, a musician known professionally as Shirley Bahn. As Bubbles Silverman, she first appeared on radio's "Rainbow House" when she was barely a toddler. At eight years of age she was in a short film, "Uncle Sol Solves It." From then on she became Beverly Sills. At ten years of age she won the popular Major Bowes' Amateur Hour radio program, and then became a frequent guest on the Capitol Family Hour. In 1945 she made her stage debut touring a dozen cities with the Jacob J. Stuart Company, doing operettas by Gilbert and Sullivan. Gilbert and Sullivan had been enormously famous composers of comic operas. Two years later she debuted as Frasquita in Bizet's Carmen with the Philadelphia Civic Opera Company. Continuing to further her career she then toured North America with the Charles Wagner Opera Company. 1953 found Beverly Sills with the San Francisco Opera as Helen of Troy in Mifistofele and Donna Elvira in Don Giovanni. In 1954 she was Aida in Salt Lake City.

But it was in 1955 at the New York Opera Company that Sills finally made it. She received critical acclaim for her role as Rosalinde in Johann Strauss' Die Fledermaus. Her reputation was secured when she performed Douglas Moore's The Ballad of Baby Doe in 1958. In the meantime she married journalist Peter Greenough in Ohio. They had two very sickly children and Beverly Sills curtailed her performances to be with her children. In 1960 they moved to Massachusetts and she performed at the Opera Company of Boston in Manon, one of her finest and favorite roles. These were followed by other successes, such as Mozart's The Magic Flute, and Queen of the Night.

Already famous, her performance, back at the New York City Opera, as Cleopatra in Handel's Giulio Cesare in 1966 made her now an international superstar. She went on to appear in The Golden Cockerel, Manon, Lucia di Lammermoor and Il trittico. Once again she received great praised for her performance in Richard Strauss' 1969 Ariadne auf Naxos. From here she became a favorite on television talk shows, such as those with Johnny Carson, Dick Cavett and Dinah Shore. With these appearances she let world know that opera was not stuffy and the performers were not unreachable. She even did The Muppet Show, and had her own Emmy winning show, Lifestyles with Beverly Sills. In 1971 her performance in The Golden Cockerel at the New York City Opera was televised. She would go on to record eighteen full operas.

Although she did perform successfully in London's Covent Garden, Milan's La Scala and in Switzerland, Venice, Vienna, Paris, Mexico City and Buenos Aires, among other foreign venues, she was most at home performing in the United States. She made the cover of Newsweek after her performance in La Scala, but she also made the cover of Time in 1971, referring to Beverly Sills as "America's Queen of Opera."

After many years of dispute with Rudolph Bing, general manager of the Metropolitan Opera, who felt American audiences only wanted Italian singers, Beverly Sills appeared there after Bing retired in 1975. She debuted in the Siege of Corinth, and received eighteen standing sustained ovations of appreciation. She went on to appear in La traviata, Lucia di Lammermoor, Thais and Don Pasquale. She still stayed with New York City Opera, performing in The Merry Widow, Il Turco in Italia, and in La Loca, which was written for Beverly Sills by Gian Carlo Menotti for her fiftieth birthday. Her farewell performance was in 1980 at the San Diego Opera with Die Fledermaus.

She began to put on recitals in mid-size cities and college campuses so that people who never had the opportunity to hear opera could. In 1979 Sills became a member of the board of directors of the New York City Opera, and chairperson in 1991, taking a struggling institution and making it wildly successful. And in 1991 became a board member of the Metropolitan Opera, later becoming its chair until 2005. She resigned due to the ill health of her husband, who died in 2006. In 1987 she published Beverly: An Autobiography. During all this time, she still managed to devote her efforts for the March of Dimes, even serving on the board of directors. The March of Dimes is a non-profit organization dedicated to the prevention of birth defects and infant death. She herself had been diagnosed with ovarian cancer in 1974, and died in Valhalla, New York of lung cancer on July 2, 2007.

Besides being granted the Medal of Distinction from Barnard College, she also received honorary doctorates from Temple University, New York University and the New England Conservatory of Arts. Harvard University not only gave her an honorary doctorate, but also its Hasty Pudding Woman of the Year Award given to those who have shown "a lasting and impressive contribution to the world of entertainment." Beverly Sills had been named Musical America's Woman of the Year, received the Handel Medallion, the Recording Industry

American Culture Award, the Golden Baton from the American Symphony Orchestra League, and the Pearl S. Buck Award. She has been inducted into the Long Island Music Hall of Fame and the National Women's Hall of Fame. She has been the recipient of the Presidential Medal of Freedom, the National Medal of Arts, and a deserved Kennedy Center Honoree.

#124- Bessie Smith (1898-1937)

Empress of the Blues

Bessie Smith was born on April 15, 1898 in Chattanooga, Tennessee, to William and Laura Smith, and went on to become America's greatest blues and jazz singer in the 1920s and 1930s. By the age of nine, she had lost both her parents and was raised by an aunt. Smith became a street singer, but she soon joined the Moses Stokes traveling troop, first as a dancer, then singing with Ma Rainey's Rabbit Foot Minstrels, doing cabarets, tent shows and vaudeville. Following this she joined the Florida Cotton Blossoms. She was a fine powerful, contralto, the deepest of the female voices.

Bessie was huge and tall and soon became the sold-out, main attraction on the African American vaudeville circuit, earning a great deal of money, and encouraging her fans to make a lot of noise. In 1923 she began a decade of recording "Downhearted Blues," selling over a million copies the first year alone. The 1920s were the peak years of her career. She had become known as the "Empress of the Blues," was the highest paid performer and had her own customized railroad car. In 1925 she married Jack Gee, and made a short film, St. Louis Blues, and had performed regularly on the radio, as well. And by this time she already had had big hits with "Nobody Knows When You're Down and Out," "Back Water Blues" and "Empty Bed Blues." Bessie Smith even did Broadway, in Pansy. The show was a flop, but Smith got good reviews. Some of her other popular tunes were "After You've Gone," "Baby, Won't You Please Come Home," "Lost Your Head Blues," and "Careless Love Blues."

All the jazz greats, such as Louis Armstrong and Jack Teagarden, admired her immensely, and would come to her shows and listen in wonderment. She even had duets with the likes of Armstrong and Sidnet Bechet. But by 1930 she had separated from Gee and her alcoholic habit, her lack of business sense, and the changing times, brought this phenomenal performer to a low point. She did begin a relationship with one Richard Morgan, who stayed with her right up until her death. She did make somewhat of a comeback in 1933 with "Gimme a Pigfoot and a Bottle of Beer," one of her truly best. But this was really the end of things. She felt she could try to make a comeback touring in 1936 and 1937.

While on tour she was in a car crash near Clarksdale, Mississippi, and larger than life Bessie Smith died there on September 26, 1937. She is buried in Sharon Hill, Pennsylvania. Columbia Records released "The Bessie Smith Story," containing forty-eight of her songs. Due to this, she became more famous after her death. And her influence in music has been shown by her inductions into the following: this great lady is enshrined in the Jazz Hall of Fame, the Rock and Roll Hall of Fame, The Big Band Hall of Fame, the Blues Hall of Fame, and the National Women's Hall of Fame, as well as being awarded a Grammy Lifetime Achievement Award. Three of Bessie Smith's songs are in the hall of fame, as well: "St. Louis Blues," "Empty Bed Blues," and "Downhearted Blues." Janis Joplin was most responsible for putting a headstone on Bessie Smith's grave, and Dory Previn wrote song about it: "A Stone for Bessie Smith." Her influence can be seen in the work of Joplin, Aretha Franklin and Billie Holiday.

Edward Albee's 1959 play, "The Death of Bessie Smith" was based on a long held misconception the Bessie died as a result of racial medical neglect. In 1994 her likeness graced a United States postage stamp, and in 2001 she was the subject of the musical The Devil's Music: the Life and Music of Bessie Smith. She had been the subject of The Band's song, "Bessie Smith," and a short story, "Blue Melody" in 1948. Queen Latifah portrayed her in the 2015 film, Bessie, with actress Mo'Nique in the role of Ma Rainey.

#125- *Margaret Chase Smith (1897-1995)*

Declaration of Conscience

Margaret Madeline Chase Smith, born in Skowhegan, Maine on December 14, 1897 to barber George and Carrie Chase, must be considered one of America's most daring and principled women of the twentieth century. In 1916 she began work as a telephone operator, and later became an executive there. In addition, she became circulation manager for the Independent Reporter. By 1926 she was elected president of the Maine Federation of Business and Professional Women's Clubs.

In 1930 she married local politician Clyde Smith, who was elected to Congress in 1936. In 1940 he died, and Margaret Chase Smith was selected to fulfill his term. She then chose to run herself and was re-elected four times. She was a member of the House Naval Affairs Committee and the House Armed Services Committee, working diligently to further the position of women in the military. She was called Mother of the Waves. She was later honored with the Naval Heritage Award for those efforts. During World War II she traveled on an investigative journey to the South Pacific.

In 1944 she was chair of the Maine Republican convention, and four years later ran for the United States Senate. Not only did she defeat two opponents in a primary battle, but went on to win the general election with seventy-one percent of the vote, the greatest in Maine history. Margaret Chase Smith served until 1973, the only woman up to then elected four times. She was the first woman to serve in both houses of Congress in Maine. She began wearing a red rose to work, campaigning to have the rose become the official flower of the United States. It was passed in 1987.

She showed what it meant to stand up for what you believe is right, regardless of the possible dire consequences. During the Senator Joseph McCarthy disruptive fear campaign, he accused a vast number of people of being un-American, communists or subversive, she went against this powerful man, in the same Republican party, becoming his greatest adversary. She felt there were no facts to substantiate his charges, causing unnecessary widespread turmoil. In her "Declaration of Conscience" speech she declared: "I speak as a Repblican. I speak as a woman. I speak as a United States Senator. I speak as an American…I think it is high time that we remember that the Constitution as amended speaks not only of freedom of speech, but also of trial by jury, not trial by accusation." McCarthy had her removed from her seat on the committee and replaced by California senator Richard Nixon. It backfired. Smith was granted the Freedom Foundation Award for Americanism in 1950.

McCarthy put pressure on to have her defeated for re-election in 1954, but she won again in a landslide, and in 1955 was given the Distinguised Service Award from the Reserve Officers Association, in which she was a lieutenant-colonel. The 1960 election broke the record again. In 1952 she had been considered as a possible vice presidential running mate to Dwight Eisenhower, and in 1964 she tried to get the Republican party nomination for president. She did not get it, but was the first woman to have her name placed in nomination.

Margaret Chase Smith represented what all women, what all Americans, should try to be. She was often "Woman of the Year" and on the lists of the "Ten Most Admired Women." In the 1998 mini-series, From Earth to Moon, Smith is depicted, as she was in the television movie, Tail Gunner Joe. She died at age ninety-seven as a result of a stroke on May 29, 1995. and was laid to rest at the Margaret Chase Smith Memorial Library in Skowhegan.

In 2007 a fifty-eight cent stamp was issued in her likeness. Her portrait is on display in the Augusta, Maine capitol building. She has been made a fellow of the American Academy of Arts and Sciences, inducted into both the Maine Women's Hall of Fame and the National Women's Hall of Fame, and had been presented with the Presidential Medal of Freedom.

#126- *Gertrude Stein (1874-1946)*

The Lost Generation

Gertrude Stein, possibly the greatest literary influence of America up to her time, was born in Allegheny, Pennsylvania on February 3, 1874, went to Vienna and Paris as a child, and grew up in a wealthy family in Oakland, California, the youngest of five children. She graduated Radcliffe College summa cum lauda ("with highest honors") in 1897, then spending another four years at Johns Hopkins medical school before abandoning medicine as a career.

When her parents died, she went to live for a while with relatives in Baltimore. But Stein, a brilliant woman of independent means, and after a while not wanting a career in medicine, left for Europe, London in 1902, and Paris in 1903. Her address, 27 rue de Fleures, was to become a salon that welcomed more famous, and beginning, artists than probably any other in history. She once stated that "America is my country, but Paris is my hometown."

Here she met and became friends with Pablo Picasso and Paul Cezanne. They influenced her way of thinking and she influenced their way of painting. And they all were friends with artist Henri Matisse. Here she became a world-class art collector and a pioneer of Modernist literature and art. Three Lives was her first important work, and in it she demonstrates her realistic style of prose, in a simple way, reflecting her deep awareness. 1914 brought Tender Buttons, a rather difficult and controversial book of poems, and establishing Stein as "eccentric."

With the outbreak of World War I, Stein worked for the American Fund for French Wounded. After the war she returned to her salon, remaining throughout the 1920s and 1930s. Every important writer and artist who came to Paris during this period visited her and sought her advice: gatherings that brought together the talent and thinking that produced modern literature and art. Ezra Pound, Ernest Hemingway, Paul Cezanne, Paul Robeson, Sinclair Lewis, Thornton Wilder, F. Scott Fitzgerald, Sherwood Anderson, Ford Madox Ford, Andre Gide, and others were among her guests.

The Making of Americans in 1925 was her greatest work, and really demonstrated her ability at character analysis, following a series of portraits of her famous friends who visited her for over a decade. This was followed by Ten Portraits and Lucy Church, Amiably (1930), Before the Flowers of Friendship Faded, Friendship Faded (1931), Matisse, Picasso and Gertrude Stein and Operas and Plays (1932). In 1933 she enhanced her already cult-like, world-wide fame with the publication of The Autobiography of Alice B. Toklas. Toklas was her partner, but in truth, this was her own memoir.

In 1934 she famously toured the United States (191 days, 37 cities, 23 states), and when it was over, Gertrude Stein was the most noted female author in the world. Her words were published the next year as Lectures in America. And to add to this her comic opera, Four Saints in Three Acts (1934) appeared on stage in New York, Chicago and Hartford. The next few years saw Picasso, another autobiography, Everybody's Autobiography, stating "It takes a lot of time to be a genius, you have to sit around so much doing nothing, really doing nothing."

After World War II, Wars I Have Seen was published, as was Brewsie and Willie, dealing with American servicemen in Paris after the war. Other works were Fernhurst, Useful Knowledge, Ida, and The Mother of Us All, an opera based on the life of Susan B. Anthony, which appeared in New York and other cities in 1947.

She died in the American Hospital in Neuilly-sur-Seine, France from surgery for stomach cancer, on July 27, 1946. In the imaginative 2011 film, Midnight in Paris, she is portrayed by actress Kathy Bates. Loving Repeating is a musical based on the writings of Stein. Stein was known to have coined the phrases "a rose is a rose is a rose" and "the lost generation." Some of "the lost generation" are those same artists influenced by her, who visited her in Paris. The influence she exerted should not be under-estimated. She loved words, and the use of words, using unorthodox methods to achieve a desired result, such as repetition, fragments and juxtopositioning. "There is no there there."

"We know that we (women) can do what men can do, but we still don't know that men can do what women do. That's absolutely crucial. We can't go on doing two jobs."

#127- *Lucy Stone* (1818-1893)

"The Lucy Stones"

Lucy Stone was born on August 13, 1818 in West Brookfield, Massachusetts to Francis and Hannah Stone, and went on to become one of the more popular feminist leaders. At sixteen she began teaching and found that as a woman she was being paid far less than her male counterparts. This affected the rest of her life, and she knew she must find a way to advance.

She graduated Oberlin College with honors in 1847, the first Massachusetts woman to graduate college, and at the encouragement of famous abolitionist William Lloyd Garrison, began touring for the Massachusetts Anti-Slavery Society. In 1850 she helped found the National Women's Rights Convention in Worcester, Massachusetts. Her oratory skills were very impressive, effective and persuasive. She had now become a well-paid speaker and leader in both the anti-slavery and women's rights movements.

In the early 1850s she traveled for thirteen weeks with Lucretia Mott to the "western" states, those west of Pennsylvania and Virginia, mostly in Illinois, Indiana, Kentucky and Missouri. In 1855 she married anti-slavery leader, Dr. Henry Blackwell, brother of Dr. Elizabeth Blackwell, and again went on a very effective and ambitious lecture tour, covering Maine, Massachusetts, New Hampshire, Vermont, Rhode Island, Connecticut, New York, Pennsylvania, New Jersey, Delaware, Ohio, Indiana, Illinois, Michigan Wisconsin, and Washington, D.C. Eventually the couple settled in Orange, New Jersey. In 1868 she helped found the State Woman's Suffrage Association of New Jersey and became its president.

However, at about this time Stone switched her primary vigor toward women's rights over anti-slavery. She became quite controversial even within her own circle. She disputed with Frederick Douglass about putting women's rights before anti-slavery. She also fought with Elizabeth Cady Stanton on the issue of divorce. For a while she also began wearing "bloomers" that were all the rage, giving women more flexibility of movement.

She was also instrumental in forming the Woman's National Loyal League to encourage passage of the thirteenth amendment. In 1869 she helped found, and was the first president of, the American Woman's Suffrage Association. She remained president until 1872. Somewhat of a feud erupted with the women's rights group and Lucy Stone split from Susan B. Anthony and Elizabeth Cady Stanton. Stone supported passage of the fifteenth amendment, even though it gave voting rights to African American men, but not to any women. She felt it would lead eventually include women. Anthony and Stanton heartily disagreed and almost came to calling Lucy Stone a traitor to their cause. But she had also founded the Woman's Journal.

In 1887 the two groups reunited under the name National American Woman Suffrage Association with Elizabeth Cady Stanton as president, and Lucy Stone as editor of the Woman's Journal, until her death in 1893.

Lucy Stone died in Dorchester, Massachusetts of stomach cancer on October 19, 1893. Her popularity was so great that feminist leaders and lecturers became known as "Lucy Stones." Her death was the most widely reported of any American woman up to that time. A 1968 fifty-cent stamp was issued in her likeness, and there is a Massachusetts park named in her honor, and she is featured on the Boston Women's Heritage Trail. In addition, there is a bust in Boston's Fanuil Hall. She is in the National Women's Hall of Fame.

#128- *Harriet Beecher Stowe (1811-1896)*

Uncle Tom's Cabin

Lyman Beecher was a preacher and abolishionist of the early nineteenth century, and the head of an outstanding family. His son was Henry Ward Beecher and his two daughters were Catherine the educator and Harriet Elisabeth the writer. Harriet was born on June 14, 1811 in Litchfield, Connecticut. For a short time she assisted her teacher sister.

Lyman and Roxana Beecher moved the family to Cincinnati where the sisters opened a school, and Harriet began to write. She joined the Semi Colon literary club and in 1834 she won a contest with her "A New England Story." In 1836 she married fellow club member Professor Calvin E. Stowe of Lyman Beecher's Lane Theological Seminary. From about this time forward, Harriet Beecher Stowe began getting more and more angry about the evils of slavery. She heard stories from agents of the Underground Railroad, and from this came the idea of Uncle Tom's Cabin. She had become on friendly terms with other abolitionist people in Cincinnati, such as the Blackwells, who would comment on her manuscript and check while she would be busy with her own child rearing and domestic duties. In 1850 the Stowes moved to Brunswick, Maine where her husband began teaching at Bowdoin College, and then two years later to Andover, Massachusetts to teach at the theological seminary there.

In the meantime, Harriet, with help from Cincinnati friends had her book serialized in The National Era, a Washington, D. C. publication, and soon after Uncle Tom's Cabin came out in book form. In the first year it sold three hundred thousand copies and in five years it sold half a million copies. However, it was not really a true picture of the southern states, but her way of writing made it so very popular and widely read, and many northerners, and even foreigners, believed she depicted a true picture. It was one of the most influential novels ever written, definitely energizing abolitionists by showing slavery to be degrading and humiliating, and plantation life only romantic for the owners. Needless to say, it angered southerners.

A play based on the book was widely traveled in the northern states, and both the play and the book were harshly criticized in the south as being grossly misleading. It certainly influenced elections. Abraham Lincoln supposedly called Harriet Beecher Stowe "the little woman whose book caused the Civil War" when she visited him in November, 1862.

After this success she continued to write. She had gone to Europe and wrote Sunny Memories of Foreign Lands in 1854, Dred: A Tale of the Great Dismal Swamp in 1856, and The Minister's Wooing in 1859.

Following the Civil War the Stowes moved to Mandarin, Florida, where they spent part of every year there, and the rest in Hartford, Connecticut. In Florida she helped found a school that was integrated, many decades before most of the southern states did that. In Hartford she helped to found the Hartford School of Art. In 1866 she wrote The Little Foxes, and in 1868 joined the staff of Hearth and Home magazine, but only for a short time. Old Town Folks in 1869, Little Pussy Willow in 1870, My Wife and I in 1872, followed by Palmetto Leaves in 1873 came later. The 1872 book was an attack on Victoria Claflin, as part of a Claflin/Beecher feud. In all, Harriet Beecher Stowe wrote over thirty books and memoirs. She also became a campaigner for married women's rights.

She wrote a goodly number of books, but Uncle Tom's Cabin was not only her most popular, but one of the most influential novels of all time. She has not only been inducted into both the Ohio and Connecticut Women's Hall of Fame, but also into the National Women's Hall of Fame. And she has a bust in the Hall of Fame of Great Americans. At times she wrote under the pen name Christopher Crowfield. Her husband died in 1886, and Harriet Beecher Stowe died of complications from what we now know as Alzeimers disease on July 1, 1896 in Hartford. Her next door neighbor, Mark Twain, saw the sad progression of this disease on her. Her home in Hartford, as well as the one in Brunswick are museums. She is buried in Andover's Phillips Exeter Academy. In 2007 a postage stamp was issued in her likeness.

Group Eleven

Maria Tallchief-
Babe Didrikson Zaharias

#129- *Maria Tallchief (1925-2013)*

First American Prima Ballerina

Elizabeth Marie Betty Tall Chief, known to her family as Betty Marie, known as an Osage tribal member Ki He Kah Stah Tsa, and known to the ballet world as Maria Tallchief, was born on January 24, 1925 in Fairfax, Oklahoma, on the Osage reservation. Her father Alexander was a very well-to-do member of the tribe, but her mother Ruth was not a Native American. The family summered in Colorado Springs where, even at the age of three, Maria would take ballet lessons. She would go onto become America's first major prima ballerina, and a trail blazer for Native Americans in dance.

Since Maria and her sister were both very much into dance, the family moved to Los Angeles in 1933 in hopes that the girls would get ointo Hollywood musicals. At twelve years of age she began studying with Brontislava Nijinski and became convinced that ballet truly was to be her life. She graduated Beverly Hills High School and left for New York City. First she was with Serge Denham and went on a Canadian tour in small roles. Choreographer Agnes DeMille took a liking to her, and urged her to change her name to something Russian-sounding. She refused, but started using a varied form of her middle name, Marie to Maria, and making her surname one word, Tall Chief to Tallchief.

Eventually she signed on with the New York City-based Balle Russe de Monte Carlo, in the corps de ballet, staying with them for five years, appearing in seven different productions. Slowly she began to get bigger roles. Here is also where she met choreographer George Balanchine and both their lives would be changed. Under him she matured and in 1944 she performed a solo in Song of Norway, and was the understudy, but soon became the second lead.

After World War ll Maria Tallchief stayed with Balanchine and performed in the Paris Ballet, in Le Bourgeois Gentilhomme and Sylvia Pas de Deux. The French loved her. She left the Ballet Russe to join the new Balanchine New York City Ballet and she was his first star. However, she also was had become in demand elsewhere and performed with the Royal Dutch, the Hamburg, the San Francisco and the Chicago Opera ballets, as well as others. In 1949 came Firebird. She was sensational, and rose to the top of the ballet world. This was followed a few years later by a then little-known ballet, The Nutcracker, where her role as the Sugar Plum Fairy alone made this to become an all-time favorite. And Swan Lake and Orpheus only cemented her as the prima ballerina in America. Maria Tallchief was now on television dancing and promoting ballet in America as had never before been promoted. Her athletic, energetic, yet graceful performances changed the American view of ballet.

Eventually she left the New York City Ballet and joined the American Ballet Theater as the prima ballerina. During this period she went on to become the first American dancer to perform at Moscow's famed Bolshoi Theatre. In the early 1960s Maria Tallchief performed mostly dramatic roles for them. She retired in the mid-1960s. In 1966 Cinderella was her last performance. In the 1970s she became ballet director of the Lyric Opera of Chicago, and in 1981 debuted the Chicago City Ballet. Until her death she remained Artistic Advisor to the Chicago Festival Ballet. She married Balanchine in 1946, but it was annulled in 1952. She then married pilot Elmourza (Elmo) Natirboff in 1952, but were divorced in 1954. However, her marriage to Henry (Buzz) Paschen, Jr. in 1956 lasted until his death.

June 29, 1953 was declared "Maria Tallchief Day" in Oklahoma. The Tulsa Historical Society erected "The Five Moons." of which one is Maria Tallchief. The documentary, Dancing for Mr. B in 1989 featured her. In 2006, the Metropolitan Museum of Art paid her special honor with "A Tribute to Ballet Great Maria Tallchief," and in 2007 PBS's documentary, Maria Tallchief, was aired. In 2011 The Chicago History Museum awarded her the "Making History Award: Distinction in the Performing Arts." The Washington Press Club twice named her "Woman of the Year," and The New York Times declared her "one of the most brilliant American dancers of the 20th century."

Of the honors she received, two were most important. In 1996 Maria Tallchief was honored at the Kennedy Center for Lifetime Achievement. On her behalf it was said she was, "both the inspiration and the living expression of the best....one of the most vital and beautiful chapters in the history of American Dance." In 1999 the National Endowment of the Arts recognized her with a National Medal of Art. And, she is, of course, in the National Women's Hall of Fame.

In December of 2012 she broke her hip, and due to the complications of the surgery, Maria Tallchief died in Chicago on April 11, 2013. There have been many biographies written on her life, as well as documentaries. Her own autobiography is Maria Tallchief: American Prima Ballerina. Her sister, Marjorie Tallchief, was also a ballerina. Upon Maria Tallchief's death, her daughter said her mother "raised the bar high and strove for excellence in everything she did."

#130- *Ida M. Tarbell (1857-1944)*

Muckracker

Ida Minerva Tarbell was born in Erie County, Pennsylvania on November 5, 1857 to Franklin and Esther Tarbell. Her father was, among other things, a small time oilman in the oil rich lands of northwestern Pennsylvania, whose business was badly impacted by the practices of the monopolistic Standard Oil Company. After graduation in 1880, as the only woman, from Allegheny College in Pennsylvania, she became a teacher in Ohio, but then became associate editor of The Chautaquan. This was the official publication of the Chataquan Institution, an adult education movement. Soon after she went to France to study at the Sorbonne (University of Paris), a school whose reputation for academic excellence dated back to the middle ages, delving into historical research. Here she co-wrote a biography of Madame Roland, a leader of the "salon" during the French Revolution, a place where politics and culture were discussed, who eventually was herself led to the guillotine, which was the apparatus designed to carry out executions by beheading. Upon returning to America in 1898, she became an editor of McClure's Magazine. In this atmosphere she pioneered what it was to be both journalist and investigator, meeting many famous and influential people. Her writing brought many new readers to the magazine. At this time she wrote a serialized biography of Napoleon. In 1900, her Life of Abraham Lincoln was published. The Lincoln information was used on a lecture circuit, as well.

A robber baron was an American businessman who used unscrupulous methods to get rich. After interviewing robber baron Henry "Hell Hound" Rogers, one of the brains behind Standard Oil and the railroads, who thought she was to compose a complimentary piece, she became aware of those business policies that hurt her father's business, which she later exposed, such as privileges allowed to monopolies, but not to independents, and the giving of inside information of independents to those monopolies for the purposes of sabotage. Ida Tarbell's History of the Standard Oil Company in 1904 made the world aware of unfair and strong-arm practices within major corporations. She depicted John D. Rockefeller a vicious money-grabber. It had been first serialized in McClure's from 1902 to 1904. This was the era of the "muckrackers," a group of reform-minded and progressive newspaper writers who attacked establishment corruption, during President Teddy Roosevelt's tenure, and she was a leader. The movement to outlaw or curtail the power of the "barons" was strengthened enormously because of this book. Standard Oil was forced to break up in 1911. This work ranked number five on New York University's top 100 works of twentieth century journalism. After McClure's she became associate editor of The American Magazine from 1906 until 1915, while continuing to write. He Knew Lincoln, The Traffic of Our Times, The Ways of Women, and The Business of Being A Woman were published during this period.

More Lincoln works followed: another Life of Abraham Lincoln in 1923 and A Reporter For Lincoln in 1927. Her autobiography, All in a Day's Work, was published in 1939. Charles Klein's play, The Lion and the Mouse, is supposedly based on Tarbell's efforts. Ida Tarbell died of pneumonia on January 6, 1944 in Bridgeport, Connecticut. The Ida Tarbell House in Connecticut is on the National Historic Landmarks list. She is also enshrined in the National Women's Hall of Fame, and in 2002, was pictured on a commemorative stamp.

#131- *Elizabeth Taylor (1932-2011)*

Maggie and Martha and So Much More

Elizabeth Rosemund Taylor was born in London, England of American parents, Francis and Sara, on February 27, 1932. Her father was an art dealer representing his uncle's interests. In 1939 she came home, first to Pasadena, and then Beverly Hills, California. At age nine she was signed to a one-year contract with Universal Studios for two hundred dollars a week, and appeared in There's One Born Every Minute. She changed studios and then came Lassie Come Home and her breakthrough performance in National Velvet. From then on her future was secured. Soon followed were The Courage of Lassie, Cynthia, Life With Father, and Little Women, in which she played the artistic Amy.

In 1950, a now much more grown-up Elizabeth Taylor appeared in Father of the Bride with Spencer Tracy. She had very successfully transcended into more mature roles, including Father's Little Dividend, and about to become one of the most publicized and highest paid actresses of all time. By this time she already married hotel heir, Conrad "Nicky" Hilton. But they divorced in 1951. A Place in the Sun followed as did a marriage to actor Michael Wilding, which lasted until 1957. She now came into her own as a serious actress with Ivanhoe, The Girl Who Had Everything, The Last Time I Saw Paris, Elephant Walk, Giant and Raintree County, for which she received her first "Oscar" nomination. In 1957 she married, for the third time, producer Mike Todd, and the next year was again nominated for an "Oscar" for portraying Maggie, The Cat on a Hot Tin Roof. Unfortunately Mike Todd was killed in an airplane crash in 1958, and soon after this the first of Elizabeth Taylor's scandals erupted. Popular singer Eddie Fisher, who was married to pretty actress Debbie Reynolds, began to be seen quite often with Taylor. It should also be noted that Fisher and Reynolds had been in the Todd and Taylor wedding party. As things developed Reynolds appeared as being terribly hurt and Elizabeth Taylor depicted as the terrible woman wrecking a happy home. Eddie Fisher was considered a cad. Reynolds and Fisher divorced, and for the fourth time Elizabeth Taylor married, this time to Eddie Fisher in 1959.

That same year she was again nominated for an "Oscar" for Suddenly Last Summer. She and Katherine Hepburn were nominated for the same film, and both lost. However, she did receive the David di Donatello Award for her work. The next year she finally did win her "Oscar," portraying Gloria Wandrous in Butterfield 8. The 1950s ended with Elizabeth Taylor starting as a new grown-up actress to being nominated for the "Oscar" four times and finally winning it. She also experienced marriage four times.

And yet there was so much more to come. In 1963 she portrayed the title character in the forty million dollar epic Cleopatra in which she was the first actress to earn one million dollars for a film. Richard Burton portrayed Marc Antony, and their spouses were ignored. Taylor and Burton became very much involved. Divorces followed and Elizabeth Taylor and Richard Burton were married in 1964. In 1965 she and Burton appeared in The Sandpiper. Who's Afraid of Virginia Woolf? came out the next year, again co-starring Burton. It would be her fifth "Oscar" nomination and second win, and for this she also was rewarded from the New York Film Critics, the National Board of Review and BAFTA. Following her "Oscar" winning role as Martha, she appeared in a number of films with top tier actors: Reflections in a Golden Eye with Marlon Brando, Secret Ceremony with Robert Mitchum, X, Y and Z with Michael Caine and Ash Wednesday with Henry Fonda. She also made The Taming of the Shrew, The Comedians, Dr. Faustus, Hammersmith Is Out and Under Milk Wood, all with Burton. As per her usual personal life, she divorced her fifth husband Richard Burton, and married sixth husband Richard Burton, and divorced him again.

Taylor again married, for the seventh time, to John Warner, a candidate for the United States Senate from Virginia, and a former Secretary of the Navy, for whom she tirelessly campaigned. He was sworn into office in 1979. But a political life was not for her. Eventually they divorced, and much later, in 1991 she married construction worker Larry Fortensky, lasting until 1996. He was her last.

She had made many television appearances on a variety of shows, and her own Elizabeth Taylor in London in 1963. She also made the television movies Divorce, His; Divorce, Hers, and in 2001, her final appearance in These Old Broads. In addition to all her Academy of Motion Picture Arts and Sciences nominations and "Oscars," she had also been honored by the Golden Globe Awards (Giant, Suddenly Last Summer, and Ash Wednesday), the National Review Board, the American Film Institute, the New York Film Critics, The Film Society of Lincoln Center and Photoplay magazine as well as the Silver Bear Award for Hammersmith Is Out, and a Cecil B. DeMille Award. Some other notable films she made were A Date With Judy, Julia Misbehaves, The VIPs, Beau Brummel, Boom!, and The Mirror Crack'd. Elizabeth Taylor even tackled the stage, appearing in The Little Foxes on Broadway and in London, and also Private Lives. She not only was made Dame Elizabeth Taylor by Queen Elizabeth ll, but was also given the Presidential Citizen Medal.

Elizabeth Taylor devoted a great deal of time, effort and money in the latter part of her life supporting efforts to find a cure for AIDS. She was presented with the Jean Hershholt Humanitarian Award, was an honoree of the Kennedy Center Honors and given a gala tribute from the Film Society of Lincoln Center. She died on March 23, 2011 in Los Angeles of congestive heart failure. During her life she had had many, many illnesses.

Elizabeth Taylor proved her greatness as an actress by rising up to and above her material. In all the films she made only six were nominated for best picture, and none won. But there is no doubt that she managed to become one of film's great actresses. In 1999 the American Film Institute named her the seventh greatest female legend. And unlike some others, she managed to cope with all those pressures of great success, hounding publicity and a turbulent very public private life, and did not quit.

#132- *Laurette Taylor (1883-1946)*

The Greatest Artist of Her Profession

Loretta Helen Cooney, daughter of James and Elizabeth Taylor, known later as the great actress Laurette Taylor, was born in New York City on April 1, 1884, and began her career in vaudeville as a child, La Belle Laurette. In 1903 she appeared in His Child Wife in Boston, and then in New York City in From Rags to Riches. Then she went on to perform in stock for a number of years. She also married Charles A. Taylor, and even though they later divorced, she kept the Taylor name. Her first appearance on Broadway in The Great John Garton, immediately brought her acclaim. Later she appeared in Alias Jimmy Valentine as Rose, and her Broadway career really began. Soon came The Ringmaster, Seven Sisters, Lola, The Bird of Paradise and then in 1912 she married British playwright J. Hartley Manners and opened in Peg o' My Heart. This was an enormous hit, six hundred and three performances, the greatest of her early career and continued in it until 1916, not only in New York, but also in London. She returned to Broadway with the play in 1921 and went on for another six hundred and ninety-two performances.

In a rather bizarre immigration circumstance, when Hartley died, since Taylor was married to him, she lost her American citizenship even though she was born in America. She had to regain it through the naturalization process. That law has since been changed.

In the 1920's she appeared in Humoresque, Sweet Nell of Old Drury, Out There, One Night in Rome, The Wooing of Eve, Happiness, and Trelawny of the 'Wells'. At this point the critics referred to her as brilliant. She would go on to make film versions of One Night in Rome, Happiness, and Peg o' My Heart.

In 1928 Manners had died and Laurette Taylor retired. But her two greatest successes came after she retired. In 1932 she appeared in a pair of J. M. Barrie plays, Alice-sit-by-the-Fire and The Old Lady Shows Her Medals. Her performances showed her great range of talent in two very different roles. It brought her more critical acclaim and was her greatest triumph to that time. She also did well in 1938's Outward Bound.

Her final and greatest triumph came in 1945 as the mother in Tennessee Williams' The Glass Menagerie. She was superb, memorable, fascinating. She won the Donalson and the New

York Drama Critics Circle awards. Many an actress has claimed it was the most memorable performance ever seen. After her death Tennessee Williams wrote, "I consider her the greatest artist of her profession I have known."

Laurette Taylor died of a coronary thrombosis in New York City on December 7, 1946, and is buried in the Bronx, New York.

#133- *Shirley Temple (1928-2014)*

"On the Good Ship Lollipop"

Shirley Jane Temple, Twentieth Century-Fox's number one star of the 1930s, was born to Gertrude and George Temple on April 23, 1928 in Santa Monica, California. She was adorable and cute, with dimples and curly ringlets, and at age three began taking dancing lessons, and by four had started a series of comedy one-reel Baby Burlesks, where children acted as adults, and then two-reel Frolics of Youth for Education Pictures, Incorporated. Her first role, a small one, in a full film was in The Red Haired Alibi. In 1934 Fox signed her to a one hundred and fifty dollars a week contract. The amount would be greatly increased as time went by.

In that first year she made Stand Up and Cheer, her breakout film, and short story writer Damon Runyan's Little Miss Marker, a marker being in gambling terms something held until you paid a debt, and she was that marker. Baby, Take a Bow and Bright Eyes (singing "On the Good Ship Lollipop.") followed . This all managed to gain this seven-year old an Academy of Motion Picture Arts and Sciences "Oscar" for outstanding and spirited personality. Already an accomplished star in the 1930s, she went on to make Rebecca of Sunnybrook Farm, Captain January, Little Miss Broadway, The Little Colonel, Curly Top, The Littlest Rebel, Dimples, Wee Willie Winkie, The Little Princess, Savannah of the Mounties and other films, becoming now an international star. In the late 1930s she was the biggest box office attraction of all. It is somewhat believed that she saved Fox from bankruptcy. There were dolls made in her image and even a sweet non-a alcoholic drink, a "Shirley Temple," made with ginger ale and grenadine, topped with a maraschino cherry. MGM even approached Fox to allow her portray Dorothy in The Wizard of Oz, but negotiations never seemed to come together.

During the Great Depression, her light and happy musicals gave some joy to people. In 1940 Young People became her last movie for Fox, and she retired at the ripe old age of twelve, with a three hundred thousand dollar bonus. She had already made twenty-four films by then. However, a year later, for fifty thousand dollars a picture, she un-retired to make Kathleen and Miss Annie Rooney. But she was no longer "little" Shirley Temple, and no longer had starring roles. But she did make Since You Went Away, The Bachelor and the Bobby Soxer, and I'll Be Seeing You.

She married John Agar in 1945, made a few more films, including Fort Apache and Adventure in Baltimore, with Agar. By 1950 she was retired again, her last film being A Kiss for Corliss, and divorced from Agar. In her short, but fabulous career she starred with such film legends as John Wayne, Spencer Tracy, Myrna Loy, Carole Lombard, Lionel Barrymore, Cary Grant, Bill (Bojangles) Robinson and Buddy Ebsen.

The next year she married Charles A. Black and moved to Bethesda, Maryland to be with him, as he was assigned to the Pentagon during the Korean War. Later in the 1950s back in California, she had two television series, Shirley Temple Storybook and Shirley Temple Presents Young America.

She had, in the meanwhile, become interested in national affairs and politics. Living now in the San Francisco area, she resigned in 1966 from the executive committee of the San Francisco International Film Festival in protest of what she felt was pornography. As a result she was awarded the Kiwanis International Award for her courage for demanding decency in films. She became so involved that she sought the Republican candidacy for Congress in 1967. She did not get the nomination, but did come in second out of ten candidates.

Two years later, in 1969, Shirley Temple Black was appointed a member of the United States delegation to the United Nations, serving on the Social, Humanitarian and Cultural Committee. She continued her efforts in the civic and political arena, becoming ambassador to Ghana in 1974, and then, in 1976, became the first woman to be Chief of Protocol for the Department of State. She was also put in charge of preparations for President Jimmy Carter's Inauguration and the Inauguration Ball. In 1989 she became ambassador to Czechoslovakia.

The little girl whose dolls were created in her curly-topped image that created a rage, and who famously sang "On the Good Ship Lollipop," showed how a woman can overcome former status to achieve new successes. She was also a co-founder of the International Federation of Multiple Sclerosis Societies, and a member of the San Francisco Health Facilities Planning Council and the Regional Board for Criminal Justice. In addition, in 1974 McCall's magazine wrote about her battle with breast cancer and having had a radical mastectomy. She was the first public figure to come out publicly on this topic. Shirley Temple wrote two autobiographies, My Young Life in 1945, and Child Star in 1988.

Shirley Temple Black died in Woodside, California on February 10, 2014. She had had her footprints and handprints in wet cement in front of Grauman's Chinese Theatre and had a star on the Hollywood Walk of Fame. She had received Lifetime Achievement awards from the American Center of the Films for Children, Screen Actors Guild and the National Board of Review, as well as being a recipient of the Kennedy Center Honors.

#134- *Sojourner Truth* (1797-1883)

"Ain't I a Woman"

Isabella (Bell) Baumfree, a daughter of former slaves, James and Elizabeth Baumfree, was born on Swartekill, an upstate New York Dutch plantation near Esopus, in 1797. She was sold at nine years old age, and then again when she was eleven. Her first language, and only language until age nine, was Dutch, and new owners would whip her because she did not readily understand English.

Bell married an older slave named Thomas, but In 1826 she escaped with her infant daughter Sophia, and two years later she sued to get her son, Peter. Her master in New York had illegally sold him to a slave owner in Alabama. The court agreed, and that was the first time an African American woman sued a white man and won. She then moved to New York City in 1829. Most of the 1840s were spent being involved with abolition, women's rights, pacifisms, and religious tolerance. 1843 was an important year for Bell. She had become a devout Christian, joining the Methodist Church and changing her name to the much more well-known Sojourner Truth, saying that, "the Spirit calls me. I must go." And she did, preaching abolition wherever anyone would listen. And she was good. If anyone jeered her she would go right back at them. She really became very popular. There was an instance when some rowdies tried to disrupt a meeting, and Sojourner Truth left and stood outside singing a hymn, "It Was Early in the Morning," and the disrupters went over to her, and calmed down after a few more songs and some prayers. Well-known abolitionist William Lloyd Garrison published "The Narrative of Sojourner Truth: A Northern Slave."

From 1851 to 1853 she joined abolitionist and speaker George Thompson traveling throughout New York and Ohio. She gave hundreds of speeches. There has been much commentary about a marvelous speech Sojourner Truth made on the topic of equality of women and African Americans, on May 29, 1851 in Akron, Ohio at a women's convention. It has been entitled "Ain't I A Woman." There are any number of variations as to exactly what she said and how she said it, but the gist of it was, "May I say a few words...That man over there says that women need to be helped into carriages, and lifted over ditches, and to have the best place everywhere. Nobody ever helps me into carriages and over puddles, or gives me the best place--ain't I a woman? Look at me! Look at my arm! I have ploughed and planted, and gathered into barns, and no man could head me- and ain't I a woman? I could work as much and eat as much as a man- when I could get it- and bear the lash as well! and ain't I a woman?...If the first woman God ever made was strong enough to turn the world upside down all alone, these women together ought to be able to turn it back, and get it right side up again!....Obliged to you for hearing me, and now old Sojourner ain't got nothing more to say." When they printed the speech they gave her a Southern accent which she did not have, and also had many inaccuracies.

In 1857 she moved first to Harmonia, Michigan, and then to Battle Creek. She attempted to vote there in 1872, but was turned away. During the Civil War she had worked with National Freedman's Relief Association and recruited African American soldiers. Sojourner Truth died on November 26, 1883 in Battle Creek. She is listed as one of "100 Most Significant Americans," and there are statues of her at the University of California at San Diego, and in Florence, Massachusetts, as well as a monument in Michigan, and in 2009, a bust in the United States Capitol. At least six states have schools named for her, and in Baltimore there is the Sojourner-Douglass College. A United States postage stamp was issued in her honor in 1986, and the 1997 NASA Mars Pathfinder was called "Sojourner." In 2020 a new ten dollar bill will feature the likeness of Sojourner Truth, as well as those of Elizabeth Cady Stanton, Susan B. Anthony, Alice Paul and Lucretia Mott. She is in the National Women's Hall of Fame and the Michigan Women's Hall of Fame, and has a highway named for her there.

#135- *Harriet Tubman* *(1820-1913)*

Moses

Araminta Ross Tubman, called Harriet, the fifth of nine children of Ben and Harriet Ross, was born near Bucktown, in Dorchester County, Maryland on a plantation somewhere between 1820 and 1825. She was a slave, and a second generation in America of the Ashanti tribe of Ghana. At fifteen years of age an overseer hit her with a two-pound weight. In addition to causing her very marked features, the skulling affected her for the rest of her life, sometimes putting her into an epileptic, coma-like state. In 1844 she married John Tubman, a free African American man, who proved to be a disappointment to her. After five years of woe, she escaped to the north without him, with the help of Quakers, and began a new life working first in Philadelphia, and then in New Jersey.

1850 found Harriet Tubman making her first trip down south to help slaves escape. She also found that her rather uncaring husband had remarried, but it did not present much of a dilemma to her. She continued her work as a "conductor" on the Underground Railroad" for many missions over more than eight very dangerous years. The Underground Railroad were routes and "safe" houses used to help slaves escape. It is estimated that she freed many slaves. If a slave got nervous or frightened or considered returning, she would pull out a pistol and threatened to shoot, and she never got caught and never lost a "passenger," even though there supposedly was quite a big a bounty on her head, that is, a payment for her capture.

The most mysterious "passenger" she brought up north was a young girl named Margaret. Some thought she was Harriet's daughter, but it was never really established or proven. Abolitionist William Lloyd Garrison called the five-foot tall Tubman the "Moses" of her people because, like Moses, she got her people to freedom. All this, while putting herself in such danger, she also spoke at anti-slavery meetings and became friendly with two very important men: escaped slave and brilliant orator and reformer Frederick Douglass, and Senator William Seward, later Secretary of State. She did support and give aid to John Brown before his infamous raid, but did not take part in it. John Brown was a fierce abolitionist who believed that war was the only way to free the slaves. He was eventually caught and hanged.

When the Fugitive Slave Law went into effect, which meant that runaway slaves living in the north had to be returned to their masters, Tubman moved to Canada, near Niagara Falls. Seward, however, helped put her up in a home in Auburn, New York in 1859. She made her last trip in late 1860. Undaunted she became a scout, a spy, a nurse, and a cook for the Union army during the Civil War at no pay. She also fought for the rights and payment of the African American soldiers. She even led part of a Union raid at Combahee Ferry that resulted in the freeing of hundreds of slaves. However, it was not until 1899 that they gave her a Civil War pension. Since John Tubman had been killed in the 1850s, in 1869 she married Nelson Davis, a Civil War veteran and bricklayer.

When Seward died so did payments on her home, and the bank began foreclosure proceedings. The people of Auburn became so incensed that they made contributions to keep the house. And Sarah Hopkins Bradford wrote Scenes in the Life of Harriet Tubman and the money earned from that also helped save the house. Later in her life she got involved in the women's rights movement, especially with Susan B. Anthony, and even accompanied her to Boston and Washington. Finally in her seventies she had the brain operation she should have had when she was fifteen. This was partly accomplished with the proceeds from a revision of the Bradford book, entitled Harriet: The Moses of Her People. Harriet Tubman died of pneumonia on March 10, 1913 in Auburn. A monument was raised in her honor with the prestigious Booker T. Washington as the main speaker. There is now a Harriet Tubman National Historic Park in Auburn, New York, which encompasses her home and a church where she had worshipped.

In a survey at the end of the twentieth century, she was listed as one of the greatest civilian Americans, only behind Paul Revere and Betsy Ross prior to the twentieth century. In the 1970s a postage stamp was issued in her likeness, the first African American woman so honored, and in 1978, a television movie, A Woman Called Moses, told her story. In 2002 she was named one of the "100 Greatest African Americans." There are statues dedicated to her in Boston, New York City, Salisbury, Maryland and Ypsilanti, Michigan. And in 2003 the Harriet Tubman Underground Railroad National Monument was dedicated on Maryland's eastern shore and there is a "Harriet Tubman Path to Freedom" in Maryland. There are many schools named in her honor and many biographies written, as well as there being the liberty ship, USS Harriet Tubman. She has been inducted into both the Maryland and National Women's Hall of Fame. The twenty-dollar bill in the future will have Harriet Tubman on the front.

#136- Lillian Wald (1867-1940)

Visiting Nurse Service

Humanitarian Lillian Wald was born on March 10, 1867 in Cincinnati, Ohio, but her well-to-do German-Jewish family, father Max and mother Minnie, moved to Rochester, New York when she was still a young child. She attended Miss Cruttenden's School for Young Ladies, graduating cultured and refined at sixteen years of age.

She decided, however, that the cultured and refined life of a society matron was not for her. She became an early advocate for nursing schools. Wald enrolled in Elizabeth Blackwell's Women's Medical College of the New York Infirmary. Upon graduation in 1891 she began teaching immigrants on New York City's East Side. For a while she worked at the New York Juvenile Asylum, an orphanage, run incompetently, in terribly poor condition, and no one much caring. With some funding and assistance from Jacob Schiff, a banker and philanthropist, and others, she set up a small settlement place on Rivington Street in 1893, which led to the present day Visiting Nurse Service, but soon there was not enough room, and she moved to the famous Henry Street house in 1895. Wald's intention was to provide visiting nurse service, and this she did, but she soon found that she was dealing with immigration problems and many other situations. In 1902 she managed to get nurses in New York City schools. In 1906 she had twenty-seven nurses; by 1913 she has ninety-two.

This also led to her seeking child labor reforms. In 1905 she visited President Theodore Roosevelt as a representative of the Child Labor Committee and proposed that there should be an agency to watch over the rights of children. Eventually, ln 1912, the Federal Children's Bureau was begun.

In 1903 she helped found the Women's Trade Union League, campaigned for women's suffrage, even help found the NAACP (National Association for the Advancement of Colored People). The NAACP's first major convention was held in her Henry Street house in 1909.

In 1910 she and a few others went on a tour of Hawaii, Japan, China and Russia espousing her reforms. Lillian Wald was also a pacifist and opposed the United States entering World War l, but she was so beloved that no one interfered with her Henry Street Settlement house work, due to her lack of support for the war, other than calling her a few names. She helped establish the Women's International League for Peace and Freedom, and had even been elected president of the American Union Against Militarism, which later became the ACLU (American Civil Liberties Union).

By 1915 they even had the Henry Street Playhouse. Wald stepped down from active settlement work in 1933, but remained president until 1937 and President Emeritus until her death of a cerebral hemorrhage on September 1, 1940, in Westport, Connecticut, and is buried in her hometown of Rochester, New York. A few months after Lillian Wald's passing, there was a tribute held at Carnegie Hall, attended by thousands, with messages from President Franklin D. Roosevelt and the governor of New York and the mayor of New York City.

Her entire life had been a kind of labor promoting the happiness and care of other people. She had written two books: The House on Henry Street in 1911 and Windows on Henry Street in 1934. The Lillian Wald Houses in New York City's East Side are named in her honor. Lillian Wald has been inducted into the Ohio Women's Hall of Fame, the Jewish-American Hall of Fame, the Hall of Fame of Great Americans, and the National Women's Hall of Fame.

In addition, Wald received the Lincoln Medallion as an Outstanding Citizen of New York. In 1922 the New York Times declared her to be one of the two greatest living American women.

#137- *Madam C. J. Walker* (1867-1919

"I Promoted Myself"

Sarah Breedlove, later in life known as Madam C. J. Walker, was born to Owen and Minerva Breedlove on a cotton plantation in Delta, Louisiana on December 23, 1867. She went on to become an entrepreneur, an activist, a philanthropist and possibly the first female self-made millionaire. She was orphaned at seven years of age, and moved in with relatives in Vicksburg, Mississippi where she probably worked as a domestic and cotton picker.

In 1882 she married Moses Mc Williams, but he died in 1887. In 1888 she again moved, this time to St. Louis, Missouri, where she started as a laundress. Throughout all this time, she had very little formal education, but while in St. Louis she discovered that many African American women, including herself, had severe hair problems, including dandruff, balding, and scalp irritations and disease. Her original products were only designed to correct these problems. In 1894 she married John Davis, but left him in 1903.

In 1904, she was an agent for Anne T. Malone of the Poro Company, and began to bring her own knowledge to bear and developed her own line. Moving to Denver, Colorado in 1905, she continued with Poro, but started her own grooming and styling business, going door to door as an independent hair stylist and a retailer of cosmetic creams. Things were going so well she started a mail order company, with her daughter in charge. In 1906 she married Charles Joseph Walker (C. J. Walker) and she, therefore, became Madam C. J. Walker. He was a newspaper advertising salesman and helped her quite a bit with getting the word out about her products. However, they did divorce in 1912.

She moved to Pittsburgh in 1908 and opened a beauty parlor, and started Lelia College to train "hair culturalists." Walker left her daughter A'lelia to run the business there, as she next moved to Indianapolis, Indiana in 1910, making it her headquarters. She had developed and successfully marketed a whole line of beauty products for African American women. It was the Madam C. J. Walker Manufacturing Company. She began to travel all around the country to promote her products. Walker became quite a speaker, not only for her products, but for political, economic and social causes. At the National Negro Business League Convention in 1912, she stated, "I am a woman who came from the cotton fields of the South. From there I was promoted to the washtub. From there I was promoted to the cook kitchen. And from there I promoted myself into the business of manufacturing goods and preparations."

From 1911 to 1919 Madam C. J. Walker's company had trained twenty thousand women as sales representatives, wearing her standard uniform of a white shirt, black skirt and carrying a black satchel, always keeping in mind, "cleanliness and loveliness." She organized her sales agents into local clubs with an area to sell, forming the National Beauty Culturalists and Benevolent Association of Madam Walker Agents. Soon, through her advertising in magazines, her products were selling in Cuba, Haiti, Panama, Jamaica, Costa Rica and other parts of the Caribbean.

In 1916, Walker left the day-to-day business at the Indianapolis headquarters and she moved to New York, and In 1917 became a member of the executive board of the NAACP (National Association for the Advancement of Colored People) in New York. She also became a philanthropic patron, donating to Tuskegee Institute, Mary McLeod Bethune's school, NAACP, the Frederick Douglass Anacostia House, the YMCA (Young Men's Christian Association), and other artistic endeavors. She moved to Harlem, New York, but built her designer thirty-four room mansion of twenty-thousand square feet in Irvington-on Hudson, New York, calling it Villa Lewaro. The name "Lewaro" was created by a guest, the world renown opera star, Enrico Caruso. Walker's daughter LElia WAlker RObinson, LE WA RO.

Madam C. J. Walker died on May 25, 1919 at her Villa Lewaro estate of kidney failure complicated by hypertension. She is buried in the Bronx, New York. At the time of her death, a combined company and personal assets had her being a millionaire, possibly the first African American woman to do it on her own. She is in the National Women's Hall of Fame, but also in the National Business Hall of Fame, the American Health and Beauty Aids Institute Hall of Fame, and the recipient of the Direct Selling Association Distinguished Service Award. Harvard Business School named her one of the "great American business leaders of the twentieth century, and in 1988 a postage stamp was issued in her likeness. Her Villa Lewaro is a National Historic Landmark, and on the National Register of Historic Places, as is the Madam Walker Theater Center in Indianapolis. In Denver there is a Madam Walker Park. The National Coalition of 100 Black Women created the "Madam C. J. Walker Business and Community Award.

Most of Madam C. J. Walker's personal papers are with the Indiana Historical Society. In 2006 Regina Taylor's play, The Dreams of Sarah Breedlove was produced, but Walker's great-great granddaughter, A'Lelia Bundles, wrote the comprehensive biography of Walker, On Her Own Ground. Sundial products has brought back Walkers products with some advanced technology, with the assistance of her great great granddaughter, calling it the "Madam C. J. Walker Beauty Culture."

#138- *Edith Wharton (1862-1937)*

The Age of Innocence and so much more

Edith Newbold Jones, later Wharton, must be considered to be one of America's greatest molder of words. She was born into wealth and privilege to George and Lucretia Jones, on January 24, 1862 in New York City, spending some time there, and some time in lavish Newport, Rhode Island. This is where the expression, "Keeping up with the Jones'" comes from. They were related to the Renssalears, one of the great patroon families of New Amsterdam. In New York, patroons were similar to plantation owners of the south. As a child she also traveled throughout Europe to France, Spain, Italy and Germany. But in 1872, she contracted typhoid and returned home.

Much of her writing dealt incisively, psychologically and, sometimes humorously, with this type of late nineteenth century society. She married Edward Wharton, a wealthy sportsman, in 1885 and they moved to Massachusetts. They divorced in 1913.

In 1877, at age fifteen she had a novella, Fast and Loose, published, and the next year her father had privately published her Verses. In 1880 she had some poems in the Atlantic Monthly, but her fame began with The House of Mirth in 1905, Ethan Frome in 1911 and The Custom of the Country in 1913. She was influenced by Jane Austen and Henry James.

During World War l, in France, she wrote for American periodicals as to what was going on at the front, and also established the American Hostel for Refugees to help Belgians fleeing the Germans. France awarded her the Legion of Honor.

In 1921 she was awarded the Pulitzer Prize for her Age of Innocence, the first woman so honored. Two years later Edith Wharton was given an honorary doctorate from Yale University.

She was also quite the decorator and gardener. The home and grounds she bought in 1901, The Mount, in Lenox, Massachusetts was designed by her, and is a National Historic Landmark. And Wharton wrote about her design abilities and knowledge with such books as The Decoration of Houses and Italian Villas and their Gardens. She was quite the traveler and a travel writer, having crossed the Atlantic sixty times. Among her writings in this genre were: Italian Backgrounds, A Motor-Flight Through France, The Cruise of the Vanadis and In Morocco.

She died August 11, 1937 in France from a stroke, having been recently weakened by a heart attack, and is buried in the American Protestant Cemetery in Versailles. She had written her autobiography in 1934, A Backward Glance. Wharton had written fifteen novels, seven novellas, and eighty-five short stories. In 1918 a silent film version of The House of Mirth was made. In 1981 a television version starring Geraldine Chaplin was done, and in 2000 another film was made starring Gillian Anderson. In 1924 there was a silent film of The Age of Innocence, a 1928 a stage version was produced, starring Katherine Cornell, and in 1934 another film version starring Irene Dunne. There was a 1993 version, under the direction by Martin Scorcese, with a phenomenal cast, including Michelle Pfeiffer, Daniel Day-Lewis, Winona Rider, Geraldine Chaplin, Jonathan Pryce, Mary Beth Hurt, and the voice over by Joanne Woodward. In 1960 a televised version of Ethan Frome, starring Julie Harris and Sterling Hayden was aired, and in 1990 there was a film. Some other novels by Edith Wharton were The Buccaneers, The Marne, A Son at the Front and Summer.

She has been inducted into the National Women's Hall of Fame, as well as the American Academy of Arts and Letters.

#139- *Phillis Wheatley (1753-1784)*

First Female African American Poet

Phillis Wheatley, the first published African American female poet, was born of the Kaffir tribe in Africa in 1753 and brought to Boston, Massachusetts as a slave in 1761. She was called Phillis because that was the name of the slave ship in which she was transported. She took her master's surname, which was common at the time. Although she was purchased to be a servant to his wife, John Wheatley and his family taught Phillis to read and write. She was very intelligent. By the age of twelve she was reading Latin and Greek classics, and the Bible. As a teenager she began writing her own poetry, including a poem written on the death of a popular minister. It was reprinted many times and she became quite a celebrity in Boston. In 1768 she wrote "To the King's Most Excellent Majesty," praising King George lll for repealing the Stamp Act. In 1772 she had to appear in court to prove she was the author of her poetry. The panel, which included among others, Governor Thomas Hutchinson, a descendant of Anne Hutchinson, and John Hancock, felt she was, indeed, the author. The Wheatleys tried unsuccessfully to get the poems published, but that happened only when one of the Wheatley sons, Nathaniel, went with her to England and did have success, with the poems being published in 1773 in Aldgate, London: Poems on Various Subjects, Religious and Moral. Not only did she get to meet the mayor of London, but Selena Hastings, Countess of Huntington, supported her poetry and allowed a volume of poems to be dedicated to her. Phillis Wheatley was now the most famous African American in England and America, and the first African American woman to have a book published. It contained thirty-eight poems.

In 1775 she wrote a poem on George Washington, and he was pleased enough to invite her to his headquarters in Cambridge, Massachusetts, and she did go. Thomas Paine published the poem in the Pennsylvania Magazine. It is in this poem that the term "Columbia" is first used as a reference to America.

> "...Fix'd are the eyes of nations on the scales,
>
> For in their hopes Columbia's arm prevails....
>
> Proceed, great chief with virtue on thy side,
>
> Thy ev'ry action let the Goddess guide.
>
> A crown, a mansion,
>
> and a throne that shine,
>
> With gold unfading,
>
> Washington, be thine."

The poems she wrote were unusually original and unique, but influenced by Alexander Pope, John Milton, Homer, Vergil and Horace. Her themes quite often dealt with Christianity and the classics. As time went on John Wheatley and other various members of the family passed away, and although now free, Phillis Wheatley worked as a maid and tried unsuccessfully to get published. She married a free African American grocer John Peters, and they tried many things, but were financially impoverished. In 1779 they left Boston and lived in a barn in Wilmington, Massachusetts, where she gave birth to John Peters, Jr. They returned to Boston in 1783 where Susie Peters was born, but both children died. Peters was imprisoned for debt in 1784 Phillis Wheatley continually tried very hard to get more poems published, but was unsuccessful. "Liberty and Peace," which she had written at the end of the Revolutionary War, was finally published, but too late, for in December, 1784, in frail health, at only thirty-one years of age, Phillis Wheatley died from complications from childbirth, along with her third baby. "A Farewell to America," "Goliath of Goth," "A Hymn to Evening," "A Hymn to Morning," "On Imagination," "On Virtue" and "Ode to Neptune" are some of her more noteworthy poems. "On Being Brought from Africa to America" is one of the few poems in which she mentions her own condition.

"...Some view our sable race with scornful eye. 'Their color is a diabolic dye.' Remember, Christians, Negroes Black as Cain, May be refined, and join th'angelic train."

In 2002 Phillis Wheatley was declared one of the "100 Greatest African Americans," and in 2003 she was made part of the Boston Women's Memorial sculpture.

#140- *Victoria Claflin Woodhull (1838-1927)*

First Female Presidential Candidate

Born Victoria California Claflin to illiterate Roxanna and con man Reuben Claflin on September 23, 1838 in Homer, Ohio, she would go on to have one of the most extraordinary, sensational, outlandish, radical, controversial and opportunistic lives of just about anyone, man or woman, in American history.

Her childhood was a series of problems, from poverty, parental sexual abuse to belonging to a family always in trouble. Barely fifteen years old she married her "doctor," Channing Woodhull. His womanizing and alcoholism brought the marriage to a rather quick end, but she retained his name for most of the rest of her life. Her strange career began as a "healer," claiming to cure illnesses with magnets. Then she was a "spiritualist," acting as a go-between for people wanting to talk to their dead relatives. In 1865 she married Civil War veteran Colonel James Harvey Blood. He would be very helpful and supportive in her further endeavors, until their divorce in 1876.

Moving to New York City at about 1870 with her sister Tennessee, they opened the first female brokerage house on Wall Street. It was rumored that Tennessee was having an affair with the Commodore, Cornelius Vanderbilt, one of the richest men in America, who also believed in Victoria's spiritual ability to know stocks. His attachment to the sisters is how they got their backing for the brokerage. They became known as the "Queens of Finance."

In 1871 Woodhull appeared before the House of Representatives' judiciary committee and argued that women already had the right to vote, based on the Fourteenth and Fifteenth amendments, which gave "all citizens" the right to vote. She was becoming a champion in the eyes of the women's rights movement. The healer, spiritualist, broker now, again with her sister, began one of the first female published newspapers in America, the Woodhull & Claflin Weekly. There had been two in the colonial era, and, of course, the of Susan B. Anthony and Elizabeth Cady Stanton a few years earlier. By this time Victoria had become interested in the social issues of the day, in particular, suffrage. Her primary purpose, however, was to promote her candidacy for president in the 1872 election. But, it being in her nature to go beyond the norm, the newspaper was the first in the nation to publish Karl Marx's Communist Manifesto in English, and also published articles on suffrage, spiritualism, sex education, licensed prostitution, the eight-hour workday, and free love. Her association with free love was how she saw the hypocritical behavior of her father and her first husband.

The very well-known Reverend Henry Ward Beecher attacked her lifestyle and writings. She, in turn, found out that Beecher was having an adulterous affair with a married member of his congregation, and the woman admitted it. She wrote about it and it became the biggest scandal of the time. But again, she used this to expose that gender hypocrisy, and although it made sensational headlines, a hung jury, undecided, was the result. To make the matter more ludicrous, Victoria was arrested because she had used the United States Post Office to send "obscene" materials, the Beecher story, through the mail.

In that election, Woodhull ran on the Equal Rights Party, with famed abolitionist Frederick Douglass as her running mate. She was now the most famous woman in America. As with all minor parties, they received no electoral votes, but just being on the ballot was a historical occurrence. She ran a few more times, and with the same results.

The Beecher "trial of the century," and the aftermath left Victoria and company acquitted, but bankrupt, and somewhat in disrepute. In 1877, Vanderbilt's son, William Henry Vanderbilt, gave Victoria and Tennessee a rather large sum of money so they could temporarily leave the country and go to England. She became a lecturer and, during this period met and married John Biddulph Martin in 1883. In 1890 she wrote The Human Body, The Temple of God.

Martin would pass away in 1891, leaving Victoria a very wealthy widow. From 1892 to 1901 she published the magazine, The Humanitarian, and then retired.

Victoria Claflin Woodhull died in her sleep on June 9, 1927 in Worcestershire, England, and her ashes were scattered at sea. In 1980 there was a Broadway musical based on her life, Onward Victoria. In 2008 she was posthumously awarded the Ronal Brown Trailblazer Award from St. John's University, and in 2017 actress Brie Larsen portrayed her in the film, Victoria Woodhull. She has also been inducted into the National Women's Hall of Fame.

#141- *Chien-Shuing Wu (1912-1997)*

Nobel First Lady of Physics

Experimental and nuclear and radiation physicist Chien-Shuing Wu was born in Jiangsu Province, China on May 31, 1912 to Wu Zhong-Yi and Fan Fu-Hua. Her father had founded the Mingde Women's Vocational Continuing School. She graduated at the top of her class at secondary school in 1929, and went on to what is now Nanjing University, where she became a student leader. Upon graduation, Wu became an assistant at Zhejiong University, and was urged to go to the United States and continue her studies at the University of Michigan.

She left China, arriving in California, never to see her parents again, not even being allowed to go to their funerals years later. Here she met Luke Chia-Liu Yuan, who claimed to be the exiled Emperor of China. Although accepted at the University of Michigan, she found that there were restrictions on women, and decided to apply to the University of California/Berkeley, and was accepted. She received her doctorate in 1940, but found there were no jobs for her.

In 1942, she married Yuan and they moved to Massachusetts, where she got on to the faculty of Smith College. Wu then went to Princeton University, where eventually she was given an honorary doctorate, where she taught naval officers.

Wu then joined the Manhattan Project at Columbia University in New York City, which was the research that produced the first atomic weapons during World War II. And after World War II became a research professor at Columbia. In 1949 she became part of the world-renowned Brookhaven National Laboratories on Long Island, New York. She also became a United States citizen.

She began working on beta decay (decomposition), and is best regarded for her Wu Experiment in 1956, which contradicted the law of the conservation of parity. She designed this experiment and carried it out with fellow physicists, which showed that radiation (the emission of energy in the form of particles) caused a decaying of subatomic particles. It had been believed that there was a preservation of equality, but her experiment showed there was a decaying in certain circumstances. In the world of physics, this was quite a finding, so much so that she and her colleagues were given the Nobel Prize in Physics in 1957. Eventually this would lead to her reception of the National Medal of Science, being named "Woman of the Year" and first female president of the American Physical Society, and being inducted into the National Women's Hall of Fame. Wu even had an asteroid named in her honor.

She was made a member of the National Academy of Science, given the Achievement Award from the Association of University Women, which named her "Woman of the Year" a few years later, and received the Research Corporation Magazine Award.

If these accolades were not enough, over the years she received the Franklin Institute's John Price Wetherill Medal, the Comstock Prize in Physics, the Achievement Award from the Chi-Tsin Cultural Foundation, made an honorary fellow of the Royal Society of Edinburgh, and was the first recipient of the Wolf Prize in Physics. And there were others too numerous to mention. Her book, Beta Decay, was published in 1965. Even after Wu retired in 1981, she continued as the Pupin professor emerita at Columbia University, and still received honors, such as the Ellis Island Medal of Honor. She passed away in New York City on February 19, 1997 from a stroke.

#142- Rosalyn Yalow (1921-2011)

Madame Curie From the Bronx

Extraordinary medical and nuclear physicist and Nobel Prize laureate Rosalyn Sussman Yalow, was born in New York City on July 19, 1921, to her parents Simon and Clara Sussman. She was to become the co-winner of the Nobel Prize in Medicine for the development of the radioimmunoassay technique (referred to as RIA), which originally studied insulin in diabetes mellitus, but has come to have hundreds of other uses, as well. This made possible the screening of the blood of donors for such diseases as hepatitis and thyroid problems. It was a process for precisely measuring substances, such as insulin, in the blood and tissue, in the very smallest concentrations that had been missed before.

After graduating from high school, she briefly took a secretarial job with bio-chemists to earn money, because there was little or no money for female Jewish graduate school students. She graduated with a degree in physics from Hunter College in 1941 and took on a graduate teaching assistantship at the University of Illinois at Urbana/Champagne. She only got this position because most of the men were in the armed services during World War ll, and got her doctorate in nuclear physics in 1945. In the meanwhile she married fellow student Aaron Yalow, the son of a rabbi, in 1943, and from then on kept a kosher home.

After obtaining her Ph.D. she returned to New York and took a position as a physics professor at Hunter College, and volunteered at the laboratory of Dr. Edith Quimby to gain experience in the possible medical applications of radioisotopes (radioactive elements that have an unstable nucleus and give off radiation during its decay). Yalow then went to work setting up a radioisotope service in 1947 at the Bronx Veterans Administrative Medical Center, just beginning her work with radioimmunoassay. This became a full-time work in 1950. The applications of her research garnered her the Nobel Prize in 1977: "We bequeath to you, the next generation, our knowledge, but also our problems. While we still live, let us join hands, hearts and minds to work together for their solution so that your world will be better than ours, and the world of your children even better."

In 1968 Rosalyn Yalow had become Research Professor of the Department of Medicine at Mt. Sinai Hospital in New York City. She went on to become the Solomon Berson Distinguished Professor at Large at the Albert Einstein College of Medicine at Yeshiva University.

Yalow's admiration for Madam Curie was so enormous that in 1976 she agreed to host a dramatic PBS (Public Broadcasting Service) five-part series on her life. Curie was the first woman to win a Nobel Prize. In 1981 Yalow was a founding member of the World Cultural Council, which encourages philanthropy and exchange of cultural values among its many members. Super scientist Rosalyn Yalow died in the Riverdale neighborhood of the Bronx, New York on May 11, 2011, following an unfortunate number of years in mental and physical decline. Her husband had passed away in 1992.

Across her lifetime of astounding achievement, Yalow was given a vast number of honorary doctorates, was granted the William S. Middleton Award for Excellence in Research (the highest honor given at the V.A. Medical Center) in 1972, the A. Cressy Morrison Award of the National Academy of Sciences, the Koch Award of the Endocrine Society, as well as being the recipient of the Dickson Prize, the American College of Physicians Award, and the Eli Lilly Award of the American Diabetes Association, and received the American Medical Association Achievement Award in 1975, was the first female honored with the Albert Lasker Award for Basic Medical Research in 1976, was made a Fellow of the American Academy of Arts and Sciences in 1978, and had the National Medal of Science bestowed up her in 1988. She has been inducted into the National Women's Hall of Fame and is, of course, a Nobel Prize winner.

"We cannot expect in the immediate future that all women will achieve full equality of opportunity. But if women are to start moving toward that goal, we must believe in ourselves or no one else will believe in us. We must match our aspirations with the competence, courage, and determination to succeed."

#143- *Babe Didrikson Zaharias (1911-1956)*

Flawless

Mildred Ella Didrikson was born the sixth of seven children of Hannah and Ole on June 26, 1911 in Port Arthur Texas. The family moved to Beaumont, where Mildred acquired the nickname "Babe." But was it because when playing baseball she could hit extremely long shots like "Babe" Ruth or because her Norwegian mother called her Bebe? She was also a basketball star for the Employers Casualty Insurance Company "Golden Cyclones" in Dallas. She once scored one hundred points in a game. From 1929 to 1931 she was named All American.

At the Amateur Athletic Union's 1931 Track and Field Championships she won seven events, tied for first in one and finished second in another, and setting world records in the hurdles and the javelin throw. In 1932, representing Employers Casualty Insurance she competed in eight events, won five events, tied for one and took third in one, breaking records in the hurdles, javelin throw and high jump, and won the championship for her team, with her being the only member of the team, and obtaining a spot for herself on the upcoming Olympic games, representing the United States. In the Olympics she was only allowed to compete in three events. She got a gold medal and set a record in the javelin throw. She won a gold medal and set a record in the eighty-meter hurdles. She was tied for first in the high jump, but disqualified for using an unorthodox method, even though she had been using it all through the competition. She had to settle for a silver medal. This "unorthodox" method was later deemed acceptable. Babe Didrikson was voted "Woman of the Year" in track and field. After the Olympics she began another legendary career, this time in golf! In 1935 she won the Texas State Women's Championship, but because of a technicality was declared ineligible, and was no longer considered an amateur. There was quite a bit of outcry over this ruling, but the United States Golf Association held firm, and she had to sit out a few years.

In 1938 she married wrestler George Zaharias, and in 1940 began her career in golf in earnest. In her lifetime she won every single tournament at least once, winning eighty-two, both amateur and professional, in all. During World War ll she did golfing benefits for charity, and in 1945, 1946, 1947, and 1951 was the "Woman of the Year" in golf. In 1946 and 1947 she won seventeen tournaments. In 1948 she helped found a women's professional golf tour, and won the United States Women's Open in 1948, 1950, and 1954, and the Vare Trophy in 1954. In 1950 she won the "Grand Slam" of women's golf; the U. S. Open, the Titleholder Championship and the Women's Western Open. Until this day she holds the record of ten wins in twenty days.

However, in 1952 she underwent surgery for a hernia and then later for cancer. She did continue to play, and to win, being awarded the Ben Hogan Trophy for "Greatest Comeback of the Year." She also managed to be president of the LPGA from 1952 to 1955. Babe Didrikson Zaharias had excelled in basketball, excelled in track and field, excelled in golf. She also excelled in bowling, once in a three-game series rolled a 268, 234 and 214. She also excelled in baseball, playing a game with women she got up thirteen times, hit nine home runs, two triples, two doubles and twenty-two runs batted in. She also excelled in weight lifting, fencing and competitive billiards. The 1950 Associated Press Poll selected her as the outstanding woman athlete of the first half of the twentieth century. She was later declared the greatest of the entire twentieth century. There really were no serious challengers to her. And considering the breadth of her accomplishments, she just might be the greatest overall woman athlete of all time. She even excelled as a seamstress, winning a sewing championship in Texas in 1931. And as a singer for Mercury records, she sang her version of "I Felt A Little Teardrop."

Babe has been inducted in to the National Women's Hall of Fame, the United States Olympics Hall of Fame, the Ladies Professional Golf (LPGA) Hall of Fame, the World Golf Hall of Fame, the Texas Track and Field Coaches Hall of Fame, the Florida Hall of Fame, the Colorado Women's Hall of Fame, and the International Association of Athletes Federation (IAAF) Hall of Fame and awarded the Bob Jones Award posthumously in 1957. In 1981 a postage stamp was issued in her likeness. Grantland Rice, a legendary sportswriter once penned this about Babe Didrikson Zaharias: "She is beyond all belief until you see her perform. Then you finally understand that you are looking at the most flawless section of muscle harmony, of complete mental and physical coordination, the world has ever seen."

Afterward

The women in this book have all proven that they were more than quite able in their various endeavors. And, of course, there were so many more. But because we honor our past greatness, it does not mean that there are not great and extraordinary women among us today. There are many, but a small sample given here, just five, five women who have done and are doing those things that will have future generations looking back with awe.

First, there is Gloria Steinem, born in Toledo, Ohio in 1934 and a graduate of Smith College. She is a journalist, writer and one of the leading movers of the feminist movement in the twentieth and early twenty-first centuries. "Imagine we are linked, not ranked." She is a granddaughter of one of the leaders of the early National Woman Suffrage Association, and she herself has written for numerous magazines, even going undercover as a Playboy bunny, writing the expose' "A Bunny's Tale." Her Ms. magazine has been a beacon for women's liberation, going back to its first edition with Wonder Woman on the cover. She has been involved with numerous television documentaries and movies, and has herself been the subject of three television documentaries, and is a founder of the Women's Action Alliance, and a co-founder of the "Take Your Daughter To Work Day." She has been inducted into the National Women's Hall of Fame, and a recipient of the Presidential Medal of Freedom.

And then there is Hillary Rodham Clinton, born in Chicago, Illinois in 1947, a graduate of Wellesley College and Yale University Law School. Early in her career she served as attorney for the congressional committee investigating Richard Nixon. Besides being First Lady of Arkansas and of the United States as the wife of Bill Clinton, where she worked hard for universal health care, she has been elected United States Senator from New York and appointed Secretary of State. At a United Nations Conference on Women she stated, "Human rights are women's rights, and women's rights are human rights once and for all." In 2008 she unsuccessfully sought the presidential nomination, but in 2016 she did become the first woman nominee for president of the United States on a major political party. Although she lost the election, she did win the popular vote. And she is a Grammy winner for the spoken word for her book, It Takes A Village. She has been selected "Most Admired Woman of the Year" many times, including from 2002 to 2016, fifteen years in a row, and has been inducted into the National Women's Hall of Fame.

Let us not forget Meryl Streep, born in Summit, New Jersey in 1949, and graduated from Vassar College and Yale Drama School. She has been called the "best actress of her generation," starting on the stage on Broadway, and then to film. In addition to garnering the most acting nominations ever, she has won two best actress Academy Awards and another for Best Supporting Actress, Streep has been honored with the Cecil B. De Mille Award and on the Hollywood Walk of Fame, has won nine Golden Globe Awards, an Emmy for Holocaust, and has won at the Cannes Film Festival. Just some of her superior and diverse performances were in Sophie's Choice, Out of Africa, The Devil Wears Prada, The Hours, The Iron Lady, Julie & Julia, Suffragette, It's Complicated, Kramer vs. Kramer, Doubt, The Deer Hunter, Mamma Mia, The Post, and August: Osage County. If those accolades were not enough, she has been given the National Medal of the Arts, the Presidential Medal of Freedom and has been a recipient of the Kennedy Center Honors. And she has been given honorary degrees from Yale, Dartmouth, Columbia, Harvard, and other universities. After receiving an award at the 2016 Golden Globe ceremony, Streep bravely stated: "But there was one performance this year that stunned me...It was that moment when the person (Donald Trump) asking to sit in the most respected seat in our country imitated a disabled reporter...And this instinct to humiliate. By someone powerful. Filters down to everybody's life because it kinda gives permission for other people to do the same thing. Disrespect invites disrespect..."

To be sure, let us appreciate Oprah Winfrey, born in Kosciusko, Mississippi in 1954. Oprah Winfrey can be accused of doing it all, of possibly being the most influential woman in the world, and nicknamed "The Queen of All Media." She hosted her own highest-rated daytime talk show, Oprah Winfrey Show, from 1986 until 2011, formed her own production company, Harpo Productions, and has her own magazine, O. She has been a worthy actress, being nominated for an Academy Award for her role in The Color Purple. She has had an important part of such other films as Beloved, A Wrinkle in Time, and The Butler, and is a recipient of the NAACP Image Award, been awarded the Presidential Medal of Freedom, the Cecil B. DeMille Award, the Jean Hersholt Humanitarian Award and been inducted into both the Television Hall of Fame and the National Women's Hall of Fame.

And finally, there is Serena Williams, born in Saginaw, Michigan in 1981, and considered by many as the greatest woman tennis player in history. She has been on a winning streak going back to 1999 and up to the present. She has won the Australian Open seven times, Wimbledon (British) seven times, the US Open six times and the French Open three times, and she was a runner-up in these tournament six times. And that is only her singles championships. She is undefeated in various doubles championships with her sister Venus, another tennis great, going fourteen wins against no losses. That is thirty-nine Grand Slam events, twenty-three in singles, fourteen in women's doubles, and two in mixed doubles. Oh, and she has won an Olympic gold medal in singles, and three in doubles.

These women, and so many others, as well as those of the past, have all faced adversity in one way or another, and they have set the example to all young women: success and equality, in whatever area of endeavor,can be achieved, in spite of...everything.

Printed in the United States
By Bookmasters